ALSO BY FREDRIK NATH,
AVAILABLE FROM FINGERPRESS.CO.UK

The Cyclist—*World War II Series, part I*

Farewell Bergerac—*World War II Series, part II*

Francesca Pascal—*World War II Series, part III*

Galdir—Rebel of the North—*Barbarian Warlord Saga, volume II*

Fred Nath

2014

ABOUT THE AUTHOR

Fredrik Nath is a full-time neurosurgeon based in the northeast of England. In his time, he has run twenty consecutive Great North Run half-marathons, trekked to 6000m in Nepal, and crossed the highest mountain pass in the world.

He began writing, like John Buchan, "because he ran out of penny-novels to read and felt he should write his own." Fred loves a good story, which is why he writes.

Catch Fred online at:

www.frednath.com

GALDIR
A
SLAVE'S
TALE

Fredrik Nath

FINGERPRESS LTD
LONDON

Galdir – A Slave's Tale

ISBN (pbk): 978-1-908824-13-4

Published by Fingerpress Ltd

Production Editor: Matt Stephens
Production Manager: Michelle Stephens
Copy Editor: Madeleine Horobin
Editorial Assistant: Artica Ham

www.fingerpress.co.uk

For Jane,
for all the support.

Acknowledgement:

Deepest gratitude to Matt and Michelle Stephens at Fingerpress for their hard work, help and perseverance, without which this book would never have seen the light of day.

GALDIR

A SLAVE'S TALE

BOOK I: SLAVE

CHAPTER 1

"Nothing happens to anybody which he is not fitted by nature to bear."

— Marcus Aurelius

A slave is not a piece of furniture, though there are similarities. If you bump into a chair you would not apologise, nor would you if you bumped into a slave. If you break wind in front of a table it is not worthy of an apology in just the same way as a slave might be considered unworthy. I knew this deep inside, but it suited me to live in denial.

I find it strange how all of one's existence can hinge upon the events of one single day, but that is what happened to me in my life as a Roman domestic fixture.

I had lived in the household of the Praetor, Gaius Licinius Piso, from the age of about six. He bought me himself at the slave market. He was not a man to let even his wife choose his slaves. He often said within my hearing that choosing a slave requires an awareness of particular qualities that lie deep beneath the surface. 'Potential' he called it. With the benefit of hindsight, I think he was right.

When I was about ten, they sent me to the country estate to work in the stables where I discovered a lasting love of horses. The stableman was one of the few people with whom

I came into contact who was not a slave. He was the only person there whom I would have considered kind. His own son had died of a fever two summers before. By kind, I mean he never beat me and he taught me about grooming, feeding, and stabling a horse. If no one was looking, he taught me how to ride when we exercised the horses. His tutelage included how to talk to a horse and when riding, to guide it with gentle little movements of my feet and legs. Most important of all, he taught me how to stay on a horse at speed—a vital skill for any warrior.

By the time I reached adolescence, they sent me back to Rome as a house-slave. I spent my time waiting at table and standing around. Endless standing. I seldom left the house unless Piso took me with him to the Forum Romanum where he judged his various court cases. I waited in wooden silence behind the curule chair to be at his instant disposal. I never understood the application of Roman law. They stood and debated all day and the cleverest speaker always won whether the defendant was guilty or not. They called it Lex Romanum, I called it unjust.

My Master socialised with a Praetor called Cassius Severus, whom I often saw at the courts. They enjoyed drinking wine together in the Master's peristylium, a large colonnaded garden. In very hot weather, the Master permitted me to stand in the shade of the colonnade.

On one sweltering summer's day, my Master and his friend sat in the peristylium, shaded by an awning, enjoying a drink. I stood to attention under the colonnade. My new sandals chafed where the dry leather ties gripped the pale skin of my muscular calves. My tunic was also new. The Master insisted slaves were like ornaments—they should always be well presented and clean. The rough wool of it rubbed me raw around the armpits, but such was my life then, I put up with such discomfort without demur.

Cicadas droned a soporific tune all around. Sweat trickled down my back as the Master and his friend drank their watered wine. They discussed matters beyond my understanding, for they often lapsed into a foreign language I assumed was Greek. To my surprise, the Master turned to me.

'Sextus, come here.' He gestured a place in front of him and his guest. 'Quickly now.'

He turned to the Praetor and said, 'Cassius, this is the slave I was talking about. A fine specimen of German Barbarian youth, don't you think?'

'I see what you mean. What muscles!' the man said.

Severus was small and plump with a clean-shaven face and fashionable sandals. His tunic was white with a red border, a sign of rank. On his left hand was a large gold ring sparkling in the sunlight. His eyes were small and dark and they darted as he sweated in the heat.

'He is a typical Barbarian,' my Master said. 'Unadulterated German stock. They are all tall and blonde, but fierce as wounded boars unless tamed from an early age like this one.'

Severus placed a sweaty hand on my leg and moved it upwards, feeling my buttocks.

'Nice, very much a Paphos not a Galatea at all, wouldn't you say?' he said.

'Cassius, I said unadulterated.'

'As you wish,' he said withdrawing his hand. 'What in the name of Juno made you buy him?'

'To be honest I admire their purity. They have a capacity for simple ferocity that makes them interesting.'

'How old is he?' Severus said.

5

'Difficult to say really. I think he would be about fifteen or sixteen years old. Do you know your age Sextus?'

'No, Master.'

'I suppose you wouldn't.'

They studied me in silence. I shifted from one foot to another, uncomfortable in the hot sunshine.

Presently Piso said, 'Sextus, we have been having a discussion about a Greek myth. You do know what a myth is, don't you Sextus?'

'No, Master.'

I felt discomfited by my owner addressing me because he spoke to me only on rare occasions, unless it was to give an instruction.

'A myth is a story one cannot verify.'

'Yes, Master.'

'As I said, we were talking about a Greek myth. It is a story about a sculptor called Pygmalion.'

Severus sniggered. He said, 'Pygmalion created something out of nothing. Are you nothing Sextus?'

I kept silent.

'We have been discussing whether we can make something out of you,' the Master said.

'Yes, Master,'

'Cassius here believes it is impossible to change nature. If you are born a Barbarian you will always be one, whether we educate you and teach you manners or not.'

'Well?' Severus said.

'I don't know about such things, sir.'

'Of course you don't, you haven't been educated yet.' The Master looked at Severus and they laughed.

Severus said, 'We have made a wager. I maintain that you cannot be educated however hard we try. Your Master believes one can mask the Barbarian nature with education and build a Roman from the dust of a German Barbarian.'

'For this experiment, I will have you educated,' Piso said.

I looked straight ahead, puzzled.

'You will have lessons every day and learn the things we Romans value. We will arrange a suitable test of the finished product in due course,' my Master went on, with, as it turned out, an odd prescience.

They sent me away to stand in the colonnade again for the rest of the day. Things changed for me afterwards.

They made me have lessons each day in which I learned Roman history and Greek language. A Greek slave taught me about the legal system and the history of Rome—Romulus and the wolves and all that rubbish. Had it not been for the fact they made me do it all outside my normal working time it would have been easy. I studied at night and before the household awoke in the morning. If I dissented they whipped me.

In a short time, I did learn a great deal. It was as if I was a sponge soaking up moisture after long deprivation. I thrived upon it. I enjoyed it in the end and it changed me, not in the manner my master anticipated, but in a subtler less obvious way. The more I learned of the Roman ways and their history, the more I hated them for what they did to mine and other peoples. It fostered a seething resentment beneath my usual, furniture-like exterior, which was impossible to vent. Slaves who disobeyed were whipped. I swallowed all those feelings and the educative process continued. By two years of this education I could speak Greek passably and could write well in Latin, but less well in Greek. I became an educated slave.

My house-slave duties continued despite my growing

knowledge. In the daytime, I waited upon the Master and Mistress and stood in corners most of the time. I ran errands for the Master as well. He now trusted me enough to send me to the Subura. It was a maze of three and four storey tenements, many of them ramshackle and falling down, but thousands lived there. Most of the street crime in the city took place in that quarter and the Night Watch seldom entered, because gangs went around the streets robbing and on occasion killing. It shows how little esteem they held me in—my errands were at any hour of the day or night in the roughest and most lawless part of the city.

When I say errands, these were sometimes unsavoury in character. My Master liked young girls. Nothing out of the ordinary in Rome one might think, but he liked to cause pain and it was never a pretty sight. They often sent me to a whorehouse to fetch the object of the Master's desire and bring her back to the house.

Although I think the Mistress knew what he did, no mention of it passed between them in my presence.

I often witnessed in disgust what he did to these girls. They were always of an age to understand and they always asked for extra money, which he seemed happy to pay. I stood in the corner partly obscured by a hanging drape, trying to be inconspicuous and staring into thin air. I held no illusions about what would happen if he thought I might be watching. I distracted myself by thinking about my own life. I withdrew within it as if cocooned. The scenes played out before me had a habit of breaking through the reverie but I always returned to my own thoughts and memories. It was all I could do, even though there was precious little in my life worth a daydream.

On the spring day in question, I was alone in the house

apart from a kitchen slave who worked in the culina at the other end of the villa. The Master arrived home from his work with a man and a small girl. The man was her father and he seemed to be a wealthy Roman citizen judging by his clothes. The girl was dressed in a fine tunic, her auburn hair tied with a clasp at the back of her head in a rather more adult fashion than one might expect for a child, but girls, I supposed, mature early. Dark eyes shone from her pretty face. They sat down and she stared at the floor, legs crossed, arms folded.

Piso ordered me to bring wine and water, which I did. I backed away against the wall and awaited further instructions. The visitor after drinking some wine, stood to depart. As he made to leave, the girl grabbed his tunic and burst into tears saying, 'Father please, I don't want to! Please!'

Her pleas fell upon deaf ears however, but unlike her father I found them impossible to shut out. I questioned how anyone could treat his own child in this way. I knew what was coming. I felt hot and flushed; my head throbbed. I could feel the blood coursing through my body.

'It will be alright, I keep telling you this nice man will look after you for a few hours and then I will come back,' the man said as he left, but I could hear his voice tremble as he spoke.

He was quite wrong. There was nothing nice about my Master and I knew it. I could feel my pulse rising. The previous objects of my Master's sexual attention always seemed willing, though I suppose no one offered them a choice. This girl was terrified and it was obvious. I noticed a choking feeling and I clenched my fists to keep myself still. I dug my fingernails into my palms hoping the pain would distract me. I could not understand why I felt like this. I

9

supposed it was because of the faint memories of how the legionaries killed my mother when I was a child, but it seemed also to stem from some deeper almost innate sense of injustice. What was about to transpire should have been a mere repetition of many such scenes I had already witnessed in Piso's house, but this time it was different.

The girl was about ten or twelve years old. As soon as she was alone with my Master, he proceeded to try to undress her. She cried and he slapped her face saying, 'Be quiet, I have paid your father a lot of money for this. Without it, you and he will be in the street. You would do well to do as he told you.'

My distress became as intense as if I urgently needed to pass water. It tore my heart to hear her sobbing. I could say nothing. If I even made my presence felt, I knew the Master would have me whipped; he owned me after all.

Piso's hands moved, kneaded, rubbed. The tension rose in my neck and my back. Breathing became a struggle. I knew there was nothing I could do for the girl. Her snivelling and whimpering were like a stabbing in my ears, a torture and violation of its own, but directed at me. I felt useless, degraded by my own indecision and fear of punishment.

'Coward!' I thought, 'coward!' as I witnessed him pulling the gown over her head.

It was like some old and cracked witch's voice in my brain. It goaded me; it stoked the fires of my anger and drove me to the brink of a precipice of action from which I knew there could be no return.

'Coward!'

This is where the similarity ends between slaves and furniture. Ash and pine do not feel. Only men—men of flesh and blood are intolerant of evil. I experienced a profound and burning fury so intense it was beyond my understanding. It was beyond my control.

My Master stood over the girl. He pushed her onto the low couch. She used one arm to cover her tiny immature breasts, and the other hand guarded her groin. He stepped back to disrobe. His tunic covered his head as he struggled in haste to pull it off.

I seized a heavy oil lamp. He never knew what hit him. I laid into him hard. I struck him so many times I lost count.

Blood ran in rivulets across the floor. It splashed all over my tunic, my face, my arms. The rage was unquenchable. I had never felt such pure unbridled emotion before but would feel it again many times in my life. It consumed me; it possessed me and it felt good. In that momentary state of exhilaration I could have killed a dozen magistrates, a hundred if they had been there.

Then silence.

Then breathless and all-consuming calm.

A finch singing in the peristylium interrupted the hush, oblivious of the Praetor's departing shade. I looked up at the little girl. The smell of blood was rank in my nostrils. I was spattered with it and breathless. I had trouble believing it, but she smiled.

Unperturbed and in singsong tones she said, 'They're going to crucify you.'

It began to dawn on me she was right. The punishment for a slave who killed his Master was indeed nailing to a wooden cross and to be displayed to all. I was scared now. None of the other slaves would help me, for if I ran away the law demanded their crucifixion in my place.

I stood up and paddled through the pool of blood on the

floor. Turning to the smiling girl, I said, 'Wait here. Don't run away, remember I helped you.'

She reached for her tunic with no apparent urgency.

I left the room, my heart beating like thunder beneath my ribs.

I washed with haste at the fountain in the peristylium and went to my quarters. There I changed my clothes as if in a dream. Still in a daze, I stole some of the Master's sandals from his room and took a knife from the chest by his bed. I found some gold coins in a small pouch and returned to the triclinium where the half-dressed corpse of my former Master lay. I noticed he no longer sported an erection; it gave me a cold gratification.

The girl was still there, but she was now dressed. I took her hand in mine and led her around the gruesome mess on the mosaic-laid floor. The mosaic was of Hercules, clubbing the Nemean lion. It seemed ironic but apt.

'I'd better get you home,' I said as we walked out of the front gate.

'I live near the Quirinal.'

'Come, you will have to show me. If I ask a favour will you help me?'

'Depends,' the child said, her little face a picture of guile.

I looked at her with curiosity; she was not behaving as I expected, but it is a fact Romans bring up their women seeing death and blood in the arena. It makes them hard. I wondered if perhaps she was not the innocent I at first imagined her to be.

'Can you tell them I said I was getting out of Rome to go to Thurii?'

'They'll catch you anyway, you know.'

My Master's experiment had reached its conclusion. Severus was right. Deep inside me, I realised who I was. I wondered with vague humour whether I had passed the Master's test or failed it.

I think he lost his bet.

The hunt was on.

CHAPTER II

"Time is a violent torrent; no sooner is a thing brought to sight than it is swept by and another takes its place."

— Marcus Aurelius

I never liked Rome very much. It is a crowded, foul-smelling, dark place. They built the houses too close together for a start so when these tall wooden buildings fell down, which they did with monotonous regularity, they killed many and obstructed the streets causing chaos. The reason the tenements fell down was that the builders bribed the building inspectors; shoddy buildings went up without proper foundations. They used unseasoned or flimsy timber and, combined with the shoddy construction and over-crowding, it made the place unsafe. They never learned and it still goes on from what I hear.

The worst area was the Subura. In olden times when Augustus Caesar ruled in Rome, he tried to clear the place out. He failed because he used the wrong tactics, or so my Greek teacher said. To make the residents move out the Senate bribed them. They razed it to the ground then rebuilt the place. Herding people out and finding other accommodation in the country allowed others to move in to fill the empty space and nothing changed.

The Subura, at the time I escaped, was the same as two

14

hundred years before. The occupants of the tenements threw their waste and effluent out of the window in the morning so it would wash down the central gutter into the sewers. That was the intention at any rate, but the sewers often blocked with detritus and backed up leaving pools of excreta in the street. They carried on discarding the contents of their overnight pots into the street anyway. The rats enjoyed it but I cannot imagine the occupants of the tenements did. I found it a mercy that prolonged exposure inures the nose to any such odours however bad they are, and life continues.

I left the little girl near her father's villa on the Quirinal and walked the long straight road down to the Subura, the only place in Rome I knew well. As an escaped slave there were few places for me to go. I knew the owner of the whorehouse where my deceased Master used to send me, but since I was instrumental in removing that particular source of income from the proprietor, I reasoned I would not find a place of refuge there. I had enough money in my pouch to pay for a roof over my head but no idea who to approach for this.

I spoke to no one. My appearance was against me and it seemed obvious. I felt as if everyone around me was staring. Their gaze seemed to strip me bare and I imagined they all knew who I was and what I had done. Not many Romans were tall and blond, but by good fortune, there were often German travellers and soldiers in Rome. The Emperor kept a whole bodyguard of German soldiers and a fair proportion visited the Subura for sexual entertainment ,and the taverns, some of which served a filthy brew called beer. This horrible bitter drink full of alcohol and hangovers was the traditional drink in all the countries across the Rhine.

I decided to have my head shaved and buy a new tunic. I

thought if I was no longer blond, I could merge better with the background. The first option on my list was easy. I asked the barber to shave my head and beard. He did so with glee. He coated me in olive oil and applied his razor with enthusiasm. He expressed surprise at the result. My whole scalp was a mass of tattoos. There was a long snake with intertwining coils of red and black, its open jaws across its tail. I did not know I had a tattoo; no one had even hinted it was there. I had seldom seen myself in a mirror and never had my head shaved, although I had often seen my face reflected in water. I presumed it was some kind of decoration from my childhood.

The image in the mirror disturbed me. It grabbed me. I could see my face—a young, strong face with hollow cheeks and a heavy jaw-line. My eyes focussed on the background as if drawn to it. I saw men on horses, warriors every one, swinging swords. I heard them cry aloud in a foreign language. It was a strange living picture portraying a battle. A large man, blond- moustached and bald-headed, bearing my tattoo, fell from a horse and a red river of men swallowed him up. I must have leaned forward because I bumped my head on the shiny surface and the picture dissolved like a bursting bubble. With a sudden shake of my head, I returned to reality. The sounds of the Roman streets came first, a man hammering on something made of metal, a horse whinnying, a child shouting at play. I was standing in the forum again and the barber was looking at me. It seemed a foolish dream, but I felt shaken.

'Are you all right?' the barber said.

'Yes...yes, fine thanks,' I said.

'Only, you looked a bit strange just then.'

'Really, I'm fine. Just tired, that's all.'

I could not explain it and so in typical Sextus furniture fashion, I put it away in my mind.

It occurred to me then the tattoo would be a good disguise, for no one would know it was there and the soldiers searching for me would not be looking for a bald man with a tattoo.

The second option was more difficult. I stopped at a stall in the Forum Boarium. It was the cattle forum and farmers herded their prize stock there to sell them to other farmers or for sacrifice. In all the fora there were stalls selling goods as varied as jewellery, furniture and clothes. An old man sitting at a clothes stall looked me up and down. He smiled and asked me what kind of tunic I wanted. The one in which I escaped stood out as a slave's clothing and I wanted to look like a free man. I had no idea what to say. I paid the man extra and he came up with a tunic he had made for a visiting Greek who failed to turn up to collect his order.

Roman law forbids anyone from carrying weapons within the Pomerium, that is, inside the old city walls. This was an ancient law to which many people adhered at first. With the passage of time, the law fell into virtual disuse and most people carried at least a knife in modern times. An unarmed man in Rome was open to robbery and worse.

There I was, a wanted murderer with a shaven head and new tunic looking for temporary accommodation. I had enough money left in the purse I had stolen from the Master to afford a room, but I was reluctant in case someone informed upon me. I trusted no one. I knew there would be a price on my head and that the denizens of the Subura would sell their own relatives to get gold. I needed to be careful if I wanted to leave Rome or it would cost me my life. The soldiers would know I could only be hiding in the Subura. It was the one place in the city where no one asked questions, but if you paid them, they would do anything.

On my first night of freedom, with shaking limbs and frequent startles I attempted sleep in a doorway. Rest was elusive for there was a nocturnal rattle and thump from all the carts passing in the streets. I felt as nervous as a hunted beast, expecting soldiers would discover me at any moment.

When I closed my eyes, memories came. They disturbed me. Faint recollections intruded of how the Roman soldiers snatched me from my mother's arms at the age of six. I will never forget the colour of her blood—it has stamped itself on my brain. I can still see it flowing onto the straw-lined floor of our hut as they dragged me away. I thought about my mother's softness and her long reassuring arms encircling me with such gentleness when I was sleepy or I needed her love. It was the only love I was to experience for a long time, for no one loves a slave. I felt tears on my cheeks as I lay in that doorway.

I remembered a man who helped me walk and sometimes carried me on my way to Rome. His rough calloused hand gripped mine with a sweaty firmness I found reassuring at the time. I recalled he was big and broad and I recalled the long, yellow, braided hair I held on to as I sat upon his shoulders on the long march to Rome.

I shifted with discomfort in the doorway as I pictured arriving at my Master's villa, a small child alone and unable to talk to anyone—I spoke no Latin after all. They gave me to one of the house slaves who did look after me physically. There was no affection in her touch. If I did anything to put her position at risk she beat me without mercy. In the end, sleep flew away as dawn caught me. I needed to move. A stationary target is an easy mark.

I obtained food from street vendors the next day but I knew I needed a plan to get out of Rome. I knew it was risky, but what did I have to lose?

I sat on the steps of the temple of Venus Libitina and pondered. Wagon traffic is restricted because Roman laws do not allow carts or wagons into or out of the city until after sunset. I thought this could be to my advantage. I decided to find a carter who would take me with him. They would not be looking for a bald, tattooed youth riding in a cart so there was some chance the gate-guards would overlook me.

I had a whole day to get through first. I knew Rome well enough from my trips out with the late Piso and I felt I might be able to while away the daylight hours by finding some hostelry where they served food and wine.

I ended up in The Old Gaul tavern—a tavern tucked away in a small cobbled alleyway at the southwest end of the Subura near the Forum Romanum. The thing attracting me was the quietness of the alley. The crude wooden door was open and the interior was small with only eight tables and rough wooden benches. I looked around the dim interior as I entered. Customers occupied two of the tables. At one of them, three men talked in loud voices. At the other were two big fellows with their heads bowed muttering to each other as if they had something to hide. It looked ideal. I sat down in the darkest alcove hoping to be inconspicuous.

The tavern was two hundred years old; established by a one-armed soldier whom the proprietor told me was an ancestor of his. He said this with an air of pride when I sat down. It had changed hands once or twice but the original owners bought it back so it had been in the Sinna family ever since the Republic. The owner however, had two arms and a ready smile. I was tired and my hand was shaking when I picked up the cup of watered wine.

He approached me again and said, 'So, you're the fellow they're looking for?'

I looked up at him. I said nothing.

He shook his head and said, 'You're so conspicuous with that tattoo—it marks you out as different. I think you'd last about twenty minutes in the street before someone started to get curious. Don't worry though, we don't ask any questions in here as long as we aren't ourselves in any danger.'

The speaker was a big fair-haired man. His dark-brown eyes stared right through me. To this day I remember those eyes for they said much. For a start they said life in the Subura had its own rules. They were welcoming eyes. You know the truth of a situation when you read the eyes of a man – it is like looking into their shade. It is just as true when you fight as when you make a joke over a cup of wine, believe me. In any event, his eyes were solid, brown and seemed true.

I was about to tell him how if I had kept my hair I would have been even more conspicuous, but we were interrupted by the arrival of five legionary soldiers who looked around the tavern with interest. One of them approached my table. I looked down. My heart was beating fast and I broke out in a sweat. I sipped my wine, trying to moisten my arid mouth.

The tavern-keeper got up. He put out a hand and guided the soldier away towards the others, gesticulating with the other hand as he talked.

I heard him say, 'Slave, eh? Thousands of 'em out there, my friend. Let's have a cup of Falernian on the house and see if we can't find the killer. German, you say?'

He poured them all a drink which they took standing up. After an animated conversation with the soldiers in which he waved his arms and grinned, he finally laughed and slapped one of them on the back. Then the tavern keeper indicated to the right, outside the tavern and gave them some directions. The soldiers left soon after. I heard little more of the conversation because the two men on my right began arguing in loud and angry tones about a woman. One of them stood up and drew a knife.

The tavern keeper walked from the bar without hesitation, wielding a heavy cudgel and hit the man hard on his right arm. The customer dropped his knife, it clattered across the floor towards me and I picked it up. It was a long curved blade with a wicked point, not much use for anything but killing.

The troublemaker was rubbing his arm above the elbow and swearing. Grabbing him by the tunic, the tavern keeper ejected him through the door to the street. Still grasping his cudgel, he sat down next to me.

'I'm Flavius,' he said, 'I already know your name, Sextus—the soldiers told me all about you.'

I stared at him and looked dumb.

'You're going to get caught if you stay in Rome. They're looking for you everywhere.'

'They don't know I've shaved my head.'

'The barber talked and the man who sold you the tunic went straight to the Town Guard.'

'Shit.'

'I can help you.'

'Why would you help me?' I asked, puzzled anyone would try.

'I just didn't like the creature you killed. He was corrupt. He once falsely condemned someone close to me—a relative.' He looked down for a moment. Presently he continued but the look in his eyes was sad. 'If you hadn't done it, I would have joined the queue of killers waiting to do what you did. Rome is a better place without that bastard. Many in the Subura think as I do, which is why no one has reported seeing you so far.'

'What should I do?'

'I'll get you a new tunic for a start. They know how you are dressed. You'll need a cloak too.'

Flavius let me stay in the tavern until nightfall and he fed me. He was an interesting man who had travelled like his forbear and he had interesting tales to tell. I absorbed it all like a dry cloak in the rain. He taught me the names of German tribes he had fought and told me what the German lands were like.

It was midnight when Flavius stopped a man with a cart whom he knew and asked him to take me out of the city. The man looked me up and down. He grunted his assent and charged me a gold piece which I now realise was as good as robbery. I was a slave after all, and had never possessed money, so I capitulated and resigned myself to the dwindling of my fortune.

I said farewell to Flavius and he wished me luck.

'If you ever come back to Rome look me up. I will be very interested to hear how you managed to escape crucifixion,' he said, in a low enough voice so the carter did not hear him. He laughed then and slapped me on the back as I mounted the cart. I did not see him again until many years later.

The man who owned the cart was one of the hairiest men I have ever seen. I remember his beard covered most of his face. The hair on his arms as he pulled on the reins was as luxuriant as that on a horse's neck. I jumped aboard and he let me sit beside him. He smelled of onions and sweat. The odour of my companion was the least of my concerns. I could see soldiers at the Salarian gate in the distance as we approached. My heart was racing as I hid beneath some sacking covered by bales of cloth in the back of the cart.

The guards stopped the cart and spoke to the man; they wanted to search the wagon. The guard lifted the first bale and as torchlight began to penetrate my thin layers of protection, the cart shuddered as if struck by lightning. Another cart had collided with us as it passed. The soldier standing in the back must have been catapulted out and although I could not see, I realised he must have been injured. I heard groans and a shout of dismay. In the ensuing confusion, we sneaked out of the city without further hindrance. Had I not been godless then I would have prayed. A few miles down the road, the man dropped me off at some crossroads. He did not even acknowledge my thanks and drove off without looking back.

I had some money for food and my only possessions were two knives and some spare clothes, but I was free and had a plan. As I walked, the vision in the barber's mirror kept returning mind. When the scene replayed itself, it was without my conscious thought and it seemed beyond my control. I puzzled over its meaning, but could make no sense of it. In the end, I put it out of mind again.

I could hear the coins jangling in my pouch as I walked. They reminded me of the murder and the theft. I was not ashamed of the killing but stealing bothered me. I believed in honesty you see. I had no inkling of where the concept came from. I only knew it was wrong to steal. Deep inside, I had a feeling that so far, my life was not unfolding as it should. The feeling was indefinable and hidden from conscious thought. I knew my destiny was not to be a thief. I found out however, there are worse things in life than simple clean thievery. Many men have things in their past of which they are ashamed and in mine it is the period following my time in Rome.

CHAPTER III

"O tempora. O mores!"

(Oh, the times! Oh, the manners!)

— Cicero

The road was muddy with the spring weather. It was cold for that time of year and I wrapped my cloak around me to keep out the damp of the drizzle beginning to fall. The moisture clung to it making it heavy, but there was a spring in my step as I made for the hills. Perhaps I would be safe there; there was no reason for anyone to pursue an escaped slave so far from Rome.

Although I had slept rough for three nights after leaving Rome and wished I could be somewhere with a roof over my head, I was content with the thought I was free. I found it exhilarating but I felt insecure. It was as if I had lived my whole life in a tiny room and all of a sudden, they had churned me out onto a vast plain whose borders I could not identify. It was a feeling close to gut-wrenching fear but at the same time I was happy.

It took some hours to get onto the slopes of the nearest hill. There were vineyards to my right as I headed north. Triangular cane tripods lashed together with twine supported the vines. The beginnings of leaves were sprouting already and it seemed to promise a hot summer. In contrast to the stench of Rome, all I could smell here was the fresh spring

25

morning. To my left, were olive groves and some green pastureland rising towards high verdant hills. I stopped and hid behind some rocks and ate part of a cheese and a piece of bread Flavius had given me before I left the Old Gaul Tavern. I was not lost but I did not appreciate distances; I had only travelled to Ariminium and back once in my life. I did not understand why I was going north in any case. I recall I had some vague idea of stealing a horse from the stables of my dead Master's country estate perhaps because I longed to be somewhere familiar.

I could see a winding track wending its way to the top of a high hill to my left. Leaving the road, I began to climb. I made good progress and within minutes stood a short distance from the summit. A scream rang out. It was not a loud scream. The sound seemed cut short as if stifled. I proceeded with caution not knowing what I might find.

I left the track and used a large boulder to hide my approach. I peered around the boulder and saw about twenty armed men; half were mounted and half on foot. They were ragged and unkempt. Their unshaven faces seemed to reflect their nature. They looked savage. Their grey tunics had tears and stains. Each of them carried arms of some kind of weapon. Some sported swords and others had spears. I had no desire to face such people. Fear gripped me. I wondered if they would notice me if I sneaked off and hid. The scene before me however kept me spellbound. I stared with a mesmeric fascination fed by my dread, like when a rabbit seeing a hunting dog cannot move; tense but coiled ready to spring.

There were three bodies on the stony ground and there was blood all around them. An enormous broad, squat man stood with a sword in his hand. Another man knelt before him. The kneeling man was crying and begging. I watched in horror as the stocky brigand stabbed with his short sword into the kneeling man's neck and a gout of blood spurted up.

I was horrified. I had seen death in the arena when my Master took me there to stand behind him and run errands. This was different in a subtle way. This was real. It was not a show put on for religious purposes. It was as if I was an interloper in someone else's world. Death in the arena was a universal spectacle. Everyone there was expecting to see it and the antagonists knew they might die. They were never helpless victims. In fact, the death of a gladiator was uncommon; they often spared each other, for they were expensive commodities. These rough, unkempt, on-looking men, laughed as the kneeling man fell twitching in death. I closed my eyes.

With the suddenness of a thunderbolt I found myself catapulted forwards with a force that felt superhuman. I rolled head over heels towards the men. I tried to rise and run but two of the men crossed the space between us and pinned me face down on the rocky ground.

'What have we here?' I heard a deep, gruff voice say.

'I found him sneaking behind that rock, spying. I think we should get rid of any witnesses don't you?' another said.

'Let's see what we've found first, eh?' the same gravelly voice said, whose owner was invisible to me since the two men held me face down. They let me up then and the armed men surrounded me with swords drawn and pointing at me.

'Lost your tongue boy? It would be a shame. I couldn't cut it out for you if that's the case.'

The men around the speaker laughed again.

He was a bald man of medium height but with a build of which any ox would have been proud. He had no neck and his ugly face seemed to emerge from out of his shoulders, which were massive. Below the hem of his dirty grey tunic were legs like tree trunks and just as solid.

He slapped me then. Not a hard blow for him, but hard enough to knock me to the ground.

'I asked you a question boy and you'd be wise to answer,' he said.

'I'm just a traveller looking for work,' I said, my mouth beginning to swell. It was not a very convincing lie but it was the best I could come up with at the spur of the moment.

'Looking for work were you? Got any money?'

'Not a lot, just enough for food. As I say, I'm looking for work.'

They searched me and found the two knives and the little gold and copper remaining. It was in the leader's pouch in the blink of an eye.

'Not much use to us is he?' a tall thin fellow said, 'Just kill him and we'll be off.'

'No,' the Ox said, 'If he's looking for work, he can work for us. We need to make up our numbers since Septimus got it last week.'

'You can join us as a slave or as a member of the team. Can you fight?'

'I don't know much about fighting but I can learn I suppose. Oh, and I can write.'

'We don't have much use for scribes do we Rugio?' he said looking at one of his men. There was a ripple of laughter.

'I can ride and I'm good with horses,' I said.

'You won't be on a horse for as long as I can help it. I don't want you to run away and bring the soldiers. Do I look stupid?'

He did look stupid, but I was not in a position to say so. I mumbled something and they dragged me to my feet. Rugio produced a rope and tied it around my neck. They pulled me along behind them and as I stumbled cutting my knees I had visions of torture and worse. We ascended a steep bank where hawthorn bushes made the going hard. I waded through, dragged by my captors and entered a gulley where they had made a rough camp. My further education began that evening.

After they had eaten, a tall man cut the rope around my neck and pulled me into the centre of the seated group.

'I'm Rugio and I'm going to give you a lesson in fist fighting.'

There were peals of laughter from the men. Rugio stood me in front of him with my fists raised and said, 'All right, throw a punch and make it as hard as you can.'

I lashed out with my right fist as hard as I could. The blow struck thin air as Rugio dodged the punch. What followed was a lesson I would not forget in a long time. It was a lesson in pain and I learned I was slow, clumsy, and as far as they could see, stupid.

Each time I raised my fists Rugio would punch me, from in front, with right hooks and with left hooks; he even head butted me on the nose and my streaming eyes blinded me whilst he danced around me and rained blows on my head, neck and body. He was not punching hard enough to injure me although he could have done so with ease. He could have ended the fight at any time with a single well-placed punch but it was sport to him. It sounds cruel but he did teach me to fight in the end. He repeated the performance almost every night and he would punch me until I was unable to stand.

On the fifteenth night, I got lucky. He was landing a right hook to my cheek, when his foot slipped and he over-balanced a fraction. It was his undoing. That moment was long enough for my opportunity to appear. I hit him for the first time. I hit him with all the force I could muster, twisting to use my back muscles as I did so. I am not a small man and the rigours of the last two weeks in the camp with these ruffians had hardened me. My punch landed on his left cheekbone with a crunch. It sent him spinning to his right and he fell in a heap. His neck looked twisted at an absurd angle.

When he did not get up, there was silence and consternation in the men around the campfire. After a few moments the leader whose name was Sartorius, got up and tried to rouse Rugio.

'He's bloody dead,' he said.

Several of the men got up then and one drew a sword.

'I knew he was bad luck,' the man with the sword said, 'let's kill him.'

Sartorius turned and said, 'Don't be daft, it was a fair fight and if Rugio wanted to pick fights with people instead of teaching them, then that's his problem isn't it?'

There was an escalating murmur of agreement from the assembled men and they dragged the body down the hillside and left it there. They returned with his clothes and sandals. No burial for Rugio. They spoke no words over his body. It was just meat, left for the creatures. I did not intend to end my life in such a way. I needed to learn to fight. No one picked a fistfight with me afterwards, but no one spoke to me either.

After a few days, the brigands moved on to another camp and they seemed to accept me in a taciturn sort of way. On occasion one of them would slap me on the back and call me 'killer' or 'champion'. The mealtimes were no longer a general excuse to beat me up or push me around and to be honest, I was beginning to enjoy life and freedom. Compared to being a slave in Rome this existence was worlds apart from the humdrum standing, staring and musing to which I had become inured.

I was scared of Sartorius. He was a big man with a temper flaring bright, especially in the mornings. He almost killed one of his men for contradicting him. All the poor fellow said was, 'That wasn't the way it happened.' Sartorius beat him with his fists until the man was unconscious and then kicked him while he lay on the ground. We had to carry him for days afterwards.

It is true to say of bullies that if you once stand up to them they leave you alone. In Sartorius' case, there was no one who could stand up to him and survive. It never happened unless it was by accident. He was a natural killer and forgave nothing. In short, he was mean to the point of being evil.

Sartorius did try to teach me how to use a sword. He needed me to replace Rugio and I would be no good to him if I couldn't wield a weapon. He taught me to parry, thrust, and strike. He showed me how to use a small round shield. The legions had taught him, but he had committed some crime of which he would not speak and ended up a brigand in the hills.

We moved north again after a couple of weeks. We had marched for four hours on the third day when the mounted brigands came back to inform Sartorius there was a farm half an hour's march to the west. They felt this would be a good target because they needed supplies and some of the better off farmers had money and horses. They marched fast, as if they were looking forward to some action. I was curious to see what was going to happen.

When we saw the farm from a nearby hill, Sartorius organised the attack. They were not expecting much resistance but they planned for any eventuality. Six of the riders were despatched to guard the road into and out of the farm.

It was a small farm with vineyards on a south-facing slope and the house was of typical Roman design. There were outhouses and a barn and there was a wall around the farmhouse itself. The spring sunshine spread its afternoon glow over the scene and there were people working in the fields planting and hoeing. It looked idyllic—peaceful, and quiet.

The brigands numbered over twenty men, ten mounted and ten on foot including me. I did not know what to expect. I had never seen these men in action and I looked forward to doing something to release me from the boredom setting in. I wondered what they would do with the inhabitants of the farm. I imagined they would tie them up and leave them. I hardly imagined they might take them along.

The five riders with us followed up the rear and were to stop anyone who escaped from the farm buildings. We walked at a marching pace, each of us armed with a sword. Sartorius gave me Rugio's sword but I had no shield or helmet because the others had taken most of Rugio's gear.

We entered the yard which formed the centre of the farm buildings. There were half a dozen slaves. They huddled together as if for protection. I could have told them. At some point you have to stop being slaves and become men. They put up no resistance at all. The brigands killed them like pigs from market and I felt unable to watch. One tried to run away and a brigand named Tunius threw a knife. It struck the unfortunate slave between the shoulders and he still ran for twenty yards before he fell, his legs twitching beneath him. Tunius complained about having to walk all the way to retrieve his weapon and he slit the gurgling slave's throat slowly to get even. I remember the sawing movements of the knife and the sudden spurt of red as his knife reached the arteries. He was holding the struggling man down all the time and laughing. I felt nauseated and I kept closing my eyes to rid them of the scene. I thought of what I had done to Piso but it did not help. I had been in a fury then and now I was not.

Sartorius led the men into the farmhouse. The farmer rushed at the brigands with a short sword in his hand. Sartorius dispatched him with a quick stab of his gladius. Blood ran red, pooling on the tiled floor.

All around were sounds of shouting or screaming, furniture breaking and ornaments crashing to the ground. I turned and saw a queue of my comrades. I assumed they were lining up to get wine. With a loud guffaw, Sartorius pushed me into line with the rest and walked into a room, where I could hear him ransacking the place. I did not have a cup but I expected they would give me one as I reached the corner. I heard a scream then and it prompted me to peer around the doorjamb. I was dumbstruck by what I saw.

They had dragged the farmer's plump wife into the kitchen area and stripped her naked. She was weeping as the men queued up to take her. I wanted to shout out. I wanted to stop them, then I realised I was in the queue too. I could not face what was happening. I staggered away from the scene. It burned itself deep into my mind in the days to come; I could even see it when I was awake.

I felt sick and dizzy with it all. It was like some waking

nightmare. There was blood everywhere I looked, smeared on the floor-tiles, spattering the walls. The farmer's wife screaming in the background added another dimension of horror to the whole episode. I understood my naivety then. There would be no prisoners. There would be no tying up. These men were evil killers and they sickened me.

There were two children in the house no more than ten or twelve years old. My comrades dragged them through the blood on the tiles of the peristylium. They were screaming and every note was an assault to my senses. I could do nothing for those children. I knew if I tried to intercede, these monsters would kill me too. I had to look away as they decapitated them. The brigands said it was because the children could identify them. I could smell the blood and hear the screams of their victims.

They left no one alive. We herded the farm animals together. They killed some and butchered the carcasses to add to our supplies. They herded some along with us for later. The brigands also took a cart full of corn and wine barrels, which they said, would keep us in grain and merriment for months.

My comrades searched the farmhouse again but all they found were a few coins and some small silver dishes. I could not imagine such a small farm taking twenty men to attack it.

They burned the farmhouse and the farmer's wife within. I could hear her screams as we marched away. Those sounds stayed with me for a long time too. They intertwined with my dreams and at times, late in the night, if I was alone, I heard that sound of screaming far off in the distance haunting me.

The men were all grinning and laughing. They thought

the rape was funny. I pretended to join in with their humour, but I hated them for what they had done. They had no honour. I determined never again to take advantage of those weaker than myself and never to kill women or children. That these men were evil was clear, but my connection with them was making me equally guilty.

To do nothing and stand by as children are murdered is as bad as participating, and it was hard for me to come to terms with it even then. I wished I could kill them all but I had no way to do it. It was foolish thinking and I knew it. It would take even more than this to provoke me, and make me put fear away for the sake of honour.

Although we often ascribe things to fate, the truth, I think, is that to be passive in life, is to be weak. The strong change their destiny by taking opportunities and I will tell you how I became strong despite the weakness and passivity my life had hitherto followed.

CHAPTER IV

"Accept the things to which fate binds you, and love the people with whom fate brings you together, but do so with all your heart."

— Marcus Aurelius

After burning the farm, the men were in good spirits. It was as if the violence and wanton destruction created a fresh bond between them. There was much backslapping and laughter in the camp that night and they allowed me to test my new sword skills by practise with one of the men. He almost cut my head off amidst howls of inebriate laughter. They had started the barrels of wine from the farm and were all so drunk that the evening ended early, which I regarded as a mercy, for I realised now how much I hated them all. I dared not show it and I knew that somehow I had to escape.

The next morning we set off amidst bad hangovers and frayed tempers. The mood of the gang was grim. No one dared speak to Sartorius, for in his present state of mind, we all knew he would erupt with the slightest provocation.

One of the riders who had been scouting returned with news.

'Sartorius, there's a wagon approaching,' the man said. 'It looks fully laden and the driver is an old man. Looks an easy target.'

Sartorius halted the little column. He planned the ambush with care because, with experience, came caution. He was always afraid there might be soldiers nearby or the easy robbery was some kind of trap. The road wound around a grassy hill in a sharp bend where it came close to a copse of cypress and olive trees. The summit was invisible from the approach below because of a slight overhang. It was a quiet peaceful place, with birdsong and the fresh smell of dew on grass, reflecting the burgeoning sun.

He positioned two men with bows on the hill and others on horseback ahead on the road. The rest of us hid behind the trees adjoining the road. One of the men almost hit me for disturbing a pheasant that flew away cackling as if an army of hunters were chasing it. There was a gentle sloping spring shower racing the wind, as the horse and cart came into view around the bend. The driver was an old man with a wide brimmed hat and a dark blue cloak of thick wool. It seemed he felt the cold, for I saw him pull the cloak tight around himself.

He wobbled up and down as the cart negotiated the bumps in the little road, but he talked to the horse as he drove. I have always liked a man who talks to his horse. It means a kind of kinship with the beast and peace with the world at large; one can only gain that from close contact with animals. Of all creatures, horses are very sensitive to it.

The riders appeared without warning around the bend in front of the cart. I could feel my heart beating. My mouth felt dry. More of the brigands came up behind the old fellow's conveyance. At the same time, my group came out of the trees.

There was no escape. The old man sat immobile as an arrow stuck in the cart seat next to him. We were about a sword's length from him when the wide brimmed hat and blue cloak flew away. The sluggish old man became a very animated old man indeed. How he had drawn the sword so fast was a mystery to me, but there it was flashing in the morning sunshine. It emerged from the scabbard so fast it struck the first blow with the same movement.

It took the man on my right by complete surprise. He could not even raise his weapon to parry. I stepped back. The curved blade struck the brigand on the throat. The tip sliced though his larynx. He made a choking noise as his airways filled with blood. He fell to the ground, limbs twitching.

The old man, still using his sword, stepped with speed to his right putting the wagon between him and the archers on the hill. He was surrounded, but kept us all at bay by his rapid movements. Each man who dared stab at him received a wound of some kind. I knew I could not fight him.

He wounded six men and killed two. The fight ended when two of the brigands engaged him at once. Sartorius sneaked around the back of the cart and threw a rock, which hit the old man on the back of the head. It stunned him. He went down on one knee and the brigands closed in.

'I want him alive,' Sartorius screamed.

The men took hold of the almost unconscious old man and bound him. Sartorius approached and grabbed him by what little grey hair he possessed and pulled his head back.

'A real fighter, aren't you?' he said, 'we'll see what you're made of old dog—but later.'

They trussed the old man's hands and feet together behind his back and slipped a loop around his throat. He remained silent, passive, and immobile. The brigands examined the wagon. It contained empty barrels and some new farm tools but nothing of value to the brigands. They thought the cart might be useful so they kept it. The horse was a beauty. It was not a carthorse at all. It was a beautiful roan mare with the nature of a purebred racing horse, a rare thing indeed. Sartorius kept the horse for himself and saddled at once. The horse refused to move. He had to remove the saddle and replace it on his recently abandoned, unhappy, moth-eaten nag instead. The mare did however, consent for them to lead it away but let no-one ride her.

They burned the barrels and threw the farm tools on the blaze for good measure. It seemed to me their contempt was borne of their own idleness which prevented them from ever doing anything requiring hard work. To me, the brigands burning a man's means of earning a living seemed symbolic.

We trudged up into the hills again and found a gulley, sheltered and hidden from the roads far below. There we made camp. Not a proper fortified camp but a place where they lit a central fire. Sartorius knew how to make a camp but he was just too idle to bother. He felt safe in the hills.

They heated some sword blades in the fire and pulled out the old man. They freed his neck loop but left his arms and legs tie together. Sartorius cut off his tunic and the old man lay naked in the grass, his clothing in strips at his wrists. Scars covered his body. Most of them were on his arms and legs, but some were on his back. The ones on his back were parallel and it was clear someone has flogged him to the bone at some time in his life. I felt a strange kinship for the fellow, for it seemed clear to me he had experienced the punishments my Roman owners had threatened me with, all through my life as a slave.

The old man said nothing, I thought he was resigned to his fate, and I pitied him. Sartorius took up a sword. The tip was red-hot. Without any preamble, he placed it on the old man's inner thigh. The victim winced but said nothing. He stared at his torturer with contempt tinged with a cold anger.

'I know you come from a farm near here. Where is it?' he burned the old man again.

'If you don't tell us where your farm is and what valuables you have, you can look forward to three days of torture then I'll take your eyes,' Sartorius said.

He stood there with the smoking blade in his hand, looking huge, dangerous, and determined.

Once again, I experienced anger like when I killed my Master. It was a feeling of revulsion. These men had no honour. They were torturing a man who had given better account of himself than any we had encountered so far and I for one felt they should have given him an honourable death and not torture and blind him.

'Don't do this,' I said.

'What?' Sartorius said, 'what in Hades are you squeaking about you little rat?'

'You can't torture him; he is a warrior. It will bring bad luck,' I tried.

'When I want your opinion mouse, I'll ask for it. If you don't shut up, I'll do you next. Now run along and play some mousey games.'

'I won't let you torture this man.'

'I told you to shut up and now I'm going to kill you. You little jam-rag,' Sartorius said.

He turned on me with the hot sword he held in his hand. He raised it and struck at me. He missed because I was waiting for it. I jumped back and drew my sword, the way I had seen the old man do it. I struck a blow at the same time as I unsheathed my weapon. I thought this was quite clever not that it reached its mark. Sartorius stepped back and thrust at me with his gladius. I parried with success. He brought the hilt of his sword up under my chin. It connected. It connected with such force and speed I fell backwards and remembered little else.

When I awoke, they had tied my hands in front of me.

'He's waking up now, the idiot.' I heard the voice as in a dream.

'Well Mouse, what should we do with you? I would torture you and blind you like I'm going to do with the old man but it's a waste of time because you can't tell me anything I don't already know and I'm busy with the prisoner. I was starting to like you—know that? I treated you like a son and you betray me like this. For that, I'll let you go. You won't ever become one of us because you're too soft. Strip him; I'm going to give him a reminder of his days with our troop.'

They stripped me naked and held me face down. Sartorius took a red-hot blade from the fire and pressed it hard onto my left buttock. I now understood the old man's courage for I had none. It was like the fiery finger of Hephaestus himself. I never knew such pain existed. I screamed and shed real tears. I bear the mark of that sword even now.

I confess I fainted. They threw a bucket of icy water over me and revived me. They stood me up, for my legs would not support me. Cutting my bonds, they shoved me naked to the edge of the camp and kicked me out. I rolled down the hill and cut my back and legs on the rocks. I began making my way down the hill to the sound of a scream from the prisoner and cruel laughter from the brigands.

The pain in my buttock was still bad. I shed tears of anger and frustration. They streamed down my face but I still had the same feeling leading me to attack Sartorius in the first place lurking in the back of my mind. It might seem foolish for I was not a fighter but I did know a trick or two and one of them was the certain knowledge that all men, even brigands, sleep. I knew also they set a guard to watch in the night and I knew where they posted him. I could not be strong but I could be clever.

I hated these men, I also knew there was little I could do naked and unarmed as I was. Maybe I wanted to prove to myself that I was not a complete incompetent. It puzzles me still why I did it but I waited until it was dark, shivering in a thicket. Then I crawled up the hill making no sound. I could be silent because they had taken my sandals along with my clothes.

If Sartorius had not been such a lazy man he would have organised his camp in a true Roman way and dug a trench around it with wooden stakes to keep out any attackers. There was nothing to stop me from entering the camp at will except for one guard who was not expecting trouble. I was not brave by nature and I cannot conceive where I found such courage, but when you are young you imagine nothing can hurt you.

Silent as the grave into which I put him, I crept up behind Titus. I used a rock, which lay nearby. I clubbed him square on the side of the head. Just like my dead Master, I kept hitting him. It was clear I was getting good at hitting unwitting people on the head for he fell with little disturbance and lay still after the third blow.

I paused long enough to take his clothes and sandals. With pleasure, I put his sword into the scabbard now strapped to my waist. I could make out the covered cart by the faint half-light radiating from the dying embers of the fire. I circled and came to it from the outside of the camp.

Cutting the canvas cover with a knife, care of the now deceased Titus, I climbed into the wagon making as little noise as I could. The old man was in a bad way. His clothes still hung in strips from his wrists where they had tied him up. There was a gag of filthy cloth stuffed I his mouth. I removed the gag first. His wide, grey eyes glinted in surprise as they stared up at me. I cut his bonds and it was clear he had taken quite a lot of burns. He smelt of burnt flesh and found moving difficult. The trick now was to leave without pursuit.

The old man's name was Cornelius Nepos though I did not know it then. He showed remarkable powers of recovery for someone who looked so ancient to my eighteen-year-old eyes. He managed to rub his arms and legs. He slipped out of the wagon with almost the same ease with which I did. I followed.

I was about to object and say it was my rescue not his, when I realised what he was doing. In silence and stealth of which I was incapable, he moved across the camp. He made me stand at the far side. He took the knife with him. Kneeling at the first man's side, he held his hand over his mouth. He slit his throat. The man tried to struggle, but once someone severs the arteries in your throat, the struggles cease very soon. He went on to the next man. He must have killed five in complete silence. He got to the end of the camp where he reached the horses.

He talked to them in soft tones as I had learned to do long ago. Then he released all but his own roan mare and the best one of the rest. The horses wandered away quietly apart from two who stood their ground. The old man left them and without hesitation, mounted his mare. What a sight he was that night; an old man stark naked, sitting bare backed on his horse with a grimace of pain. The look on his face gave way to a faint smile of triumph, visible in the yellow flickering firelight.

The next thing that happened surprised me. The old man just rode the two horses across the sleeping men. A horse will not step on a man even if he is lying down in the dark, but one can train them to bite and kick, as a warhorse must in battle. These horses did no intentional harm to the confused men, but as they awoke in alarm, at least one received a kick in the face. The old man held the reins for me to mount the second horse and in the ensuing confusion, I jumped off a rock onto the horse's back. We rode through the camp again, causing further disorder and knocking down any in our path. We took the horses down the rocky slope and within minutes were on the road. I gave the old man the cloak I had taken from Titus' blood smeared body as we rode and asked him where we were going.

'You mean you had a plan to rescue me and didn't know where to go afterwards?'

'Well no,' I said. I felt I was as green as the grass either side of us as we rode.

'We need to lead them astray first then we cut across country to the Aretium road and then to my friend's farm. I cannot risk going home. They may follow us yet. By the way, who taught you to fight? Whoever it was he deserves flogging, you're hopeless! At least you can wield a rock!' He laughed at that and it was a pure clear sound piercing the frightening night with an inexplicable relief.

I could wield a lamp too, but I did not want to tell him that.

CHAPTER V

"Whether they give or refuse, it delights women just the same to have been asked."

— Ovid

We rode south for almost an hour. My horse was not fresh because of the previous day's riding and began to tire so we stopped for a little while. Before turning north, we swam the horses south in a small river then stuck to the opposite bank hoping we left no hoof prints on the bare rock for the brigands to follow.

Neither of us spoke. I was still smarting from the man's comments about my fighting abilities. I thought I had done very well considering he was facing torture and blinding, and I had returned to help him out.

The direction we took was north-west, towards the coast at Aretium. It was a long ride and took several hours. I had distained taking Titus' under garments out of some finer feeling which would never trouble me now and the result was that the horse upon which I rode, rubbed me raw. I was delighted when this torture ended. The burn on my buttock was well above the saddle area as luck would have it, but it also rubbed incessantly on the clothes, which became agonising in the end.

'Where are we going?' I asked during a short rest for the horses. We had not dismounted.

'I have a friend who lives between Aretium and the coast. We will be safe there. No long rests.' We rode on as the day dawned and the rising sun on the pink skyline threw hopeful shadows across the fields. The birds awakening in the dawn joined in a chorus, rising in volume until it was audible above the clatter of the horse's hooves. The warmth of a sunny, clear spring morning gradually replaced the cool night air.

The sun was well risen by the time we arrived. Cornelius and I dismounted as we approached the farm buildings. It was a large farming estate by Roman standards and the house was much grander and bigger than the one the brigands had destroyed. We approached the wall surrounding the farm buildings and dogs barked to announce our presence. We dismounted and approached the gate. A short, bald, stocky man in his fifties opened it brandishing a sword. He took one look at Cornelius, lowered his sword and embraced him.

'What on earth is an old war dog like you doing on my doorstep and dressed like that too?' he said in a deep and friendly voice.

The embrace had made Cornelius wince which was why our host, whose name was Valerius, had realised there was something wrong.

'Here hold the horses,' was all Cornelius said to me but I realised the old man was now falling towards me. I think he had managed to keep himself together up to that point by sheer will power and now the danger was past he just switched off.

Valerius and I carried the old man into the farmhouse and laid him on a couch. The farmer's wife was younger than he was. She was about forty and although her name was

Flavia, the Roman name for yellow, she had long, brown hair she wore swept up at the back of her head. She had been a beauty at one time, that was clear, and she was very nice to look at for a saddle-sore eighteen year old with no underwear. She had beautiful hazel eyes and a slim waist.

'Gods of Olympus, what have they done to him?' she said with tears in her hazel eyes.

'They tortured him with red hot sword blades,' I said, and anxious to show I was part of events, 'I managed to get him out though.' I should not have said that I suppose, but I was unable to resist appearing manly in front of the beautiful farmer's wife. The truth was that if the old man had been incapable of killing another five brigands and sneak across their camp undetected, then steal two horses, we would both have been dead. I did tell the truth when they fired questions at me as Flavia cleaned and tended Cornelius' wounds. Some of those burns were terrible.

'How Cornelius could have survived after what they did to him is a complete mystery to me,' I said. 'I only had the one burn and I screamed when they did it, I can tell you!'

'Here let me see it,' Flavia said to my abject horror and teenage embarrassment. 'I think you are very brave, so do not be embarrassed.' I soon found myself baring my burned buttock to this mature and beautiful woman. Although I felt the injury was an honourable one, I was red as a ripe cherry by the time she treated it with ointment and a dressing. I said nothing about the saddle sore; that would have taken things too far even for me.

'Cornelius managed to fight because he was once the most skilful gladiator in Rome. His previous life toughened him up and that hardness never goes completely. As you say, it is amazing he made it this far,' Valerius said. 'I'm sure he will tell you all about himself in time. So what's your story then?'

Unprepared for that, I mumbled about being caught and forced into the gang, but kept things as brief as possible. I did not tell them about being an escaped slave.

The burns took a long time to heal. I never understood why Cornelius did not seek vengeance for the suffering. I think it was because he had already suffered so much in his life, another episode meant little to him. One can expect a dog to bite or a cat to scratch because it is their nature. Cornelius told me later that experiencing torture from scum like Sartorius was what one must expect. It was just his nature and like anyone of limited intellect, Sartorius was unable to overcome what he was; a vicious, cruel, and greedy man.

'You must be very good friends,' I said to Valerius.

'Yes, very. I owe him much.'

'Owe him?'

'Yes, when we were new here, we had a farm hand. He worked well but after a few months, he approached me and told me he worked for the tax gatherers. I told him I did not care. I had always paid my dues and thought I had nothing to fear. He said he would report back to his Masters I was withholding taxes.'

'But you could prove you were in the clear, surely?'

'No, I was new to this farming business and many of the records were incomplete. The man threatened to ruin me and take the farm. I was in a quandary. Cornelius was visiting and I told him, in my distress, about the tax spy.'

'He killed him?'

'No, next morning, he called us out into the yard at the front of the farmhouse. He tied the man across a horse, then threatened to cut off his manhood amongst other things, if he did anything to us. I have never seen a look of such abject terror on a man's face as I saw on that spy's. I don't know what Cornelius said to him as he led him away but he never bothered us again.'

'Would he have killed him?' I asked.

'Cornelius would have killed him with no more thought than flicking away a fly. He is a hard man but a loyal friend. I owe him everything I have.'

'I know that. After what the brigands did to him I'm surprised he could ride here.'

'We'll see how he gets on now. Flavia is very good with wounds, even burns. She has patched him up before.'

'Before?'

'Yes, there was a time when he came back from Gaul and he had a bad wound in his leg. It had gone septic and one doctor had offered to cut it off, which he refused. We looked after him and he healed.'

Each day I sat at Cornelius' bedside and fed him broth, which Flavia prepared. I helped her change his dressings and he recovered from the general effects of his wounds in a week. Spending this time so close to an older and lovely woman was an exalting experience for a young man like me.

I had never had a woman then. I had fooled around a little with a female slave at the stables but it never came to any real sexual acts because they sent me to the house in Rome just before anything could come of it. Witnessing the carnal pleasures of my late Master had given me a revulsion for sex when I was in Rome, but human nature is kind, and allows us to change with our circumstances. It did not stop me having thoughts about Flavia.

At night, I went to sleep thinking of how it might feel to

touch her naked flesh and sometimes I would dream I lay next to her naked body. I had never had such an inspirational woman near me. She was always kind and friendly. My thoughts of admiration surfaced all the time. I looked at her with the wide eyes of youthful first love. I followed her around the house basking in her smile.

I made a stupid mistake then. The rashness of youth perhaps, or my own clumsy stupidity. It could have become a disaster, had it not been for the generous nature of my hostess.

Cornelius was sleeping and I sat in the peristylium on a couch, sipping wine that one of Valerius' slaves had brought me. I began to ponder my situation. This place was the best place I had ever been to. The people here treated me like a man. I was no longer a piece of furniture. No longer a slave.

An owl hooted far off to my left and I looked up at the starlit sky. The round globe of the moon looked down upon me and I wished it would grant me my wishes. There was a sound of a soft sandaled tread behind me. I turned to see Flavia, her figure outlined in the moonlight like some silver goddess to my young eyes.

'I can't sleep. I'm surprised you are still up Sextus.'

'I couldn't sleep either.'

She sat then next to me and smiled.

'I am so impressed with how you have cared for Cornelius. I know from what he said, he thinks you are very brave. You must forgive him if he does not express his gratitude. He has been through so much in his life I think he seldom expresses his thoughts.'

'I don't mind,' I said.

She reached forward and patted my hand. I took hers in mine and leaned forward to kiss her lips, my eyes closed. Her reaction surprised me. I felt a smart slap on my cheek. She stood up.

Looking down at me she said, 'What in Elysium were you doing you silly boy?'

'I, I…'

'Sextus, I am a married woman. Not only that, I am a Roman married woman. What were you trying to do? My husband is sleeping upstairs and you are trying to kiss me downstairs. You should be ashamed of yourself!'

'I… I'm sorry,' I said. I did not know where to look. I felt the heat of my cheeks and wished I were elsewhere, anywhere. 'Really, I am so sorry. I meant no harm. I think you are wonderful.'

She looked at me without speaking and I could not meet her gaze with mine. I studied the floor in abject misery. The silence was gloomy and dark.

Presently, I looked up. As she regarded me her face softened and she sat down beside me again.

'Sextus. I like you but not in that way. I can understand how you must feel. Perhaps you are inexperienced. I don't know, but you are very young. I will be a friend to you but I would no more want to kiss you like that, than I would run away from Valerius whom I love. I am very flattered but you cannot continue thinking of me in that way.'

I looked at her in silence.

'One day you will find a young woman of your own age and that will be right. You will know love too. Life is long and here and now is but a short moment in the pattern of our lives.'

I could still not bring myself to swallow the disappointment. I turned away and stood to leave.

'This will all be forgotten in the morning and we shall be

friends again Sextus. Good friends like before, you'll see.'

She left me there in my turmoil. I was hurting. Pushed aside by a woman I imagined I had loved. I sat for a few minutes before I took my shattered hopes to bed that night. My tired mind wandered, listless, between anger at the rejection and an understanding of the huge gap between my hopes built on nothing, and reality. How could I have been so stupid? A fine lady like that would no more feel attracted to a boy like me, than she would to a slave or a piece of furniture. Nevertheless, I thought I was a man, at least until that moment. I began to drift into sleep with the thought I could not face her in the morning. Perhaps I should pack my bag and leave before the house was awake.

In the morning, I awoke feeling tired. It was a fresh morning and I could hear birds beginning to raise their chorus outside the window of my cubiculum. There was a smell of baking bread and the sunlight shone through the open window. I began to wonder if I had ruined it all. How could I have imagined a woman like Flavia would accept the advances of an escaped slave?

Flavia was still friendly and kind. In my youthful truculence I resented the rejection and she must have realised why I was so taciturn. I did not run away and we stayed two more weeks before Cornelius was fit to travel to his farm.

On the morning of our departure, Flavia and Valerius stood at the gates and waved as we rode away. I looked over my shoulder and realised I still had feelings for that woman. It was not a missed opportunity for such unrequited lust has nowhere to go, in truth. It was a lesson I needed to learn but one I had to relearn many times in my long life.

We rode at a moderate pace hoping not to tire our mounts. I rode the horse we had stolen from the brigands.

At midday, Cornelius stopped to rest the horses. It was typical; he did not stop to rest himself or me. The day was overcast but bright and warm enough to ride without a cloak. We stopped at the side of the road to Ariminium in a green pasture where the horses could move around on a long leash. I sat on a rock, my feet damp and muddy as they dangled. A faint smell of jasmine wafted across the hills nearby and we sat at first in near-silence the only sound coming from a brook below us at the base of the hills. We ate cheese, bread and a handful of raisins provided by Valerius who had given us enough food for the three-day journey.

We ate in silence at first, and then we both spoke at once. He held his hand up for me to be quiet and said, 'You had better tell me about yourself and this time be honest or you may endanger us both. Is there anyone after you?'

I told him my tale. I told him everything including the murder of my master and the miserable things I had done to stay alive since then.

'Well that's a relief,' he said smiling.

'What's a relief? They must still be after me and could catch me anytime. I have no proof of who I am and they may have spread the word even this far from Rome. My Master was an important man.'

'No, I meant that at least there is no one dangerous after you. We can avoid the Aedile's soldiers easily. They may well search farms and send word to the cities but they are not looking for a man on a horse let alone two men. We can pass you off as my young nephew who lives with me on the farm. It is an isolated place and no one will question me. I owe you my life and it is a debt I will repay. I will teach you how to defend yourself; in time, I will teach you to kill in battle and in the arena for both are necessary and useful skills in a young man in your position.'

'Where is your farm?'

'Three days ride from here. My main concern is in case those brigands find it. They may want revenge and I have more there to protect than you know.'

'Know?' I said, 'I don't know anything because you don't tell me anything.'

'Perhaps that's because you haven't asked. I will tell you when we stop this evening, but now we ride.'

We mounted up and rode for another five hours at a reasonable pace then made camp in some fields. We ate a hot oatmeal porridge which Cornelius showed me how to make.

'In the legions we ate this all the time. We make it from oats or wheat flour, whichever is handy. It gives energy and on a march, there is always a risk meat will give you dysentery,' he said.

'Never had much meat before. Mostly we got scraps from the Master's leavings or a mash of vegetables and corn.'

'Didn't do you any harm. You seem to have grown big enough.'

'I was always hungry though.'

'My heart bleeds for you.'

'Well it wasn't nice.'

'Here, have a fig and shut up,' Cornelius said.

We ate some dried fruit and drank a jug of wine and water. The night air was chill and a gentle breeze started to blow across the field; the long grass leant in swirls and eddies around us. Cornelius told me part of his story, at least, as much as he felt I needed to know.

'I started life on a farm near Aretium and joined the legions at the age of sixteen. I signed on for twenty years and during the ten years I was with them, I fought for Rome in

Thrace and on the Rhine where there were many aggressive German tribes whom we stopped from crossing over to Gaul. They promoted me to Centurion after only five years because of my fighting skills.'

'Is that where you learned to fight? I saw what you did against those brigands. I've never seen anything like it even in the arena.'

'Wait on, I'll come to that. The way the legions fought has not changed much since Marius reorganised the army, although the cavalry are better armed and armoured than in Julius Caesar's time. Soldiers wear chain mail now but the centurions still stand separate from the ranks, so they're much more vulnerable to the enemy than men of the front rank of the century who shield each other as they advance. The centurions do a lot of one-to-one combat for that reason and only the strongest fighters survive a centurion's rank for long.'

'What happened then?'

'If you can hold your water a bit longer, I'll tell you, you young pup. In one battle, my Tribune ordered me to withdraw. He was a jumped up salesman and didn't know ass from elbow. It was an inappropriate order. I refused because it would have exposed the whole right wing of our legion. Refusing the order turned out to be in vain and the battle was lost. Afterwards, the Tribune had me court-martialled. I think they knew I was right and so they spared me the death penalty but they sent me to the Galleys for ten years to row my life away under the lash.'

He reached forward poking the fire with a stick. I could see on his face that the stirrings of his memories caused him pain.

'What happened?' I said.

'Damn your impatience!'

'Sorry, I only asked.'

'I will tell you but be still. Anyway, not many survived the galleys for more than five or six years but I was very patient. I think I lived for revenge and when they released me I found that Tribune and exacted my revenge by killing him and all his family. It remained unproven who had committed the crime. On suspicion I had done it, they still arrested me on a false charge and found me guilty. They sentenced me to the arena as a gladiator. I fought and killed in the arena for six years until I won my Rudis.'

'What's that?'

'You've never heard of it?'

'No.'

'It's a wooden sword awarded to gladiators who distinguish themselves. With it, I obtained my freedom. The Emperor Antoninus Pius presented it to me himself.'

'You must have killed a lot of gladiators.'

'Not really. Gladiators are expensive to replace. They take years to train. Usually when we lost, we spared each other. An almost fatal wound and they dispatched you after the games with a pointed hammer. I never got hurt too badly but I got cut a few times.'

'So you left the arena then?'

'No. I continued to fight in the arena and by betting on myself through intermediaries, with escalating amounts of money, I became rich. After I retired from the arena, I bought my farm and hoped I would live a quiet life for the rest of my days, but it was not to be.'

'No?'

'No. I had a brother who farmed in Gaul and I received word he had been killed and his farm taken over by a local governor. I went to Gaul for vengeance. I took revenge for my brother and brought home my only relative, my niece Livia. It is to protect her that I need to return to the farm as quickly as I can. That was also the reason they could never have persuaded me to tell Sartorius where the farm was, whatever they did to me.'

I reached for the wine. 'Sartorius won't give up you know. He's an evil man,' I said.

'My farm is only a day's journey from where the brigands attacked,' he said, 'So you can see the need for haste.'

'Do you think you can teach me to fight?'

'Of course I can. I was taught in one of the best gladiator schools in Rome.'

'Who taught you?' I asked. I was really just making conversation but his answer surprised me.

'A big blonde Gaul, who was called Barbato in the arena.'

'Is he still around?'

'No he's dead, killed in a match at a private party.'

'Who killed him then if he was the best?'

'I did.'

'You killed the man who trained you? Why?'

'You ask too many questions. I killed him because he would have killed me if I hadn't got him first. There would have been no hard feelings I'm sure,' he grinned as he spoke. 'For my part if he had got lucky, I don't think I would have borne a grudge either. We all knew any of us could be fighting each other at any time, which is why we tended to dispose of friends as quickly as possible if we had to, without all the exhibition you see in the arena these days. Sometimes they use a pig's bladder full of blood to make it look like they're dead. It's not like the old days you know—mind you, maybe it never was.'

There was a pause while I took in the meaning of what he had said and I know now he was describing the acceptance among true warriors that death will come in the end. I now think it is the manner of one's death that matters. Honour and courage are what mean most to me even now.

CHAPTER VI

"If you wished to be loved, love."

— Senneca

We rode for three and a half days. On the fourth day at midday, we crossed the crest of a green hillside and looked down into a broad expanse of cultivated farmland. On the opposite south-facing hill was line upon line of vines, all supported on canes and string supports. There were no obvious grapes visible yet from the distance at which we were looking. There were well-tended pastures and square irrigated fields in which the beginnings of a crop were growing. I looked for a farmhouse. I could make out a copse of old oak trees spreading up the far hillside, dense at the top. At the foot of the hill stood a heap of charred wooden stumps. There must have been some kind of structure there once, for there was a wall around the ruins that seemed untouched.

I looked at Cornelius and he said nothing. For moments, he sat motionless staring at the remains of the farmhouse below. The visible strain on his face told me to keep silent. He dug his heels into his horse's flanks with a suddenness that made me jump and we rode down the farm track as if Valkyries were chasing our souls to Valhalla.

We rode into the walled area around the burned-out house where they had torn the gates from their leather hinges. Three neat graves, recently dug, nestled outside the compound.

We dismounted and examined the area. Cornelius said nothing. There were fresh footprints around the graves, but I knew the brigands did not bury their dead. Someone had been here, even I could tell that. Cornelius remounted his horse and said, 'Thank the Gods she's safe.'

It was all he said to me but I followed him as his horse climbed the slopes to the oak copse behind the farmhouse.

'Livia! Livia, it's me!' he called. 'Sextus, go back down, she's probably spotted you and won't know whether you are one of them or not.'

He called to her again as I rode out of the copse. I dismounted and waited with my horse. I spoke to him, rubbing his face with my hand and I ran my fingers through his plaited mane. He was a good horse that—steady, but no good for a warhorse since he was too small and his legs a little too thin.

Presently Cornelius emerged from the copse with a girl carrying a bow and a quiver of arrows. I have never seen her equal to this day. She was tall and slender, smaller than I was, but tall for a Roman. Her long blonde hair hung to her shoulders and strands of it lifted in a gentle motion in the spring breeze. She wore leggings like a Gaul and a short tunic of green wool with a red, decorated, embroidered hem. Her face was thin and angular but when she smiled it made her look like Venus herself. Her brown eyes held an impish humour when she looked at me. It hit me like one of Jupiter's bolts from above. I became tongue-tied, awkward and clumsy in her presence and wanted nothing in the world more than to have her smile at something I said or did.

'What's a boy like you doing riding with a warrior like Cornelius?' her voice was deeper than I expected but its timbre added to her attractiveness. 'Have you come to work or just passing through?'

'He saved my life when I was captured by the filth that did this.

She smiled at me then.

'Sounds like you have a tale to tell too. They came three days ago. I shot one but realised I couldn't fight against all of them, so I hid in the place we made and told the others to scatter. I found their bodies yesterday. I had to stay hidden in case they were watching. I buried what was left of the slaves. They raped Julia.'

Her eyes moistened and given half a chance I would have put my arms around her. She would probably have punched me on the nose if I had tried so it is as well I was too dumbstruck by her presence to move.

'I have to go to the Aedile. He might send some equites to ferret them out. They know where we live now and they will most likely return. I killed some of them and they must have wanted revenge.'

'Agreed,' I said, my with voice a little too loud. I flushed and with my pale freckled skin, it would have been obvious to both of them. Livia looked at me with puzzlement.

'I need Sextus to learn to fight or he won't be much use to us. I'll teach him to defend himself first and you can teach him to use a bow. Sextus my lad, you're going to become a warrior.'

We camped inside the farm compound that night and the next day, Cornelius left to go to Ariminium to arrange to have the house re-built. Cornelius built the original house himself out of wood and he had intended to have it rebuilt properly with stone even though it would take longer. He needed to purchase the stone and obtain the help of a builder, which would necessitate going to the city. Cornelius also intended to inform the authorities of the burning. There was he said, not much hope of anything coming of it but it was worth a try.

Before he left, he gave me some exercises to practise; he showed me the first part of a twenty-part exercise in sword-play.

'Practise and practise until it becomes a reflex—it is as simple as that,' he said.

He rode away and left me sword in hand, practising drawing my blade and striking straight in front of me in one move. This was what I had seen Cornelius do when the brigands attacked and I remembered the speed with which he had dispatched the first of them. I repeated the moves as Cornelius had instructed.

Livia spent time trying to salvage anything she could from the debris of the burnt out house. There was very little of value and in the end, she gave up and watched me practise my sword-work. She gave me occasional pointers since, although she was not a sword-maiden or anything like that, Cornelius had taught her to look after herself with such a weapon.

At midday we ate and she looked at me with curiosity. She said, 'What's that mark on your head?'

'I've no idea what it means. I have had it there all my life but only recently saw it when I had my head shaved to try to look inconspicuous in Rome.

'You shaved your head and you thought it might make you inconspicuous? Not a very impressive disguise was it?'

'It was the best I could think of at the time.' I said.

'It looks like one huge encircling snake,' Livia said examining my scalp, 'I have seen something like that before on a

German warrior when I lived in Gaul but it was much smaller and only on one small patch. He was reputed to be a prince of the Franks.'

'Who are they?'

'A German tribe way up in the North just on the other side of the Rhine. Don't you know anything?'

'They didn't teach me much about my people, but maybe that was to stop me wanting to escape. I do remember a tall blonde man with plaited hair carrying me most of the way to Rome when they first took me there, maybe he was German but I really don't know,' I said.

'Sounds like we are working out a little of who you really are, maybe you are German.'

'When do you think Cornelius will be back?'

'Maybe after sunset.'

'I'm glad he trusts me with you, a lot of people wouldn't.'

'I can look after myself thanks, even with a big goat like you!' she laughed and indicated I should stand. 'Attack me.'

'That wouldn't be a nice thing to do,' I said.

'Go on, try to strangle me.'

I tried to grab her by the throat and she just evaded me with ease as if I was a three year old.

'Come on, try harder!' she was getting impatient now.

When I did try harder, she took my wrist and bent it up and back in such a way I could neither strike her with my other hand, nor could I straighten my wrist. She forced it further and further over my shoulder until I was flat on my back, in agony. She let go then and laughed.

'It's a simple trick my uncle showed me. It can control any size of person, because it puts your attacker's wrist in a position where he can't use the muscles. Try it on me.'

With delight, I tried it on her, but she pulled me in such

a way that she tripped me over her leg and we both fell laughing on the green turf. Our eyes met and all at once the laughter was gone.

What I saw there startled me. It was a rare, real beauty and it paralysed me. She must have felt something too for she also became silent. We remained like that sharing a moment in time and then she looked away, embarrassed. She said, 'You had better get on with your sword practise and I will do some bow work.'

We said very little after that for quite some time but it was clear something had passed between us and I suppose we both realised there might be consequences. I began to think about what I felt and that feeling kept coming back to me whenever I looked at her. The Gods play tricks on us sometimes and for sheer mischief they do well. I have never experienced such strong emotions for a woman since the time I spent with Livia. For a young man of my age, being with her was exhilarating.

She showed me how to use a bow and how to shoot at targets with accuracy. It was not so much a process of aiming but more a feeling of kinship with the target, which once achieved allowed you to point and shoot. A certain feeling comes to a good archer when he releases the arrow. He knows it will reach its target as soon as it leaves the bow.

We practised various techniques all day until, after an evening meal of oatmeal and fruit with watered wine, we fell asleep at opposite sides of the fire. I went to sleep with my mind filled by vivid images of her and thinking I would always want to be at her side.

Cornelius returned during the night. He did not wake us but lay down by the fire. Next morning we ate fruit with bread soaked in watered wine whilst the birds around us sung a greeting to the early morning sun.

'So did you go to the Aedile?' I asked.

'Yes but he says he has too few men to let them go out into the hills chasing brigands,' Cornelius said.

'So what will you do?'

'We will have to ready ourselves in case they return.'

'Three against eleven? Not very good odds are they?' Livia said.

'No, but defending, we have a chance.'

'You think they'll come soon?'

'I hope it won't be for a long time, Sextus here needs to learn how to fight, and it is not a skill acquired quickly, or easily. Years would be better'

One of us kept watch all the time. We divided the nights up into three equal shifts. None of us slept on watch because we knew our lives depended upon remaining vigilant.

The time passed. I learned how to handle a sword and shoot a bow and I was making progress after a month. The training was intensive. I occupied the mornings with stretching and stamina training. I spent the afternoons learning specific exercises with a sword in a set pattern. I practised each move until I had perfected it and then added to the ones learned before. This continued until I could perform twenty strokes of different types consecutively. The secret is not just to have set moves, but also to know when to put two or three together depending on your opponent. The practise made me fast in the end, but I knew it took many years for most people. In my case, I was beginning to learn in almost three months.

'Sextus my boy, you have learned much, but it's only now we can start sparring. I'm going to teach you to defend yourself,' he said. He threw me a sword and stood with his blade gripped in both hands in front of him.

The last stage of my training came when Cornelius taught me how to kill with a sword. It is a lesson I have never forgotten to this day.

'The throat, the neck, the groin and almost anywhere on the chest are killing points providing you are stabbing,' he said, 'but if you want to slow your opponent down the back of the knee is a very good wound to inflict. There is also an artery and if you wait your time, your opponent will bleed out enough to weaken and slow him down. If there is no helmet, a direct blow to the head is quite good too. Avoid stabbing in the abdomen. It leads to a slow and painful death but they can still fight a long time even with entrails hanging out. Remember that.'

He showed me how to obtain a kill even when you are lying down and your opponent is standing above you. We sparred and practised in slow motion until my arms were leaden weights and my legs trembled with fatigue. The weeks passed in this way; fighting, running, training and each session became more rigorous and wearing. After several hours of this weapons training, Cornelius would leave me with Livia to practise archery and at the end of the day, to run for an hour with her. As I ran with the moist grass beneath me I remember thinking this was all foolishness. I had never fought anyone and perhaps the brigands would never return. It would mean I would never have to fight or kill. It was a false optimism. We live in dangerous times and a man must know how to defend himself, something I learned with the passage of time.

It was on one of those fitness runs I first came closer to Livia. We had run for half an hour or so. She stopped, breathing hard and I was pleased to have a chance to catch my breath too. We stood looking at each other. Our eyes met and it solved the puzzle existing between us since the first day I saw her. We both understood what we wanted. I reached forward with both arms and drew her to me. She resisted a little at first then tilted her head back and our lips met in a moist, breathless kiss making my heart sing. We stood in the forest with bird song in our ears and hearts.

We explored each other's bodies and lay in the green sward holding each other and making love. It was the purest and most genuine love I have ever felt and I despair of ever feeling those emotions again for it was the expression not only of love and lust, but also of youthful naivety.

We lay in each other's arms and talked, caressing each other as we did so.

'Sextus, I'm afraid. If those brigands come again they'll kill us all.'

'Cornelius knows what he is doing.'

'He says he does but his age is against him. I think he is slowing down and I don't want to lose him.'

'I'll help.'

'You? You are learning fast but my uncle always says experience counts for more than strength or speed. He has that but he is definitely slowing down and maybe he thinks he is more dangerous than he really is,' Livia said.

'I think he is the most dangerous man I have ever met. He moves with his sword like a cat and he strikes like a snake. I wouldn't like to fight him with any weapon.'

'Perhaps you're right.'

'Cornelius is not thinking about vengeance or punishment; he is trying to protect you. He loves you as I do.'

'You? You think you love me? We've made love once and known each other for a few months and you think you love me? You're as mad as Caligula!'

She stood up, dressed, and began running back to the farm. I dressed and followed but was baffled by her behaviour. One moment she was making love to me, the next she was running away.

I ran through the wood and into the open field, down a slope of loose rock and onto the farm track that led to the beginnings of the stone buildings Cornelius had commissioned. The walls were part-built and we could see the farmhouse taking shape a little more every day. The builders came almost every day and I often wondered if it was their presence keeping the brigands away. Perhaps Sartorius would never come back.

CHAPTER VII

*"Since love grows within you, so beauty grows.
For love is the beauty of the soul"*

— Saint Augustine

Livia and I communicated less over the next week. Every time I came near her, she shied away. I wanted her again desperately but I was unable to come close enough to begin any kind of physical contact and she hardly spoke to me.

With the three of us living together, moments when Livia and I were alone were rare. Cornelius had to travel into town once a week to make payments on the building work and it always left Livia and me surrounded by the builder's slaves who glared at us and could see anything we did, or hear any conversation around the rising brickwork.

It so happened that Cornelius was in Ariminium and the builder's slaves were having a rest day. For once, we were alone and the only company we had was the horses in the paddock and the sound of birds chanting the approach of autumn. We sat on opposite sides of a small fire on which our midday meal was cooking. I should say burning for neither of us paid it the attention it was due.

'Livia, what is happening?'

'You just can't understand because you are a man.'

'Please talk to me; I want to understand, if you will just tell me.'

'I cannot love someone who thinks of nothing but killing. All you do all day is practise swordsmanship and killing. It's ridiculous. You aren't even a soldier. It will get you killed in the end and I don't want to be left on my own. You and Cornelius talk about protecting me but you don't see what will happen to me if neither of you survives the attack from the brigands when it comes.'

'They may never come back! Anyway, Cornelius is the cleverest fighter I can ever imagine meeting. He can fight, plan and make things happen. I have no real fears, because I trust him. I can't understand why you don't.'

'Naturally I trust Cornelius, but I can't help feeling something bad will come of all this. We should leave here until the Aedile can remove the brigands. I don't want to die here and I don't want either you or Cornelius to die either.'

'I can speak to him, maybe we could move into Ariminium until the house is finished?' I said.

'Will you promise?'

'Of course I will,' I said.

She crossed from the other side of the fire and sat next to me, putting her head on my shoulder. She began to weep and her tears felt to me as if she tore them from my heart as well as hers. We began to caress each other and sank into each other's arms gaining comfort from the closeness. It was a long night and we made love many times but it was always the closeness which seemed to matter not the physical pleasure.

I remember that dawn still. All those years have passed yet I remember it. The burgeoning sunlight crept into the valley. It lit up the opposite slope in golden hues and the shadows in which we sprawled seemed longer and longer as the brightening sunlight approached. We lay in each other's arms warm and content in each other's silence, as if no other place existed in the world. The cool, green, valley surrounded us and its beauty made our love seem almost tangible. It enveloped us. We walked hand in hand, naked in the sunlight, enjoying the warmth and the closeness only two young lovers can enjoy.

We ate then dressed almost reluctantly and I felt as if I was in a dream, a beautiful dream and I wished it would never end.

We tried to practise with our weapons but it seemed a thankless task and within a short time, we found ourselves making love again. We both slept afterwards, the night's pleasure taking its toll.

I awoke with a blade at my throat. I hardly realised what it was, but a voice soon appraised me of the danger.

'Don't move you little rat!' the voice held clear malice. 'Get up slowly. If I have any trouble, I'll fix you nicely. There's a show to watch.'

As I rose, I saw there were three men. I recognised two of them, a third was a stranger, but he had no less malice in his eyes.

The two nearest to Livia grabbed her by the arms. She was silent. They pulled her a few yards away and pinned her to the ground. Their intentions were obvious. One lay across her top half. The other was exposing himself, ready for the rape. He knelt next to her.

Again, I felt a rage akin to that which led to my Master's death all those months before. The man holding the blade to my throat was watching the evolving rape with mesmeric fascination. His distraction gave me an opportunity.

I moved fast, raising my left arm and deflecting the blade at my throat. A superficial cut on my forearm was, after all, better than a cut throat. I twisted. My clenched right fist flew upwards. I hit him with all the strength I could muster striking him full square on the tip of his chin. His head jerked backwards. It was a blow worthy of Rugio. In one second, I took his blade and turned to the two would-be rapists.

The brigand holding Livia down did not even look up. The man undressing tried to stand. With a speed now second nature, I slashed the blade across his throat. A great gout of blood, with part of his windpipe flew away to my left. He made a gurgling sound. His face turned purple as his lungs filled with blood and no air came to him to relieve his choking.

I swung the sword with a single continuous movement reversing my grip, to my right and down. The third man looked up. The last thing he ever saw was the point of the sword entering his eye socket. It penetrated and buried itself in the base of his skull. I kicked his dead, twitching body away. Stooping, I helped Livia to her feet. The fight had taken seconds only. It was only at that moment I realised I had killed two men with no help, completely naked and with only a cut on my forearm.

These stupid men had no expectation I would fight back. They left me alive to make me witness the rape, but they were so impatient they had failed to tie me up.

'You're hurt,' Livia said.

The note of tenderness in her voice brought back all that had gone before since Cornelius left. I put my arms around her and felt the ultimate in relief at the lucky escape.

'You were so brave,' she said.

'No, I was angry and it is not a wise thing to give in to, according to Cornelius.'

'There is a difference between losing your temper and battle fury. It is battle fury making you fight; losing your temper obscures all the training and makes for weakness. Here, you're bleeding, let me clean the wound.'

'I would rather lie with you and that would take all pain away.'

'Don't be silly. Let's get you patched up before we even talk about such things.'

'This one is still alive. We'd better tie him up,' I said.

We trussed him up in the same way I had seen them tie Cornelius. I made sure he could not wriggle free. Livia bound my wound and it stopped bleeding. There was no serious damage. The bone of the outside of my forearm had taken the force of the cut and there was no damage to nerves or tendons.

'What do we do with him?' asked Livia.

'Keep him like that until Cornelius gets back, he may want to question him.'

'You don't mean torture?'

'No, of course not. I may have a killer instinct but I never was one of those brigands. They would do it of course, but Cornelius isn't that sort of man.'

'I can't stop shaking,' Livia said.

I put my arm around her and said, 'Maybe it's because you're completely naked?'

She punched me affectionately and the humour seemed to dissolve some of the horror of what went before. She was a strong woman that one.

After we dressed, we sat waiting for Cornelius. The sunlight faded from the sky and clouds on the horizon showed red and pink as we lit the fire for comfort as well as cooking.

We ate well that evening, as if the danger had whetted

out appetites. We roasted a pheasant Livia shot the day before. It was a little too soon and we would normally have hung it for a week or so. It tasted very good anyway. We ate bread with it and drank watered wine.

We had to water and feed our prisoner and he needed the latrine so we allowed him to walk and removed the gag. His name was Minius and he was an unprepossessing man, with long arms and short bowlegs. Beneath his beard lurked more lice than I have had in my lifetime and he was constantly trying to rub his chin on his shoulder to itch his face since we had tied his hands. His squat stature and his barrel chest matched his ugly face.

He had joined the brigands in the hills after an enemy had burned down his farm. He acquired the enemy through not paying his gambling debts and he had hoped he would make enough money after Sartorius took him in to establish a normal life. I almost felt sorry for him until it dawned on me he was the one who had held the sword to my throat and was unable to take his eyes off the two trying to rape Livia.

We tied him up again, watered the horses, and fed them. Dragging the two bodies up to the edge of the oak trees, we left them for the animals.

Two of the horses were just nags, but the third was a stallion, broad in the chest and tall with sturdy legs. It was not a great horse because it had a hip problem making it look cow-hocked but it was clearly a creature with stamina if not speed. I rubbed the horses down for it was not their fault their riders were wicked. The stallion had a saddle sore, which I could smell from several paces. I made a paste of moss and herbs and dabbed it gently on the sore. The horse enclosures were still standing so I put them in there for the night. The stable had burned with the rest of the farm buildings.

The prisoner denied us any privacy. The situation felt artificial. We talked for a while during the night and I stood watch for the first few hours and Livia for the next.

The next morning, Livia woke me with a hot cup of water and wine. Cornelius had not arrived during the night and we began to be concerned. We ate and tended the prisoner. Having this ugly man trussed up with us became more and more of a burden and an inconvenience but neither of us could see a way to release him and ensure he would not merely return to Sartorius and bring the whole gang back to us.

'What do we do with you?' I said to Minius. 'I can't let you go and there is no promise you could give that would persuade me to release you.'

'Please let me go. I beg of you. I will go back to Ariminium and I won't bother you again. I give you my word, but please don't kill me.'

There were genuine tears in his eyes and I once again felt sorry for him. Livia and I looked at each other.

'If we let him go he will go back to Sartorius, he'll bring them back here. We ought to kill him,' I said.

'But we can't just kill him, trussed up like a rabbit. We have to let him go. Perhaps we can take him most of the way to Ariminium and leave him on foot,' suggested Livia.

'I still don't trust him,' I said. 'I suppose if we take him to Ariminium he won't have any way of getting back and if we blindfold him he will have less idea of the way back.'

It sounded like a good idea. So in our naivety, we blindfolded him and sat him facing backwards with his hands tied behind his back on one of the nags. I mounted the stallion and Livia rode her own horse, another roan mare similar to

Cornelius' horse.

Livia rode behind and I tethered Minius' horse to the back of mine. We rode east until a signpost indicated the way to the town. We dropped the man off in the outskirts of town. I now know I should have killed him like the dog he turned out to be.

CHAPTER VIII

"Festina lente"
(Make haste slowly)

— Emperor Augustus Caesar

There was a warm sun in the sky by the time we turned our horses round to return to the farm. The road we followed rose sharply in places but proceeded in a straight line to the west. It took two hours of easy riding to reach the valley in which Cornelius had made his home. We talked all the way there and enjoyed each other's company. I told her about life in Rome. She for her part told me of life in Gaul and described the local people and the customs. We laughed a lot I recall. She was wonderful company, witty, beautiful, and interested in me, more than anyone had ever been. I love her still.

I could hear a chaffinch warbling in a thicket as we rode past. The dusty road meandered beneath our horses' hooves, and for once I had time to look around. It was still verdant land, olive groves and vineyards, fields of corn and small farmhouses all around us. I imagined how it would be living here with Livia and the prospect seemed idyllic. To work and produce for oneself is a privilege only a slave or an ex-slave can truly appreciate. Perhaps the freedom to choose is all that matters. As a slave, I had no right to decide anything and perhaps that was why I valued my time here so much with Livia and Cornelius.

We chatted about many things as we rode and it was like listening to Juno herself. I began to idolise Livia. How could I help myself?

She explained about the politics and the tribes in Gaul and we discussed how the Divine Julius had conquered almost all of Gaul, his campaign culminating in the great battle at Alesia against Vecingetorix. Her description of how the Romans had treated the defeated Gauls stirred deeply submerged emotions in me. The true story made me feel very sorry for the Gauls. It all seemed strange to me. I had no experience of life anywhere but Rome and the estate at Ariminium. I still did not feel free. I had spent all my life as a slave. The thought I could now go anywhere my fancy took me, seemed strange beyond my wildest imaginings. Such things can happen with enduring slavery. Slaves think there is no other world but the one their Masters allow them to see in the fetters binding them to their owners. I felt as if I was setting sail on a vast ocean with nothing to guide me apart from my love for Livia. That was my only anchor apart from Cornelius, but I had not expected my relationship with him to be permanent until now.

'Will you always stay with us on the farm?' Livia asked.

'Anything, as long as I am with you,'

'Do you think it is wise to stay here so close to where your Master and his people have land? You could be spotted any time at all and the future is not comfortable for an escaped slave.'

'I don't care, I would risk a hundred deaths to be at your side,' I said, sounding to my ears at least, like a hero.

'You're silly,' Livia said, smiling, 'you need to go north and find your own people. I think they will welcome you because the mark on your scalp must mean something to them. In any case you need to know if you belong with them or with the Romans.'

'There are a lot of tribes in Germania, Livia. I don't have the slightest idea who my people are and I know even less about how to find them. I can't just march up to a German town and start saying do you have tattoos on your heads, can I?'

'You could always be a bit more subtle and make some tactful enquiries. You will need to learn the language.'

'The only language I need is Latin; I hardly remember any of my native tongue. I do recall a few words but they mean little to me.' I said.

'Don't you remember anything about where you were born?'

'I remember my mother, she was soft and gentle. I remember a little of my father, he was big and strong and used to pick me up with one hand and hold me up over his head. I remember the village I grew up in and some faces but nothing else really. I was very young.' I said.

We entered Cornelius' valley. There was still no sign of the old man. 'I hope nothing has happened to him, I said.

'Me too,' Livia said. 'Do you think he has been attacked?'

'If I know him he's the one doing the attacking and he should be doing it with me. It's not fair to leave me out!'

'All we can do is wait. I don't like the idea of staying inside the wall to-night, after this morning I think we should hide.'

'Warriors don't hide,' I said, 'it isn't honourable.'

'Well, honourable or not, we hide in the oak trees to-night when we sleep, otherwise we have to stay awake all night.'

We cooked, ate, and made love by the fire. As the stars appeared we packed up our gear and found places in the oak trees where, from the hill, we could observe the walled area around the growing farmhouse. We alternated watches and as the dawn approached and Livia slept, I saw him.

Cornelius approached the farm compound slowly; he looked around and waited a short distance from the gate. Faint silver moonlight illuminated him and I could make out his shadow as he dismounted. For what seemed an age he simply stood waiting and listening. I called to him and he looked up. Mounting his horse, he rode up to the copse. He looked old and tired but I knew it was only a thin veneer.

'Well I'm glad to see you. I hoped you would have been sensible and hidden. I think the brigands may be coming. I saw three of them. I recognised one from when they entertained me at their camp. They saw me and ran. I tracked three of them coming in this direction but the trail ran through a river and I lost them. I spent most of the day looking for tracks but had no luck until just outside the valley and I began to fear the worst.'

'We've had our little adventure too,' I said. I told him about the three men and the result of our encounter with them.

'You let him go? Why?'

'We felt sorry for him. There isn't much he can do to us from Ariminium and he has no transport.'

'They are all dangerous. You should have killed him. Did he tell you where they are hiding?'

'We didn't ask. We assumed he wouldn't tell us and we had no way to make him say. We couldn't use torture. It would be dishonourable,' I said, with pride creeping into my voice.

'Curse you for a young fool,' Cornelius said. 'They would have tortured you if the positions were reversed, wouldn't they?'

I looked at him in silence, then apologised. We woke Livia.

'They've split up, so perhaps they won't come here,' Livia said.

'We can't take that chance,' Cornelius said.

'I think we should go to town and stay there until the Aedile sends soldiers.'

'You are laughably naïve. The Aedile has no men to send on wild goose chases in the hills.'

'Then what do we do? Wait here for them to come and find us?'

'Exactly. There can't be more than eight of them now. You killed two and the third won't be back you assure me. If Livia takes down even two of the remaining eight it leaves three each. Are you up to it?'

I swallowed. I had no real concept of what it would be like to fight superior numbers. I had no experience. All I did was nod.

'You're mad Uncle!' Livia said. 'Sextus can't fight those numbers even if you can, and you're getting old. This is lunacy.'

'We have little choice. If we hide in Ariminium, we will never know when it's safe to return. We have to fight. Our backs are against the wall and I think bad odds or not, we have little choice,' Cornelius said.

'How do we do this?' I said, 'We can't just stand in the open. They are probably mounted anyway.'

'We narrow the odds. We don't need to make it easy for them. We can stay up near the tree line. Livia can use her bow and I'm not a bad shot either. What about you?'

'Yes I can use a bow, ask Livia.'

She nodded and I could see she was tense. My mouth felt dry just thinking about a battle. I could feel my bladder demanding attention. I said nothing about my anxiety to Cornelius. I knew he would make a joke of it and I was now too worried to be tolerant.

'We have a little work to do before they arrive,' Cornelius said.

'How do you know when they will come?'

'I don't, but we need to assume it will be soon. Better to have a plan and not need it, than need one and not have it.'

'What do you mean by work?'

'You are digging a trench, Livia is going to keep watch, and I will direct operations.'

'Direct operations?'

'Yes, I'm an old man. I can't dig,' Cornelius said, rubbing his back.

'You look pretty sprightly to me.'

'Now, now, Sextus.'

'All right, where do I dig?'

Cornelius' plan was simple. We fortified the entrance to the tree line. I dug deep trenches on the approach up the hill. They were narrow holes really but deep enough to make a horse trip or break a leg if the rider took it fast over them. I covered each trench in turf and they were invisible at ten paces.

Livia strung ropes across the spaces between the oak trees so a rider could not pass through except in one area, which we were to use as a killing ground. The plan would work, as long as our attackers did not come over the hill behind us. Cornelius said we had only to run down the hill and the horse trenches would do their work anyway, but I had my doubts.

Evening came and I was tired and my back ached from the digging. We lit a fire in the compound near the partly constructed house and retreated to the copse. I looked at the flames, their warmth inviting, and the thought of hot food was compelling too, for the temperature was dropping at night now autumn was setting in. I heard an owl hooting. He kept up his call most of the night to my intense irritation. I spent a sleepless night. It was only on my watch that I felt like sleeping. I stayed awake, needless to say, for our lives depended on forewarning.

Nothing happened for three days.

Then they came.

CHAPTER IX

"Anger is a short madness."

— Horace

Donar, the God of thunder, battled giants in the sky above us as we sat among the oak trees, watching the farm. I did not know that was what was happening then, for I was a stranger to the true Gods in those days. I confess the thunderclap above and the sheet lightning lighting up the entire hillside frightened me. The suddenness made me jump. Rain fell in torrents so thick we could barely see in front of us. Our heavy, wet, goose-greased cloaks emitted a musty horse-smell and my leggings clung in sodden grips to my thighs like so many fingers squeezing my legs. We had wrapped our weapons in cloths soaked in olive oil to protect them from rust, but I was aware we would use them soon enough to prevent that. The scar on my buttock ached and I wondered whether the old man's scars ached too.

We tethered our mounts among the trees behind us. Cornelius felt it was a wise precaution in case things went awry. The booming thunder made the horses nervous, so I walked over to them and gently stroked my stallion's neck, talking in a deep voice that he found comforting. I had not named him. I began to ponder what name I should give him as we stood there in the dripping wood. The man I became in years to come would have called him Sleipnir to honour

Wuotan but I was a Roman then and could think of no honourable name apart from a Roman one. I decided to call him Ursus, which in the Latin tongue means bear, for I imagined he was fearless, which he was not.

I was wet and not a little cold. Dusk was approaching when Livia saw them. Her keen eyes could spot a hare running three hundred yards away in the dusk and I knew it was no false alarm. Panic grabbed me and my heart began beating as if it wanted to escape from my chest. I tried to swallow but no spit came.

We could see them approach the wall around the farm-house. Three of them dismounted. I counted seven men and wondered why they were one short. None of them looked like Sartorius. The three men emerged from the building and remounted. They began to look around in the rain, which was slackening off now. Presently, one of the men shouted. It was too far away for me to make out what he said but he began pointing up to the tree line and they all began to ride up towards us.

Our plan was going wrong already. The rain had soaked the bowstrings and I doubted whether my bow would function at all. Livia had spares tied in parcels of oiled skin but my hands were so wet that mine rapidly stretched beyond its normal tension as I strung my bow.

We stood there hoping we were out of sight and waited. They were twenty paces from us and I knew I could not miss. Livia fired her bow and a man fell from his horse. The others began to ride harder. Two of them stumbled on my pits. One horse lay screaming unable to stand and in its struggles must have damaged its rider, for he did not get up. The second fallen rider was up in a second and had drawn a curved sword. He dodged and weaved through the bushes keeping low. I thought him an impossible target. I heard Livia's bow twang and that brigand fell with an arrow projecting from his face.

The odds were narrowing. Four men left, they were still mounted, and only a few paces away. Cornelius brought one down with an arrow. I did not see where the dart hit him. Livia, as planned, ran to the horses. She hid behind a broad oak trunk. A rider was upon me. He reached down with his sword extended. I sidestepped and parried as he rode past. With my heart in my throat, I cut his horse as it flew past me. I hated that, but I wanted to live. The horse slowed but did not stop. I was vaguely aware of Cornelius swinging a spear and a man falling to the ground. Falling from a horse can be a long tumble. The man did not get up. Cornelius felled a second with his spear. I was dimly aware of him pulling it bloodied, out of the screaming, wriggling man.

The last rider had passed us both. He turned his mount. He rode straight at me. I ducked fast behind the tree. He did not come around it. Cornelius had thrown his spear with an accuracy I could never have mimicked. It skewered the man through the chest from behind. I came around the bole of the tree to see Cornelius grinning in the gloaming. The man whose horse I had injured, was still mounted but was almost stationary. His horse had slowed and it was limping towards us. I waited for him.

It was still raining and I was aware of drops of water running down my face. I was ready. I knew I could take him. Nothing happened. He just sat there. The horse limped forwards. The rider remained motionless. I saw Livia behind him. I realised then why he was immobile. The point of an arrow projected from his chest. I lowered my sword and began to relax.

I stepped forward to speak to Livia when I heard it. I had never heard a sound like it before. It was a distillation of sheer bestial fury. A deep and growling noise. I looked up the slope to seek its origin. I realised then why there were only seven men.

Sartorius had ridden around us and was charging down the slope. In his right hand he held a cavalry spear and in the left a shield. His helmeted head sat upon his shoulders as if he had no neck and the bulk of his huge, broad, squat, frame seemed an impossible weight for his mount. He held the reins in his teeth.

A sudden comprehension of something I should have known dawned in my stupid mind. Livia stood there. In his path. She was smiling and looking at me as if oblivious to the war-cry behind. Her outstretched hand beckoned me. I called out, I know not what. I moved. I ran towards the flying horse.

Cornelius turned at once. He knew what I knew. He saw the same as I did. Her lithe figure flew towards us. The impact thrust her forwards. We both ran towards that mounted horror. Sartorius was screaming. A guttural anger filled his voice in a frenzy of revenge and hatred. I stopped short. I swung the long German sword Cornelius insisted I use. Not at the rider. Not at that mounted flying Fury approaching from the underworld. I hit the horse square on the throat and stepped aside. My rage mounted. I was Hades-bent. I was fast, strong and angry. I did not fear the consequences.

The falling horse threw Sartorius clear. It was almost headless from my cut. He regained his feet fast, rising from the ruin that had been his mount. He stood, shield in one hand and short Roman sword in the other.

'Come on Mouse, let me cut you,' Sartorius growled.

'I've had some lessons, you bastard.'

'It won't help you, Mouse.'

I knew what to do. It was why Cornelius had trained me. Beyond that, there was an instinctual feel to my movements. It was past training, past teaching. It was as if I was in tune with the world around me. I felt my blood coursing. I heard the sounds of the woods, felt the sky above, all at once. I was more alive in that moment, than ever before. I was glowing. Bright in the gloaming. Battle fury, anger and a strange pleasure to know I controlled my limbs and I could kill. I felt like a man who after long absence, has come home at last.

He leapt forward, pushing his round cavalry shield before him. He stabbed with his gladius. I was not there. I had rolled away to my right and regained my feet in an instant. I stabbed with the sword as I arose. I contacted his leg below the knee. In a normal man, it would have been crippling. To the tree trunks holding up this monster, it was nothing. He came on.

The shield flew forward at me. I sidestepped and struck with my sword. It was longer than his gladius. It was a German sword. It was part of my ancestry and I knew how to use it. Cornelius had taught me but I already knew. I had it in me to use this wonderful weapon. It was a knowledge given not by my teacher, but by Wuotan himself.

I swung my weapon as my opponent stepped forward. It struck the top edge of his shield. It dented the rim. Sparks flew. I saw him shudder. His arm dipped a fraction. I felt I could kill him. I swung the blade over and over again. Sideways, from above down, diagonally. I kept hitting his shield. Sparks flew and I saw his arm begin to tire. I kept my distance. He could not get close. His sword was too short to get to me.

Roman armies win, because in a tight press of men, the short blade stabs and wins. A long sword can do nothing if your arms are pinned at your sides and so the legions kill and win. But you know, I would take a long-sword any time in single combat. With room to move, the force of the weapon is incomparable and the reach phenomenal.

Anger raged in my head. Blood red anger. The farmer's wife, those children, and Cornelius' tortured body all thrust themselves into my head, filling my senses. I could hear that poor woman screaming as she burned. I heard the wail of a child as they struck her head from her body. I wanted his death more than I wanted anything in the world, for such is blood lust. Unreasoning, uncompromising and unrelenting.

Sartorius was forceful. He charged like a bull. I backed away, striking with my sword all the time. I was much fitter than he was. He had not run a step for years. I was young and strong. I had more stamina than he knew.

It was not a good time for the Gods to play games with me. Loge must have had some hand in it for he tricked me then. As I stepped back, a tree stump reached up and tripped me. I swear it reached up, I would have seen it I am sure. I fell backwards and I could hear Sartorius exhale with antici-pation. For his bulk, he moved fast.

He tried to use the edge of the shield to hit me on the neck. He was too slow. I had rolled away. I struck upwards and backhand. I caught him on the knee. This was not the glancing little blow like before. I drew my blade towards me as I struck. It almost carved through his leg. I felt it slicing bone. I continued to roll. I stood looking at the man. He was on one knee. He had dropped his shield. I approached. I raised my sword and brought it down, two handed, with all the force I could muster.

It must be understood that I am a big man. I had the muscles youth and training imbue. I do not boast. The blade struck the brigand square on the top of his helmet. The blow was so forceful it clove the leather helmet almost in two. My cut sliced into his head like it would a ripe fruit and he fell, unrecognisable, at my feet. Blood and brain dripped from my sword.

I wanted more. I wanted to kill him over and over again. My blood was up. I stabbed and sliced at his limp remains until I could raise my hand no more. My arms like lead, the anger began to fade.

A vivid picture came into my head. It thrust itself into my brain. Livia, smiling and reaching out towards me. Then, her limp body flying towards me. Panic set in once more. I turned from my task and ran to where I could see Cornelius kneeling. He was weeping.

CHAPTER X

"Woe is me. I think I am becoming a god."

—Emperor Vespasian

'No, no, no, no!' Cornelius said. 'How many times do I have to tell you? You can't fight a legionary with a huge shield like that! The only way to do it is by stabbing with the point of your sword. You won't see them slashing and hacking like you did to Sartorius. They push you off balance with the shield and then stab you with the point of the gladius. Now try it again.'

It was one of those training sessions where he was trying to teach me the rudiments of battle skill. The lessons had intensified. It was as if by fighting, by teaching, he was assuaging his pain, as if he could numb his tortured brain by bringing my standards of killing close to his own. I knew that and complied, however long each session took, however hard it became. It was helping me too.

I had mastered the Thracian blade and the long sword and now was trying to use a gladius. It was an impossibly short blade to use in hand-to-hand combat but in a long line of shields, it was deadly.

'If you were a sensible Barbarian,' he went on, 'you would use cavalry. You engage the Romans with your infantry and then attack on the flanks with cavalry who should be heavily armoured. The legionaries can't defend their flanks as easily

91

as the front.'

'What about horse archers?' I asked.

'Ah yes, there was one battle against the Parthians almost two hundred years ago when all they had were ten thousand horse archers and they demolished seven Roman legions. They took out the Roman cavalry and just rained arrows down on the infantry until most of them were dead. We never fell for that one again. Next time, we were in lines and spread out. We also had enough cavalry of our own to surround the Parthians. We picked the terrain. Flat terrain is ideal for horse archers where they can chase at speed and fall back with ease. In hills or woods, they aren't much good.'

I was sweating in the sunshine. Although the autumn was fast approaching, the sun retained some heat. The colours of the fields were browns and yellows and it reminded me of something I could not place. I still did not know where it was, but Livia's words seemed to come to my mind often. There were long summer evenings when Cornelius and I would talk about where I might be from, but neither of us knew enough from my scant childhood memories to hazard even a guess.

I was getting restless. I was very young then and remaining in one place seemed difficult. Everything around me still reminded me of Livia and my loss was becoming more and more painful with the passage of time.

At first I had been numb. I had felt nothing as we burned her remains. Cornelius wept and it was the only time I ever saw him do that. The constant reminders of her presence hurt the most. It is often so; the smallest things bring back grief. I came across an old bow of hers in the woods when I was running. I picked it up. It had mould on the handle and no string. I imagined her hand, as she would have held it; it hit me hard then. I sank to my knees and could not leave that place for what seemed like hours.

Every time I ate a pheasant, I thought of her and how we had shared that moment before the first brigands came. The memory became more vivid with each remembrance. I dreamed of her and she was as fresh in my mind a year later as when we had carried her limp body back to the farmhouse.

My mind returned to the present as we took a break and ate some fruit for our midday meal. I remember looking up and seeing a hawk in the September sky as it soared high above us. It hovered then plummeted like an arrow, to strike some unseen quarry. The farmhouse was built now and the four new hands Cornelius returned with on one of his trips to Ariminium, had done the actual farm work. He tended to keep himself pretty much to himself on those trips and the news he could gather was limited.

'We have two new Emperors,' he said to me after one of his trips. 'One is Marcus Aurelius, and the other is his half-brother, Lucius Verus. They are both joint heirs to the empire now Antoninus Pius is dead. Word has it Verus is off to the east to fight the Parthians but Aurelius mopes at home writing philosophy. I don't think either of them will ever bother us here.'

He looked up and put a hand to his face to shade it from the sunshine. He stiffened.

'We have company,' he said. 'Go and saddle the horses and stay under cover. Don't come out until I call you. I thought I was being followed on my way back!'

'Weapons?'

'Of course. Pack the saddle bags and expect to leave in a hurry, it looks like a troop of cavalry on their way here from the dust cloud on the horizon.'

How the old man could see so well remains a mystery to me, since all I could identify was a cloud of dust rising in the early afternoon sunshine. A corncrake sounded nearby as I ran to the barn, and chickens scattered in my path, squawking indignantly and leaving a wake of flying feathers. I did as he suggested and sat upon my horse in the barn. Cornelius stood outside in the yard waiting. I could see him clearly through the partly open door and I waited in the gloom for him to call or not.

I saw them then. There were about twenty Roman equites, mounted, carrying spears and long swords. Each man had a small round cavalry shield and a plumed helmet. They looked as smart and pretty as if they were going to a parade. The Roman cavalry always looked smart but it never stopped them falling off their horses when they charged, since the only thing holding them in place was the saddle with its high front and rear.

As I looked, my heart skipped a beat. There was a squat, bearded man on one of the horses. He had long arms and a face I recognised. It was Minius of course. The ungrateful man had clearly sold us out. Livia and I had let him live and yet he repaid us by going to the authorities. I confess I was losing the slender thread of control I had on my temper. If there is one thing that makes my blood seethe, it is betrayal. I swore to myself I would take his head before the day was done. I listened, for even at the age of nineteen, I had enough sense to see I could not charge twenty mounted men and survive.

'This is my farm and I demand to know what you mean by this, riding in with all your men and horses,' Cornelius said.

'Don't listen to him,' Minius said, 'he is with the boy and the girl. The boy is the one you're after. He had a snake tattoo on his head when he first joined those brigands and he has blonde hair. Don't let the old man warn them.'

'Has it come to this in Rome now? You take the word of a known brigand against that of an honest farmer?' Cornelius said.

'I'm sorry sir, but we have to take you to the Aedile in Ariminium for questioning and I would like to know where that nephew is,' the commander of the troop said.

He was a small man of middle years and he had a brown beard trimmed short in the military fashion. He was looking around the farm and buildings. He paused for a second or two looking directly at me but I was deep in the shadows inside the barn and it was impossible for him to make me out.

Cornelius for his part stood stock-still. He still wore the sword he had been practising with and I began to pity the man who stood within range when he drew it. I had no doubt we would end up fighting; it was just a matter of time. I felt as if I had seen it all before. The look on Cornelius' face and the grim way his old wrinkled mouth was set. I had put both shields and weapons on the two horses, and readied myself for action. Cornelius simply stood there, to my surprise. The cavalrymen milled around him and two of them dismounted with ropes to tie him up. The commander directed the rest of his men to search the house and barn, for they were really looking for me.

Then it happened. The horsemen had dismounted except for their officer and four others. Some were in the farmhouse and some had gone around searching the grounds inside the farm compound. Three of them walked towards me and one began to open the stable door. Cornelius moved faster than I would have thought possible for an old man. He punched the officer's horse in the mouth with his fist and it reared, throwing its rider to the ground. At the same time, out came his sword and he called to me. I rode out, sword in hand, scattering the three men who had been intent on entering the stable. Cornelius mounted his horse as it ran past him. I have never seen any man of his age as nimble.

As I rode past Minius, I swiped at his head with my drawn sword. It missed the side of his head where I was aiming but caught his face. It sliced his cheek to the bone and took half of his nose. There was a gush of blood, to my satisfaction, and I shouted 'Livia!' as I rode past him.

The four mounted equites gave chase, but the others were in total disarray. It might still have gone awry, but Cornelius had taught me well. As we rode hard up the hill path to the oak copse where I had first met Livia, I turned my horse. The first of the riders was upon me with his spear. I parried with my sword. I came back with a backhanded blow. My blow struck the unfortunate man on the neck. He fell from the saddle. There was bright red blood coursing through his fingers as he clutched at this throat, rolling on the brown oak leaves beneath him.

The point of turning my horse was the rider-less horse was now between me and the other soldiers. It bought a moment of time in which I could assess where my next enemy was. Cornelius also turned but on the opposite side and he had dispatched his assailant. There was only one each now, but we could hear their comrades fast approaching.

We parried their spears. We managed to cut or kill them both. We rode on up the hill and as we left the valley behind, the sound of pursuit gradually began to fade. Our horses were fresh and theirs had ridden for four hours from Ariminium.

I gave Ursus an encouraging pat on the neck as we slowed our pace.

Cornelius was out of breath but smiling.

'Well done my boy!' he said, 'You are definitely improving.'

'Praise from Caesar,' I said.

I still do not know why I said that, it must have been something I had heard but I still cannot place it. We rode north. There was nowhere else to go. South was Rome, and now we had killed Roman soldiers we were both hunted men. I could not help but think we had suddenly become like Sartorius, but I knew I could never be as dishonourable as he had been.

We rode until evening and stopped long enough to eat, rest the horses and feed them. They had worked hard for us, but they still had much more to do. It was common sense to head north and if it were obvious to us, it would be equally obvious to the pursuing soldiers. We had to shake off the pursuit somehow. Cornelius suggested we turn south and double back as it was the last thing they would expect us to do, but I felt the sooner we reached the mountains the more likely we were to be safe. He acquiesced in the end, if only because he could see I wanted to go as far north as possible in search of my origins.

Livia was in my thoughts all the time. It might seem ridiculous, but all the time I fought the Romans, all the time I fled with Cornelius beside me, I had her in my thoughts. She was my one true love, a love that comes but once in life to any man; a love that is eternal. I care not what the witches or soothsayers or priests say about it, love is the one thing that keeps the world held high and buoyant in the arms of the giant who supports it. Without it, we might as well all perish. I tell you, it burned within me then as bright and vivid as it does now, though many years have passed and my life has changed as to be almost unrecognisable.

CHAPTER XI

"Deos fortioribus adesse."
(The gods are on the side of the stronger.)

— Tacitus

We rode north resting the horses as much as we could and still made good time. The countryside changed again as did the colours. Yellows and brown and russets replaced the green of summer all around us. There were yellow haystacks in the stubble fields and they smelled of recently cut hay. Trees were shedding their leaves and a carpet of gold surrounded them, blowing up here and there in the breeze. There was a quality of quietness about that autumn and it radiated a beauty I was not to experience for a long time. The weather changed too as we began ascending the lower slopes of the mountains. A cool wind sprang up and as the dawn came, it began to rain. Our cloaks began to weigh heavily on our shoulders and we realised we would need to find shelter even though it was early in the season.

We stopped in the half-light and ate some dried fruit and stale bread from our saddlebags in the shelter of some tall aspen trees. After drinking a little wine and water, we both slept. I had dreams of Liva and a house on fire; I heard my mother screaming. It was still dark when I awoke. Sweating, I collected my gear together in the dark and we rode on. Cornelius felt we had no time to lose with the inevitable pursuit.

There are inherent problems in riding in the dark. Horses do not respond well if they cannot see ahead. The danger of course is that if they step into a pothole they can break a leg. I should have taken better care of Ursus. We were riding off the road to stay away from any people who might still be out and as we descended a hill disaster struck. Ursus stepped right into a hole and fell, throwing me headlong onto the turf. He lay struggling but could not get up and when Cornelius and I examined him we found he had a clear fracture of his foreleg. The bone glistened white in the moonlight where it projected through his hide. It was obvious what I needed to do.

I had killed men and thought nothing of it as if it was natural for a warrior to do so, but killing that horse broke my heart. I was truly fond of him. Not only did he possess stamina, he was obedient and easy to manage. I suppose it may not have been that, but perhaps because I had acquired him when I was with Livia, I was overly attached to him. I took my knife and slit the main artery in his neck as fast as I could and because I did it gently, and spoke softly to him as I did it, he did not show alarm but seemed to relax. In the flickering torchlight, I saw his pupils dilate, huge as lakes. His eyes closed as I stroked his muzzle.

'What do we do now?' I said, wiping an unwelcome drop of moisture from the corner of my eye. 'We can't travel all the way to Germania with just one horse.'

'We will have to steal one,' Cornelius said.

'If I knew how to get there, I might be able to find the stables where I worked for the Piso family. They have horses and I know every inch of the place. When I left Rome, I always dreamed of going there to take a horse. I felt they owed me that after keeping me as a slave all those years.'

It was a stupid thing to say really. Of course, they owed me nothing; in fact, they paid good money for me and it was in all probability me who owed them something in compensation. I had after all battered my Master to death with an oil lamp.

I held a burning obsession to see and ride those beautiful chariot-racing steeds again as I had during the only happy times of my childhood. We walked to the road to get our bearings, discussing where the Piso farm might be. Cornelius had a good knowledge of the land and I recognised a hill in the distance but it was a long time since I had been there and there was no guarantee I was right.

We walked for two days but Cornelius seemed to know where we were going, so I was content to follow his lead. Climbing a hill we looked down on a large estate nestled in a range of green hills.

'There is only one big estate near here,' he said pointing north.

'How far?'

'A day's walk maybe. Of course if you're too tired you can sit on the horse and I'll lead you.'

'Funny man,' I said, shifting uncomfortably under the burden of my saddle.

'Actually, if you sat in the saddle she wouldn't move a muscle. I trained her only to move for me.'

'I noticed that when you were captured.'

'I can't bear the thought of anyone else riding her to be truthful. Livia's horse was trained like that too.'

The mention of her name was enough for us both to fall silent as we trudged down the hill. Our loss felt as fresh as if she had died days before and not a whole year. In the afternoon, we climbed another hill and then I saw the villa. I recognised it. It might have been the Norns spinning my future and having another laugh at my expense, or perhaps it was Cornelius' knowledge of the land, I cannot tell.

We waited until after sunset before we made our move. In the dark, we tied the roan mare to a tree. I placed my saddle next to her and we continued on foot. The grass was damp and soft underfoot and the moon shone brighter than either of us would have liked. We dodged from fence to fence as we approached. There was a light on in the stable. I wondered if the same old stable hand was still there or if it was another man now. As we approached we heard voices.

'By Jupiter if you don't do as I say I'll have you whipped you insolent fellow,' said a man's voice.

'That horse won't take another of those races yet. He is simply not fit for it.'

'He goes with me tomorrow and that is final. I want him ready to travel in the morning and may the Gods help you if you don't cooperate.'

A man walked out of the stable and stamped to the steps of the villa. He glanced over his shoulder in our direction and paused for a moment. I froze wondering if he had seen us, but he must have been looking at something else for he turned away and went inside.

We approached the stable and entered in silence. We saw no one by the light of the oil lamps that cast a dim, smoky light across the floor of the building. Whoever had been there was not in evidence. We stood outside the circle of light and the man came back whistling to himself and carrying a pitchfork laden with hay. We entered the light together and drawing our swords, we gestured him to silence. There was a look of abject terror on his face but he

102

remained silent as we both took a step forward towards him.

His expression changed suddenly and I realised it was indeed the same stableman who had been kind to me all those years before.

'Sextus?' he whispered. 'Is it really you? What are you doing here? I heard you were dead or something.'

'No, but I killed the Master and ran away; he was a cruel and evil man you know.'

'They'll crucify you lad, if they catch you. You must get away from here.'

'I intend to, but I need a horse and a spare mount and then I will go south. We have a boat waiting to take us to Sicilia.'

'Now you're a horse thief as well! I can't believe what's happened to you. You've turned into a brigand in such a short time.'

'Which horse is the freshest?' I asked.

'Take the two stallions. Marcus wants to race them but one of them has just recovered from a fever and I don't want him to race. The one with the diamond mark on its head is the fittest. Marcus is the Master of the house now and he thinks the Emperor will think better of him if he wins the races next week in Rome. The Emperor of course, thinks of nothing but burning Christians and cares little for chariot races. I won't say anything, but you'd better tie and gag me and it'll look better. My wife often asks after you. What on earth can I tell her now?'

'Tell her I'm free. Where are the saddles?' I said.

The old stableman indicated a stall where the saddles were stacked. We selected two and left the third horse without. After we had stroked them and breathed in their faces to tell them who we were, we tied them tail to tail and led them towards the door. We tied the old man up, for there would be a dire punishment for him if Marcus suspected him of helping us. We mounted and rode out of the stable with the hooves clattering. As we were leaving the low gate in the wall, we heard a voice cry behind us 'Thieves, thieves in the night!'

We rode harder and as I glanced over my shoulder, I could see Marcus Licinius racing towards the stable. He would be furious when he realised his racing horses were missing and it made me smile.

When we reached the roan mare and Cornelius changed horses we each tied a horse to the one we rode and I saddled the spare stallion. It was the most beautiful grey and white stallion I have ever seen in my life. He stood tall and straight and had the wide chest and straight hips seen only in the best Parthian horses. I could have stood admiring him all night and probably would have, had it not been for Cornelius' urgent warning.

'They're after us!'

I looked towards the villa and could see by the moonlight how four men on horseback were heading in our direction. We took off towards the hills from which we had emerged only an hour before. My horse was exhilarating to ride. He flew like the wind. The other stallion ran alongside with ease, tied to the saddle with no rider to bear. Their training was to run together anyway and I doubted they even needed tying to one another. Up on the hill we stopped to survey the scene behind us. There was no sign of pursuit. We turned our horses and rode slower now in southerly direction. There was a noise of hooves to our left as we rode down the hill. The pursuing horsemen must have taken a short cut and were attacking with swords drawn.

Surprised, we drew our weapons. I recognised Marcus Piso as the man in front wielding a long cavalry sword. As soon as he was in range he swung the sword. I had to lean back almost flat in the saddle to avoid the blade. My horse was a racing horse and subtle commands with my feet and knees as one would give to a warhorse were of no use. I remembered what the old stable man had taught me about these horses and the commands came flooding back.

I turned my horse to my left as Marcus came past and the two horses collided. I swung at him as I regained my upright position, but he ducked with practised ease. He had clearly trained in this type of fighting.

I had little experience, but Cornelius had taught me well. As Marcus circled to my right and swung his blade at me again, I parried and leaned forwards and to my right. With both hands, I pushed him. The move unbalanced Marcus. Neither of us had any way of staying firmly on our mounts apart from the raised back and front of the saddle. If you push hard enough from the side, any soldier will fall. I was lucky too and I must have caught him off balance for he slid from his saddle onto the sward beneath. I rode away and glancing over my shoulder. Cornelius had killed one man and injured another and the third rider held back. Sensible fellow that.

Cornelius rode towards me as Marcus tried to mount his horse. We turned tail and ran. Our horses were much faster, so it was a short chase. We distanced ourselves from them in minutes and were out of their sight in an hour.

We turned north with our prizes and laughed. It had been dangerous but fun. I felt the Piso family had repaid the debt they owed me for the beatings and the sheer misery of being enslaved. I began to feel like a man and for the first

105

time since Livia's death, I began to look to the future. We were heading north. I had no idea where we were going but I felt free and curious.

I had a strange dream that night. I saw myself on a horse, waving a huge sword. I wore no helmet and my tattoo was visible for all to see. The horse whinnied and reared. I rode from inside some kind of settlement towards gates and a group of men similar to me followed. I ducked low to avoid the lintel and as I emerged, there was another wall with Roman archers upon it. They fired at me and I rode towards them. I found myself in the midst of a battle with Roman soldiers all around. One dragged me from my blood stained horse and I awoke in a sweat. Each time I closed my eyes I could see myself on that horse. In the end, sleep took me but I remained restless and sweating.

CHAPTER XII

"Quod di omen avertant"
(May the gods avert this omen)

— Cicero

I awoke early. We had been riding north for five days and the previous night camped high up on the slopes of the mountains. It was almost dawn when I awoke and I lay for a while unable to go back to sleep. The air was cold and the pre-dawn light allowed me to see the still sleeping shape of Cornelius. He lay on the far side of the almost extinguished fire, which sat whispering, grey and unwelcoming on this late autumn morning.

Cornelius snored then turned onto his side. There was silence then apart from the soft drip of water from a nearby water-pool under the rocks. It had rained overnight and I could feel the black cloak in which I lay wrapped was heavy and damp.

I arose and walked to the edge of the escarpment upon which we had made our camp. I sat in the drizzle, wrapped my woollen cloak around me, and looked out on the valley far below as the dawn light began to spread. We had chosen to camp high to be able to see if there was any pursuit below. As I looked down upon the yellow, russet, and brown countryside, I could see smoke rising in an errant spiral from a far off farmhouse. Six crows were circling in the morning air as

107

the sun peeped out on the horizon between grey clouds.

It was a still and thoughtful morning and as I sat there I pondered on the events of the last two years. The transition from slave to escapee and then to descend as low in my estimation as any man could, made me almost shudder with shame. I had no yardstick by which to judge these things except my nature—the essence of who I was. I had inherited that nature from my parents and ancestors, but I had no chance to understand then, for my shade was wandering, with no base from which to start and no anchor in reality.

I had to become.

Become what? I puzzled over this for long minutes but I failed to notice the crows had changed direction and now flew towards me. As they passed overhead, I noticed their presence, for one of them dropped the contents of his bowels on my head. I looked up and cursed, shaking my fist at the black and grey creatures.

I took a small cloth from the saddlebag and tried to wipe the grey mess from my hair. It stank. I would have used water from the water skin but we only had a few mouthfuls left and I thought Cornelius might be annoyed if I wasted it. I tried using wine, of which we had plenty. The local wine was a dry unpleasant drink, fit more for cooking than drinking. It made matters worse. I smelt like a drunk with a hygiene problem. The furtive scrabbling about woke my companion.

'What on earth are you up to?' A deep and sleepy voice murmured from the blanket.

'A bird just shat on my head! It stinks!'

'A bird? What kind of bird?' Cornelius said in obvious good humour; he was smiling.

'Bloody crows!'

'Well the Germans think the crow is a lucky bird you know; they believe it is supposed to be a sign you are chosen by their chief God'.

'If that is how they choose people, then frankly, I'd prefer to not be chosen,' I said.

'No, really, their one-eyed God, I don't recall his name, uses two ravens to carry messages to people when he wants them to do something. Maybe it's a sign of something.'

'Yes, it's a sign your brain is rotting in your skull you old goat,' I said, 'and anyway they were bloody crows, not ravens.'

'Maybe it means you are a bad tempered, irritating, child then!'

Cornelius began to laugh and he continued to laugh for most of the morning. He even made comments to the effect that he thought maybe I was becoming a Christian, for they poured water on their heads to clean away all earthly troubles.

I became more and more morose and glared at him from time to time, as we rode north. By late morning, we had been travelling a forest path and around midday it opened out on a wide field of green grass with a clear stream scampering and giggling past us to our right. The land rose away from us and at the side of the stream and high on the hill there was a small farmhouse. It had no wall or gate and we wondered if the inhabitants would be friendly.

We needed fresh food and both agreed that resting under a roof would be pleasant, so we rode up the hill, approaching slowly. We had no wish to alarm the farm's occupants. As we neared the door to the house, a large man with short hair, a beard and a limp emerged carrying a legionary's sword.

'What do you want?' he asked in a deep and serious voice, frowning.

We looked at him as he limped into the sunlight.

'We are travellers and horse-traders,' Cornelius said. 'We would welcome shelter for the night. We have been on the road for many nights. We would also value some food for the next leg of our journey north. We are happy to pay for both.'

'Who are you?' the man said.

'My name is Lucius Percennius and this is my nephew Postumus. As I said, we are horse-traders.'

'I am Veridius, late of the Third Legion Hispania,' the man said. 'I have farmed here since I retired from the army of Antoninus Pius, may the Gods smile upon his just and kindly face.'

'I too was in the army,' Cornelius said. 'I also fought for the dead Emperor. I was in campaigns in Thrace and in Germany until I returned home through an injury.'

'Thrace? Then we were contemporaries. I too was in Thrace and helped put down a rebellion there. We smashed them and the rebels ran before us.'

'You must be older than you look. I was about thirty-five when that happened. We must have been in the same army. Do you remember a tribune called Metellus? Big man, much bigger than me with a scar across his whole face from eye to mouth?' Cornelius said.

'Yes, that was one of our tribunes, he was a stern leader that one.'

They twittered on about things I did not understand and soon the farmer invited us in and gave us food. We saw to the horses and were able to let them run free in a wooden enclosure adjacent to the house. Cornelius and the farmer began drinking wine and although I joined them, I took plenty of water with mine. I had suspicions there was something not quite right about the friendliness shown by this farmer. I thought he should have been much more cautious of us, yet he seemed to accept who we were without question. I think his eyes told me to beware. You can always judge the truth in a man by his eyes.

As evening fell, we ate again and drank more wine with the farmer.

'Have you no children?' I asked.

'Yes I have a son, but he is away in Patavium on an errand, and my wife is staying with her mother along with my daughter. They will be back in a couple of days.'

'Who is doing the farm work then?'

'There is not much to do in these months apart from preparing for winter. We make sure the grain is stored properly and the hay is in and dry. But apart from that, we have to get the animals into shape for the winter and get them well fed.'

'You must be lonely.'

'No, not at all, I have the farm animals and my family will be back in few days.'

'Well, it's time for me to sleep,' I said yawning. The farmer showed me to a straw-covered area in the barn and Cornelius followed shortly after. I was just going to sleep, when Cornelius shook my shoulder.

'Are you really going to sleep? We are in serious danger, my young friend.'

'You mean that retired soldier?' I said.

'He might be a retired soldier but he was never in Thrace. There never was a tribune called Metellus, whether he had a scar or not! This is a trap. I think he has sent word to Patavium for help and from what he let out about the distance, we can expect company by morning.'

'I agree; I had worked most of it out for myself, so I figure we take some food and get out of here.'

We packed our gear and went to the house. As we entered, the farmer seemed to have left. I called his name but no answer came. I stepped into the room and like a fool, assumed all was quiet. The descending blow to my helmeted head brought the floor crashing towards me or at least it seemed that way. I had the presence of mind however to turn as I fell and dim visions came of the farmer, gladius in hand, trying to stab at my companion. Cornelius, sword drawn in an instant, parried. Twisting his weapon, he disarmed my attacker with no more effort than if he was dealing with a child. Then stepping forward, he tripped the man as he body-checked him to the ground. The farmer lay on the hard earth floor looking up, with the point of Cornelius' sword at this throat.

I sat up, my head clearing.

'When are they coming?' Cornelius said.

'Who?' the man said, his voice a dry rasp.

'Don't play this old man for a fool. Have you sent your son for the soldiers?'

'Yes. We saw you in the distance and like everyone around here, we knew to look out for you.'

'When do you expect them?' I asked.

'Probably in the morning, maybe before.'

'Why did you betray us? What happened to hospitality? Even we Romans believed in that.'

'I need the money, times are hard here. It was easy in the legions, all found and money too. Now I'm stuck here on this barren soil trying to raise crops and a family. You

112

wouldn't understand.'

'On the contrary,' Cornelius said, 'but you have lost your pride and your sense of decency. We would not have hurt you or your family. Why didn't you know that?'

The man said nothing as we tied him up. We took food and fodder, leaving a few coins on his table for payment.

Saddling the horses, we tied the two exchange mounts behind and fled. We rode north, ever north, unsure whether we were now too late to cross the mountains before winter approached. We stopped to eat and make plans as dawn came.

'The entire countryside is looking for us and the reward seems to be attractive. I might turn you in myself!' Cornelius said.

'Thank you for your kind thought.'

'Seriously, one option would be to go towards Patavium in the north-east and then turn north to Luvavum in Noricum. There is a small garrison there, but it's not a popular place, because of the Dacian war bands raiding in the area. From Luvavum we can cut north-west and eventually reach the Rhine valley.'

'Cornelius, I will be guided by you; I know nothing of this land.'

We rode hard after that since we now knew the soldiers would follow. We had fresh mounts with us and they were all four fast, reliable beasts, the best of horses. The early morning sunshine felt weak and cool and we realised a cold autumn approached. The ground underfoot was firm and the horses were clearly comfortable even at our fast pace. It took another eight hours of hard riding to reach the outskirts of Patavium.

Patavium had been a Pannonian town many years before.

Some three hundred years before, the Romans fought a great battle there and defeated the local inhabitants. Afterwards, they took all the Northern part of Italia as far as the Alps until later they moved into Cisalpine Gaul and finally Julius Caesar took all of Gaul, from the Rhine to the western sea.

We were both anxious to stay as far away from Roman lands as possible and felt bypassing Patavium would be safest. We headed north through the province of Noricum. We picked up some food from a Gallic trader who was travelling in the opposite direction and left the smoky, dull walls of the city behind us without having to expose ourselves to anyone's greed for the reward.

We travelled for more than two months. It became a tedium of riding and camping. We provisioned ourselves as we travelled, stopping at farms and small villages to buy food, wine and fodder for the horses. The cold made us change our clothing. Cornelius made me adopt the leggings Gauls and Germans wear, despite my protests. As the weeks went by the weather worsened and it was during a snowfall that we came to the town of Luvavum. It was small enough to be home to a few hundred people who varied in origin from Roman, Pannonian, Dacian, Greek traders and some Germans.

We rode into the town, our high stepping horses lathered from the ride. We found our way through narrow muddy streets winding between wooden houses to stables where we obtained feed and shelter for our horses. The stableman offered us accommodation in the hayloft and we consented, since it was the best way to guard against anyone interfering with our horses. It was not a pleasant place. There was a midden outside the stable; so mixed with the smell of horses and hay, we experienced occasional wafts of human detritus as well.

We had no option but to stay. Journeying in that cold time of year was not possible unless one had a source of feed for the horses and we therefore needed a place to lie low until spring or at least the tail end of winter.

'A cheerless place,' Cornelius said after we had tended the horses.

'Yes but there doesn't appear to be any pursuit and I must say it feels good to be under a roof, despite the smell.'

'There are a few taverns in the main street, maybe we can get some wine there and something to eat,'

'Is it safe?'

'I think the chance of anyone following us this far from Rome or even Patavium is remote. Sextus, it looks as if we may yet make it without capture, so we need to make longer term plans.'

'We could join a war band as mercenaries. Then if we have some money, we can travel north in the spring and find out what German tribe I belong to. Maybe they will be welcoming. I wondered if maybe I have relatives surviving still and they might take us in. I don't know what we can do then, but I can turn my hand to most things I think.'

Cornelius looked at me with sad eyes. 'Perhaps you would be happy with a life amongst the German Barbarians but I most certainly would not regard it as any pleasure. It is better than being fed to the lions in the arena with my hands tied behind my back, but that only comes a close second.'

'Cornelius, it's not that I have any idea of why I want to go there. I just have a feeling it is my destiny and I must follow it. Livia told me to go you know. We neither of us knows what the future holds, so why don't we look forward to the unknown?'

He considered for a moment then he said, 'All right, you win. We will do as you wish and it will be good to stop running. Let's talk about it over a cup of wine.'

We made our way through the narrow streets beneath the thatched houses, wrapped in our cloaks and slipping on the slush. The night was dark and we had to ask directions from an old man leading two sheep along the street. After taking one or two wrong turns we found the tavern. It was crowded, perhaps because at that time of night it was the only warm place in Luvavum.

We had to elbow our way to the bar stepping over the damp straw that they used as flooring overlaying the bare earth and vomit. The tavern had an unsavoury smell but was warm. Inebriate men occupied all the tables, so we remained standing.

The owner was a fat Pannonian with full, black beard and dark gleaming eyes. He smiled to us and said, 'Wine? Well no, we don't have any. The last wine we had was in the summer and an Egyptian who asked an enormous price carried it. Of course since we get wine so rarely I bought the lot and the soldiers drank it all in a week.'

He seemed to find this so funny he had to hold onto the bar with his hand while he shook with raucous laughter. The only drink he was serving was a local Dacian beer. It was filthy stuff, all bitter hops and a scum on top making it look like cold urine. The taste was as one might expect urine to taste, but it warmed us despite our finer sensibilities. We ended the evening having drunk enough of it to make its taste seem almost bearable. Even I could have drunk more. On the way out of the tavern, a tall heavily built Dacian stood up and pushed me to one side. I was, I confess, a little over-refreshed from the beer, and overbalanced before regaining my stability.

The Dacian was drunk and belligerent. He stood swaying in the lamplight and said, 'You Roman swine, why you here? Spying on honest folk? All I wanted was to have a quiet drink and I have to put up with your snooping, so you can inform the military. I know you!'

It was a stupid thing to say to a wanted criminal and he most certainly did not know me, which demonstrates with abject clarity how beer is a drink a normal person would only consume in small quantities. I kept quiet hoping he would calm down, but his anger escalated when he failed to obtain a response.

'Well, what have you got to say for yourself?'

'Nothing, friend,' Cornelius said. 'We are only travellers and have no connection with any soldiers.'

'I'm not your friend. I didn't ask you anyway, old man; I asked him,' he said jabbing at my chest with his finger.

I began to feel angry. I did not intend to give ground to some Dacian farmer so after he poked me once or twice, I grabbed him by the beard and forced him hard against the wall. I was, after all, a tall and strong young man who had killed men in fair fights and in his inebriate state, he found it was impossible to break my grip.

'If you want to fight I'll kill you and use your skull for a drinking bowl. Now get out of the way.'

I let go and he fell, off balance, onto his knees. A look of rage came into his face. I recognised what he was feeling for he and I seemed to share this battle temper. Once released from the depths within, it has unfortunate consequences for the perpetrator as well as the victim. He got to his feet. He swung a punch at me. After my experience with Rugio in Sartorius' campsite it was as slow as watching my dead

117

Master reach a judgement in the forum. I ducked and placed a neat punch on his nose making his eyes water and then he was mine. I thumped into his face and body as if he was just a straw punch bag like the ones gladiators use.

He fell to the ground and lay there completely out of things. Cornelius and I looked at him and I think we both felt ashamed. It is not an honourable thing to defeat a man in his cups and even though I was drinking the filthy beer they served in the tavern, it was really no excuse for laying out the Dacian.

Cornelius and I looked at the bleeding form beneath us. We exchanged glances and both understood this was not a good way to endear us to anyone, let alone to remain unrecognised and undiscovered. We picked him up, each of us supporting him by his arms and took him outside. He refused to awaken and I must say it gave me some pleasure to slap his face a few times.

'I think he is so drunk he needs to be taken home or at least to the stables to sleep off the beer,' Cornelius said.

'You really want to trawl all the way across Luvavum carrying this smelly bunch of ox hide?' I said.

'It will prevent anyone asking questions tomorrow and he could always be useful to us if he knows the geography around here. Don't forget we need a winter resting place. Maybe he has a farm?'

We dragged him to the stables and resigned ourselves to having acquired a companion for the night. I must add however, he could snore in competition for Rome and the sleep I snatched as a result, was intermittent and brief.

CHAPTER XIII

"Remember upon the conduct of each depends the fate of all."

— Alexander the Great

I awoke to the sound of a horse breaking wind. With the headache I was suffering it sounded like thunder. My recall of the previous night seemed sketchy to my fuzzy mind, to say the least. I felt nauseated and the world was spinning.

That morning was my introduction to the after effects of beer and Dacians. I still view both with great care and it is a caution I have applied ever since, unless forced by politeness to partake of more than a reasonable measure of either.

It was only with difficulty I regained my feet. I looked around. Cornelius was sleeping like a baby and next to him, almost cuddled up, slept an enormous brute of a man with bruises all over his face and a snore loud enough to awaken the Gods.

'Hey, old man!' I said nudging Cornelius with my foot. I did it with my usual tact as I always employed with my teacher.

'Hey, you awake? Were you poisoned too?'

'Oh Jupiter Optimus Maximus my head,' was the only response I obtained. I continued to try awakening my friend but to no avail.

I went outside and washed my face in a barrel of icy

rainwater standing near the door. I looked up at a clear blue sky but the sun radiated little warmth. There was frost on the ground. I was glad of the leggings Cornelius had insisted we wear for disguise. They were warm and comfortable, and I began to understand why the Barbarians wore them. I stood looking around me, pensive, tired, pondering my future again. It had become almost a habit. I was lost in thought when I heard a soft hesitant footfall behind me. I looked round.

The Dacian was awake and looking at me from the stable doorway.

'You have a strong arm for a punch. If I had been sober I don't think you would have found it so easy.'

'Well you asked for it you know. I apologise. It was a stupid and pointless fight. It is not honourable to fight someone who is drunk.'

'Drunk, who was drunk? I can take my drink. It was you who was drunk.'

I did not feel like getting into another brawl so I acquiesced. The Dacian seemed to be an argumentative, disagreeable man but I had such a bad head he could have said anything and I would not have argued.

'Are you a farmer?'

'A farmer? A bloody farmer? Are you stupid? I am a warrior. I am part of a war band and as soon as my head clears, I will find my armour and ride back north to join my men. We are raiding the northern Roman borders, and before you ask why, I can tell you it is because there are great riches to be had. I only came to Luvavum because my horse went lame and I ended up walking. I need a horse.'

'I see no armour or weapons,' I said, for he had only leggings, a tunic, and cloak. He did not even have a sword.

'Hmm... I remember now, I may have lost them in a dice game.'

'So you don't have money either? How do you expect to buy a horse, with no money?'

'I didn't say I was going to buy anything. There are some very nice horses in this stable.'

'Four of them are ours. If you touch them, you will be very sorry. They crucify horse thieves in this part of the world. Remember you are unarmed.'

'I wouldn't steal from you. Why, we are almost comrades!' he laughed at that. He had a deep voice and his laugh sounded like a huge barrel hitting the ground. He was a hairy man, almost a head taller than me but not much older. He had a shock of tousled and unkempt black hair. His long beard stretched down to where the hair on his chest peeped out of the top of his tunic and he stood with his thick muscular arms akimbo as he looked at me.

'Comrades don't usually insult each other. I seem to recall your introduction last night was far from civil.'

'My name is Duras, and I am a king's son. If you lend me a horse to use I will take you to my home and we can feast the winter away, fighting and womanising. Some of the Dacian women are very beautiful you know.'

'I don't have any interest in women right now. I only fight when I have to and there is as much chance of me lending you a horse as there is of Dacia becoming the next ruling empire.'

Cornelius who had awakened now, stood next to the Dacian and must have heard all of the conversation, for he inclined his head and said, 'Let us not be too hasty, Sextus. Duras here has made a good offer. We have nothing to lose by accompanying him and much to gain; especially if his father is a rich monarch. He might buy our spare horses.'

'Are you sure we need to have business in Dacia?' I asked.

'We are headed north so there is no reason not to help this young man to get home,' Cornelius said. 'The alternative is to stay here in Luvavum and have nothing to do for three months.'

We discussed the alternatives and in the end, I agreed to take the advice of my friend. We provisioned and set off with the Dacian riding with us. The major burden for the animals was the feed they would have to carry since it was a two-week journey even in good weather and with the prospect of snow on the way, it was unlikely the horses would find any grazing.

Although we spoke little while travelled, when we set up camp, we were able to get information from Duras. He told us how although much of Dacia was a Roman province, the northern border remained free of Roman rule and it was here he and his family lived. They were close to the Scythian border, and his people had cultural and language ties with the Scythians and Sarmatians.

The change in the landscape was dramatic as we rode north. The forested mountain slopes and hills of Noricum gave way to huge, thick tracts of mixed trees and pine forest. We came to a huge river that Cornelius called the Danubus and we had to search the bank for a ferry to take us across at what seemed to me, an exorbitant fee.

We camped on the other side in a hailstorm. The horses took a long time to settle for they do not like hail. I stood talking to them for what seemed to me, to be an age and after a while, Duras joined me.

'Here, let me help you, I believe the same as you, a man who does not communicate with his horse is a poor horseman indeed.'

So saying, he walked up to the horses and crooned to them in a voice I can only describe as guttural. It did seem to do the trick however, for they soon settled where we had tethered them, under a tree.

'We Dacians are like the Sarmatians. We are great horse people. All my life I have been around horses and have never been let down by one. I wish I could say the same for people.'

'What do you think of these beasts then?' I said, indicating the stallions we had stolen from the estate.

'They are fine animals but I suspect for all their speed they have less stamina than the ones we breed. We breed warhorses and train them to show no fear in battle, to be fierce, kicking and biting when the right rider commands them.'

'Horses are not naturally aggressive,' I said. 'If it isn't in their nature to fight, then I don't see how you can train them to be vicious.'

'Maybe you are right or maybe Roman horses are weak and don't like fighting any more than their Masters do,' he smiled at that, but I did not bite, for I was becoming used to his irritating teasing.

'I am no Roman,' I said. 'I am a German and I am trying to get home to my own people, having been away since I was a child.'

'Which tribe of Germans do you belong to?'

'I don't know, but I know they use tattoos to mark their scalp and I know one or two words of the language.'

'You mean your parents never told you the name of your tribe? I think that most odd,' Duras said. 'I don't know of any who use tattoos on their heads, but perhaps my father can tell you. We are now only two days ride from my home.'

Cornelius called us for the evening meal of dried fruit and a wheat porridge he had concocted. We ate and then drank the last of the Noricum wine. It was to be a while before either of us drank wine again.

If you had asked me then what single thing I missed most about being in Rome, or with Romans, then I would have said it was wine. Beer is bitter and makes you flatulent, but a good wine is like a gift from the Gods.

'I would put out the fire if I were you. This area is not safe so close to the borders of Roman influence. There are plenty of German raiders who attack travellers and traders in these forests too,' Duras said.

'I think we can look after ourselves,' I said.

'Maybe Duras is right,' Cornelius said. 'He does live here and I don't fancy being caught by a German war band out in these forests.'

Because of that, we spent a damp, cold, and rather miserable night with no fire at the edge of a dense pine forest in the hope we would escape detection by any passing marauders. The following morning however, we came across some fresh hoof prints and wondered whether it might have been Germans or not.

Duras examined the track. 'These are not tracks made by my people. We usually file a small cut into the horseshoes so that we can identify each other's tracks, but these have none.'

'We are better to follow them than try to go around. As long as they don't turn around we will know exactly where they are,' Cornelius said.

'They went into the forest through that path there. We can follow at a distance and keep well behind them. However many they are, they can only come at us two abreast at most. If you lend me a sword and shield I can help fight if necessary,' Duras said.

'You had to borrow a horse and now a sword. Perhaps you would like to borrow my clothes too?'

'That would be very handy,' laughed Duras, 'it's getting quite cold and an extra layer would be nice, although I think your clothes may be too small. But if you insist little one...'

'Very funny, you great Dacian goat.'

We were both smiling. I felt I was at last beginning to understand this great, big Dacian oaf.

A thin layer of snow had fallen overnight and the weather felt freezing cold. The tracks of the men we followed were clearly visible in the fresh snowfall. The snow could not penetrate the thick forest either side of us as we rode, though the path we followed seemed paved in white. It was like a white pointer to the travellers who rode ahead of us. We followed their tracks for perhaps an hour but saw no sign of anything but trees.

We halted, for we heard a woman scream off to our right. The laughter of men accompanied that scream, a sound of utter terror.

The tracks led us to the right where there was fork in the path. The right-hand fork led us to a clearing. As we approached, we could hear voices and then another scream. We dismounted with caution and tethered the horses with slipknots so they would be easy to free if we needed to flee. We kept to the tree line and flattened ourselves to one side to reduce our outlines.

In the clearing, I could make out about ten men who were standing in a random order, laughing at one of their number raping a young girl, while two of them held her down. That they were German seemed obvious to me. Their flaxen hair was tied in braids and those who were still dressed wore tunics and leggings. They were all big men and had long fair beards, and pointed helmets. Their weapons were on the ground and a pile of shields and armour stood in the far corner of the clearing. A similar collection of weapons, swords, and axes stood next to the shields. A fire blazed in the centre of the clearing and its heat melted the snow into little streams that ran in trickles across the ground, leaving shining ice-trails reflecting the flickering yellow of the roaring flames.

I was more experienced than in my previous fights and realised that for three to take on ten must be suicide though half of them had their breeches around their ankles and the other half had disarmed in preparation for the fun ahead. They lacked discipline—unforgivable in a fighting man. They should have posted at least one lookout.

Holding my shield close and with my sword drawn, I rushed into the clearing. I took the first man with a full midline strike across the forehead. I hit him so hard, my sword stuck in his skull as he collapsed in front of me. I wrenched the blade free from his bleeding head. I turned full circle to my left and my sword followed. A horizontal cut struck another across his throat. He was down, clutching at the wound; gurgling sounds came from his throat. I brought my blade down on an arm. I saw in a blur, out of the corner of my eye, how Duras had similar success. Cornelius effortless as ever, dispatched two of the Germans too with a surprising speed for any man over sixty years of age.

The remaining four men managed to get to their weapons and shields. They faced us with the anger and hatred. Between the snarling Germans and us lay the girl who had now turned onto her side attempting to crawl away to the edge of the clearing.

The four warriors moved as one. With lightning speed, they crossed the clearing. They charged us all at once, no doubt to take advantage of their slight numerical superiority. They had reckoned without the speed of Cornelius' sword arm. He stepped forward and met them. His sword parried an axe cut; it went from axe to throat in a second. The man to his left then tried to hack at him with a sword. Cornelius avoided it. He stepped forward and to the side. He knelt and struck a double-handed blow, across the first and dying warrior. It contacted the unfortunate man's midriff on his left side. He howled and fell writhing to the ground.

I suppose Cornelius finished him off but I had my hands too full to follow. I was dealing with an enormous warrior as big as my Dacian comrade. The fight was a short one, because although he rushed me and tried to unbalance me with his shield, I sidestepped. Using the already bloodied point of my sword, I reached around his small shield, stabbing him with the point somewhere in the side. He turned and raised his sword. I managed to deflect the blow with my shield. I twisted my blade inside him. This time I must have found a vital area in his chest for he dropped his sword arm and fell forward. He began to twitch as his brain died and I remember the look on his face better than any of the other events because he looked up at me and stared straight into my eyes as if there was some kind of recognition in them. It is probably just fancy but I could have sworn he knew me.

We stood panting; we looked around us at the mayhem created in the time it takes to describe it. Such a skirmish lasts a short time and it can be difficult to recall details because of its brevity. The tiny clearing, strewn with bodies, leaked blood and death; so still now, seemed to me then like a burial mound; a place of mourning, despite my fading battle-joy. I was sure we all three had experienced that wild elation, which only battle can bring. That fury that takes your soul as you fight and kill, ending and replaced by the great joy, not a joy for life but a joy of death. It is something that sits ill upon any man, but it happens because Tyr pushes these feelings upon us and laughs with us on every battle-field. It is the laughter of the God of War filling us and making us love the slaying.

Yet for me, at that moment, I saw it for what it was. It was a scene of death and destruction. Those mounds of blood-soaked flesh abandoned by their shades would never hear the spring-thrush, the night owl or smell the odours of a beautiful morning. Calm came to me then and I understood the buried passion within me, the true nature with which I had been born and how it contained some lesson; a way of learning about whom I truly was and what I might become if I continued to tread this path. The path of war and destruction.

A movement to my right roused me to the reason for all this slaughter. She lay curled up at the side of the clearing. Her tattered clothes offered only meagre protection from either the cold or our eyes. I crossed to the weeping figure and laid a hand on her shoulder. She pulled away with a vigour that startled me. I felt like a man who after some great and magnanimous gesture is rejected by the very object of his charity. My hands were trembling from the exertion of the fight and it was only with difficulty that I placed it again on her shoulder and spoke in the gentlest of tones.

'It's alright, we're here to help. They are all dead.'

'Sextus, leave her alone for a while, can't you see she's in shock?' Cornelius said.

I stood and looked at my companions. 'What do we do with her?'

'She's probably from one of the villages around my father's town. If she recovers, we can take her there and send word to her people. By Donar! These Germans are nothing more than animals. I'm glad we killed them all, but it would have been fun to take one or two prisoner. At home, we geld them and burn them slowly when we catch them marauding on our land,' Duras said.

'You know I'm German don't you?'

Duras said, 'Err... Well, didn't mean any offence. It's just when I see my own people...'

I stared at him and puzzled over why I was bristling, but I said, 'I guess I'm Roman. Just don't insult my ancestors.'

Cornelius said, 'If you two have finished? We need to get away from here. There may be more of them scouting the forest. Give her some time to recover and then we must go.'

After what seemed an age, the girl began to regain her senses enough to get up and cover herself with a cloak we had left near her. We readied our fourth mount and helped her into a saddle taken from one of the German mounts. We had trouble catching some of the German horses but we managed to tie together a string of seven and that was indeed a prize for they were good horses, small but strong. Since Duras had fought with us, we decided to give him two of the horses and a proportion of the arm rings and torques we had stripped from the dead Germans.

We packed all of the German raider's goods and weapons on the spare horses and made our way along the track to the far end of the forest. We had to make one more camp in the forest. The girl seemed unable to speak. That she had suffered an unspeakable ordeal was clear, even to insensitive warriors like us but we could do little to help, apart from being as gentle as possible.

Cornelius had the most success. Maybe his age made him less threatening, but he was able to sit next to her and put an arm around her. The physical contact appeared to cause revulsion at first but he persisted and after a while, she put her head on his shoulder and cried long tears of sadness. We had no idea at that time, what people she was travelling with, or what had happened to them. There was little more we could do. She slept that night in Cornelius' arms and all I could think of was how the last person Cornelius had been tender to in that way, was Livia. It jogged all those thoughts of grief lurking deep in the back of my mind. I went to sleep thinking of Livia and the short moment we had together.

I still cannot understand how a man can get pleasure from rape. The rape itself ruins the whole point of the sexual act. The thought of violating another in that kind of intimate way is abhorrent and I have often wondered if it is a means of injuring someone in some mental way as well as a physical one. I have seen men, whom until then I had respected as warriors, indulge in violently taking the women of a defeated city and it has always nauseated me. I had faint childhood memories of my mother's death; how she had fought to protect me and how the Romans stabbed her as she died screaming. They spilled her blood as they tore me from her arms, red-soaked, crying. Perhaps that is why I feel this way. I had lost her to violence and at the hands of the Romans. I knew if there were Gods, they would grant her vengeance one day. They would suffer for what they had done.

I was not however, unaware of the contradiction. Cornelius was a Roman, yet I owed him much. He had brought out the dormant fighting ability in me and had asked for nothing in return but friendship. Perhaps not all Romans are bad, I do not know, but I had a wish for vengeance all the same. Such schisms reflect the irony the Gods employ for their entertainment; they must have many hours of amusement over us mortals. We love and we hate almost at the same time, yet we come through it with one or the other dominating and making us the people we are, good or bad.

CHAPTER XIV

"Summum ius summa iniuria"
(more law, less justice)

—Cicero

We reached the Dacian town of Lovosice in the late afternoon. It was a bigger place than Luvavum and it sprawled across a valley with black, thick forest all around and a central compound of buzzing activity. The king's town stood next to a river, tumbling by in a leisurely fashion as ferrymen and bargemen plied their trade on its banks. I did not know then that there were many tribes in the Dacian country and I had no inkling that there were so many kings either.

I was impressed by the way we entered the city. Duras announced who he was to the gate guard. The guards opened the big wooden gates immediately and bowed to him as he rode past on my Roman racing-stallion. They remained bowing as Cornelius and I rode past. It felt strange for an escaped slave like me to have men bowing as if I was a lord.

The town was a wooden conglomeration of huts protected by a wooden wall. The streets however, were wider than Luvavum's. There was a tempting smell of food cooking but mixed with an odour of animals. Most of the middens were outside the town walls and that meant hygiene was better than most places in Germania or Dacia.

There were markets, street vendors, crowded taverns, and

the atmosphere, although nothing like Rome had a busy and bustling feel to it. The locals wrapped themselves warmly in thick woollen clothes heralding the approach of winter and children played in the streets where cattle and horses wandered. Many such towns had places for the animals to sleep but they often shared the accommodation of their owners, since they were a source of warmth during the night. I felt it gave the locals an aroma that was less than sweet, but all people are different I suppose.

We rode through the crowded streets in a slow procession. The locals stared at Cornelius and me. I have no idea why, for we were dressed like them. It may have been because compared to most of the town's inhabitants we were armed to the teeth.

The King's Hall stood in the centre of the town and had a wall of its own rather like a rough broad stockade. The Dacians appeared not to use any stone, or bricks, in their buildings and the whole impression was of a crude and misshapen architecture. The hall in the centre of the palisade was wood-built and tiny compared to the great stone buildings of Rome that I was used to looking up at. We dismounted and a servant or slave took our reins and led the horses away to be tended. Two spearmen stood guard outside the wooden columned entrance. Steel bolts studded the thick wooden doors hanging from massive wooden hinges. The columns either side of the door displayed carvings of intertwined snakes.

A soldier came to lead us into the hall of the king. The main hall was a single storey with a thatched roof and a long barn-like aspect. There were tables set out along the walls on either side, I assumed, for feasts and they had strewn the earthen floor with clean straw. At the far end, we saw what they intended to be the kingly throne, but all I could see was a wooden chair on a raised platform. I was used to Rome, after all.

The place was empty. The soldier led us on through a doorway at the back of the hall, which led into a surprisingly pleasant garden. It surprised me, because the hall we were walking through was only worthy of very barbaric people but the garden we entered was tidy, well-tended and had plants that flowered even in this cold weather.

The king had his back to us as we entered. He turned and saw Duras and crossed the garden courtyard, his steps rapid and eager. He embraced his son with obvious affection. He was a man of medium height and I began to wonder how Duras had reached the size that he had if his father was as small as he appeared. One might also wonder, under the circumstances how large his mother was if his father was only of average height. All these thoughts passed through my mind in a moment and when the embrace of father and son was done, the king turned to Cornelius before me and said in surprisingly good Latin, 'Greetings, my friend, how comes it you accompany my son today?'

'We accompany your son,' Cornelius said, 'because he had no horse and no weapons and needed to be brought home.'

Duras said, also in Latin, 'Father, these two men have helped me. Without their help, I would have been left stranded by ill luck in Luvavum and still waiting for help to come to me. On the way here, we managed to fight and kill a massive band of German warriors and we rescued one of our young female subjects who we have with us still.'

'So you lost everything gambling and you ambushed some German rapists and you expect me to believe you are now a hero. You know quite well that you left in disgrace, with gambling debts that I had to pay. There are still creditors after you despite my best interventions.'

'Am I not your favourite son? Am I not the best warrior you have? Father, I have brought a beautiful stallion for you as a present. We have tethered it in our stables and my companions, Sextus and Cornelius wish you to have it as a gift in exchange for them wintering with us. For my part I have captured a German horse and wish you to have it, even if all you do is eat it.'

The king smiled at that. He was a man of pleasant demeanour. He had a short beard and dark hair like most of the Dacians. He tied his hair in braids like the German people. He had a long nose and eyes that seemed sharp, if not shrewd, but a ready smile. There were laughter wrinkles at the corners of his eyes and he grinned at us.

'So you have brought me a Roman horse, have you? They don't make good war horses but they do tend to win our races. There is a race in six weeks, and if you have brought the winning horse, I will reward you richly. If your horse loses then I will expect some recompense. Reasonable?'

'What recompense has the king in mind?' asked Cornelius.

'Why your lives of course!' the king said. He burst into laughter that seemed to rattle around the enclosed garden.

'Perhaps we should leave now, if that is the hospitality that horse-traders get amongst the Dacian people?' Cornelius said.

'My dear fellow,' the king said, 'allow an old king his joke. You are welcome here if only because you brought my son home. You must tell me about the fight you had. Where is this girl?'

135

'We left her with some people at the entrance to your noble hall,' Cornelius said.

'Well, we could perhaps have a wager on the race? Your Roman horses against our doughty Dacians? The plunder you took from those Germans might be a reasonable thing to bet over?'

'I'm not sure…' I said.

'Come, if you wish to winter with a king you must make kingly sport. Can I not persuade you?'

It sounded to me as if this was a way of ensuring we would stay, even if we lost the race.

'Your Majesty honours us,' I heard Cornelius say. 'My young friend here will ride, and in exchange, we can stay here for the winter. If we lose, you can have the German horses.'

I looked at Duras. He refused to meet my gaze. I think he felt thoroughly ashamed after the kindness we had shown him. Despite his arrogant and teasing manner, he was an honest and honourable man, and having no way to reward us for the help we had given him, he must have felt beholden.

We left the king's presence with a feeling of anger and foreboding. Duras was contrite for the first time since we had met him.

'I'm very sorry. I had intended my father to reward you, not treat you in this way. I think the horses you have, will win the Yule race without difficulty—if you have an experienced rider, but if you pick someone who does not know the course then it may be a problem. I would be more than willing to ride the horse for you, should you so wish. Of course, I cannot guarantee to win, but I promise you I will do my best.'

136

'How could you have repaid us by giving away one of our horses? The horse doesn't even belong to you! Duras, since we met you nothing seems to have gone right. Maybe I should ride the horse and you can just tell me about the course?'

'I will be pleased to, but you know, the penalty for losing could prove to be expensive.'

'I am not afraid of losing the German plunder, but the race is another thing.'

'Then we will concentrate on the race,' Duras said, 'it will be more relaxing!'

I think he meant it but he was a Dacian after all and I now know they are not famous for common sense. I often thought of Duras as stupid, but when it comes to it, he spoke three languages fluently and could plan a fight better than almost anyone I knew, barring only Cornelius.

We walked to the entrance of the hall. The rescued girl was there, sitting on a bench, her head in her hands. She stood as we entered and positioned herself next to Cornelius. At the doorway, a ray of sunshine cut through the gloom and I noticed Cornelius had his arm around the girl. He seemed protective of her and I understood that in him. Livia pervaded both our thoughts. I wondered perhaps whether his care of this girl was symptomatic of his own loss. She still seemed shocked.

'Cornelius, what do we do with this girl?' I said.

'Can't stay with us, can you?' he said turning to her, a soft smile flickering across his lips.

She looked up at him, large brown eyes opened wide, as if she was about to speak but no words came. I felt sorry for her. She had lost everything.

'I will take her,' said the guard, 'my wife will care for her.

This hall is always full of feasting warriors and it is not a fit place for a young girl.'

The guard escorted us through the hall and showed us to our quarters. He took the girl by the hand and led her away. He seemed a gentle fellow and so we acquiesced. She looked over her shoulder at us but followed meekly. Cornelius gave a reassuring smile and raised his hand in silent farewell. We never saw her again and considering what the future held for us, it was just as well.

To give the king his due, our quarters were among the best in the King's Hall. We shared a tiny room adjacent to the main feast-hall and there was even a door ensuring privacy. We unloaded our gear and decided to take a stroll in this new Dacian city. We stepped out of the door of the hall and walked in the snow along what must have been the main street. Duras, who was following, pointed out the little there was to see. Within an hour, I found myself in an alehouse. This was different from a Roman tavern for everyone inside appeared to be busy getting drunk or picking a fight with anyone who came within striking distance. We stood and ate bread and skewered meat we had bought from a street vendor outside. For my part, I felt the atmosphere in the alehouse explained our original introduction to Duras. Clearly, after a few jugs of beer any Dacian gets belligerent with anyone in his path.

Determined not to fall into the same trap as before, I was modest in my consumption. I wish I could say the same for our Dacian companion. We had no more than three drinks before he began to cause trouble. One might be tempted to think that having experience of drunkenness would allow one to curb one's behaviour. Not so in Duras' case. He picked a fight with a group of men who looked, for the entire world, like the brigands whom Cornelius and I had dispatched only a year before. Each of them was tall and looked as unkempt as our host did.

The fight spread rapidly. Every man in the place was soon punching and kicking. Cornelius and I tried to stay on the periphery but brawling drunks have a way of involving anyone within reach and we were soon in the thick of it. I landed a punch on one of Duras' assailants and it felt like punching a rock. He punched back and caught me on the chin and I remembered no more until someone tipped a bucket of water over me in the street. How long I had been lying there I could not tell, but Cornelius and Duras were standing over me and laughing.

Cornelius was the one who had assaulted me with the water. It was freezing and smelled of horse. No wonder the Dacians had the odour of animals. It was enough to make me smell like them, which in retrospect was possibly the most pleasant part of my day.

They helped me to my feet. 'You seemed to walk right into that one,' laughed Duras, who looked about as good as I felt. He had bruising and swelling beneath one eye and he was limping slightly. I had a sneaking suspicion he was the one who hit me, by mistake, but I never confirmed it.

'You seemed not to have done too well yourself,' Cornelius said.

'Cornelius is the one who did well. I don't think he got hit even once,' Duras said admiringly.

'Even at my advanced age,' he said, 'I can dodge the odd punch you know.'

We walked back toward the King's Hall feeling considerably worse for wear than when we left. I thought they had broken my jaw, but happily, it was only bruised. We sat in the empty hall at one of the long tables they used for feasting.

'What we need now is a woman each,' Duras said.

'Sorry but I'm not interested at the moment,' and I told him about Livia and the events leading up to our meeting in Luvavum.

'That is a bad thing to have endured,' he said, 'but surely you don't intend to be celibate all your life simply because of one woman who is dead.'

It was obvious that he had no more understanding of human nature than he had of gambling.

'Duras, why don't you go and find a woman for yourself and Cornelius and I will stay here and rest. It has been a long day. Tomorrow you can show me where they are holding the race.'

After he left, Cornelius looked at me and said, 'I think we will be comfortable here as long as you win that race.'

'I can ride, and ride fast but I have never ridden in a horse race before. Have you?'

'No, but I'm sure you can do it.'

'Has everyone suddenly become stupid? You seem so calm about me risking my life, I can't believe it.'

'Stop panicking. The worst that can happen is you lose our plunder.'

'I'm not panicking. I just think that in six weeks' time we will have our hands full just trying to hang onto the little we have.'

'I am calm because anything we lose we have stolen already. If you believe in that sort of thing, you might speculate that the Gods are telling us we cannot hang on to property that rightfully belongs to others. For my part, I think that since we did not have those horses to start with, and it cost us nothing to get them, then if we lose them, then we have lost nothing.'

We retired for the night. My head was full of thoughts whirling around like a tempest. The impending horse race, losing Livia and the forthcoming journey in the spring. It all seemed oppressive. My thoughts faded in the end and I drifted into a deep, dreamless sleep.

CHAPTER XV

"To have begun is half the job: be bold and be sensible."

— Horace

It was bitter cold in Lovosice that winter. I had not realised our journey had taken us so far north we would feel this frozen. It is an odd thing about travelling to an icy land that when one is warm, as we were most of the time in Rome, one cannot imagine being cold. When I lived there in my enslavement days, I would never have understood the chance that in the future I would awaken in the night and need to brush ice from my cloak. Lovosice was like that, even with a roof over my head; my first experience of true, biting cold came home to me that winter.

The weeks passed without trouble or signs of pursuit and Lovosice seemed a very good choice of winter quarters for us in many respects. When I now compare hospitalities in my past, the Dacian King did provide a good table and excellent entertainment most of the time for his people and for his guests. There were regular feasts and the entertainment ranged from jugglers and acrobats to singers and mortal combats in which eager participants demonstrated their aggression in front of the bloodthirsty gathering in the King's Hall.

The forthcoming race had been on my mind throughout

however, and it took more than such entertainments to distract me. In the first weeks, I rode the course often, to familiarise myself with the terrain. Duras took me some of the time and sometimes I went alone.

The race was about five Roman miles in length and went from outside the King's gates to the south towards the surrounding forest. It then took a left turn, heading east, along a narrow path through the pine trees. After that, it circled around through the forest and back north along the river and then to the finish outside the gates of the King's Hall. The problem was not the distance, but the width of the track in the forest. It would at most only accommodate two riders abreast and although I did not, everyone else found it easy to see what was going to happen there. Out of sight and close up riders would exchange blows and a rider who fell would be left behind.

'The best way to stay on your horse is to make sure the others don't,' Duras said, 'I have ridden this race many times.'

'Have you ever won?' I asked.

'No, but I came second one year when I was just a lad.'

'If you never won, how can you give me advice? I need to talk to a winner, not just the runner up.'

'I'm only trying to help,' Duras said.

'It's thanks to your help I'm in this mess,' I said. 'If you'd kept quiet about the racing qualities of the horses, your father would never have made me race.'

'Actually, if I hadn't talked about racing he might have taken everything you own. I'm afraid that's the sort of thing our kings do, you know.'

The night before the race, I slept badly. All I could think of was winning, to salvage my pride. I was as well prepared as I could be. I had ridden the course enough times to know the vagaries of the landscape and the only unknowns were my opponents. I had gone to the trouble of corn feeding my horse for weeks in the hope the extra nutrition would give him stamina. This was a longer race than any he had faced in Rome and I remained uncertain what the heavy going in snow would do to him. It is a fact you can take a horse from one type of terrain to another and he will lose all his expected performance simply because of being unused to the conditions.

My stolen horse was a black stallion, a tall beast with a wide chest and a proud demeanour. He was well trained on the Piso estate for what he had been bred for—chariot races. I spent the time well, in training him and he was used to wearing a saddle. He was also used to my style of riding, for the horse and I had the same teacher. I often thought of the old man whom we left at the estate and wondered if he had suffered because of our theft. I hoped he had not, for he had always been kind.

Cornelius, I think, was enjoying my discomfort. He spent most of the time teasing me about the scar on my buttock and enquiring whether it would slow me down in the race to come. I never understood why he failed to take the race seriously. It may have been that he trusted me to win or perhaps he had no real cares about losing our new-found wealth to the King. I began to wonder whether all he had been through in his life had detached him from material things and now the only thing that mattered to him was enjoying the moment.

I felt tired and drawn on the morning of the race. The start was early and I ate a good breakfast of bread, meat and fruit to keep my strength up. As I crossed the hall's threshold, I realised this was an important event to the Dacians. They were a nation of horse breeders and as such, had a great interest in the result of this race. The winner could be certain of selling his horses and to put the winning horse out to stud in the coming years gave the chance of money in the future—a strong incentive to the owners.

A huge crowd gathered in the winter sunshine. The light reflected bright as a summer sunrise off the fallen snow, which lay compacted underfoot by the huge number of spectators. It was then I saw the competition. There were six others in the race. All of them big boned men with the same black hair as the typical Dacians. They all sat astride their mounts at the starting point. Dacian horses are small but broad and have thicker legs than the Roman animals. They train them to be warhorses and they can be vicious when roused in battle.

I mounted and sat feeling sleepy and tired. It was cold and frosty. Steam issued from the nostrils of the horses. Some of them were highly strung and their riders could barely keep them still. I talked in soft tones to my horse whose name Cornelius insisted upon choosing. He called him Bucephalus, after the great warhorse ridden by Alexander the Great all those years ago in Macedon. The crowd quietened for they knew too much noise around these beasts, would cause them to panic. The spectators were packed with such density they formed a kind of human funnel along the first part of the course. I could see their eager faces, ruddy and expectant. Their anticipation was almost palpable and the tension was rising.

Cornelius walked up to me as I mounted.

'Here, take this,' he said.

He handed me a small shield such as certain gladiators

used in the arena. It was no bigger than a plate, but it was used as much as a weapon as a protection.

'What for?' I asked.

'You will need some protection, won't you?'

'What on Olympus for? It is a race not mortal combat! I'm not fighting anyone.'

'My dear boy,' Cornelius said, 'if you think you are racing with women then don't take the shield. I think you will need it when the going gets tough. You didn't think this was just a bit of horseracing did you?'

The news unsettled me. It occurred to me perhaps Cornelius was right, when I considered the narrow track through the forest. Two riders abreast meant a number would be left behind to fight it out. I had already worked out how the fastest part of the course was the return along the river. I needed to be in front by the time we reached the forest, in order to make the most of my horse's speed later.

One of the gate soldiers was to start the race by dropping a red cloth in front of the lined-up riders. He stood quite still and I could feel the tension in the air. I looked at the crowd. Their faces were intent and the expectation in them was clear. A horse next to me bucked and whinnied. My nervousness evaporated.

I focused on the apex of the human tunnel in front of me. People waved and cheered as they stood below the eaves of their thatched wooden houses. They waved cloths of different colours according to their factions and called both abuse and encouragement.

He dropped the cloth. All of a sudden, it was mayhem. The riders seemed all to have the same idea. There was a good deal of jostling and elbowing as we began to accelerate. The compressed snow in the hall's courtyard led to slipping hooves and unbalanced riders. Bucephalus was a hardheaded horse; he neither gave way to the others, nor did he falter as we picked up speed.

I was through the throng in moments. I was third in the group as we headed to the forest. This comforted me; I had to keep up with the leaders. If I could get through the forest fast, I stood a chance of overtaking them. The course was flatter and faster towards the end and there Bucephalus would fly. I could see the two leaders ahead of me. I had no chance to look behind. Ahead, I could see the edge of the forest looming dark and threatening.

The riders turned the bend. We reached the forest track. Another horse came from behind and drew level. I could just make out the look on my adversary's face. He was smiling with pure joy. He began to pass me on my right. As he did so, his left hand shot out at my head. A leather glove with spikes enclosed his hand. He aimed directly at my head. I jerked forward. He missed me completely. As I righted myself, I reached behind. I grabbed his wrist and pulled. He was badly off balance, having missed his punch. The effect of my pulling on his arm was to draw him bodily off his horse. I had no qualms about that at all. If he had not struck at me, he might have passed me, instead of lying with his unconscious head in the bushes.

The world moved up and down with the motion of Bucephalus' stride. The sound of his hooves on the brittle white road rang in my ears. I focussed on the second-place rider. The ground was slippery even here in the forest. I breathed as hard as my horse. Tree roots reached up for us. Low branches stooped to strike me. I tried to gain a little ground. I had to close the gap.

We entered the woods in a line. Bucephalus was enjoying

the ride. He showed no signs of fatigue. I drew forward and tried to pass. The rider took his mount into the middle of the track. I talked to my horse. Bucephalus had to remain steady and balanced. His hooves thundered on the snow-primed track. He leapt over tree roots and logs like a winged steed. He was ready to fly away as soon as we left the forest. I kept tight rein on him. I had no wish to soar through the air.

The track widened as the trees opened up and the path was a little wider and smoother. Bucephalus and I saw our chance. I spoke to him in a cool, clear voice and encouraged him. He needed no more from me. He forged ahead. Unless you have ridden a powerful horse in a race, it may be hard to understand the thrill and the exhilaration of that feeling. The icy wind rushed past my face and my heart leapt as we began to force our way towards the leader. I really was flying now, as the forest swept by in a blur and the frozen ground roared to the sound of Bucephalus' iron-shod hooves. I could win this. I knew it. I could taste the victory on my lips like a sweet wine, like the soft touch of a woman's lips. It was all there for me now.

I drew level with the man in second place. He was not smiling like the man whom I had pulled from his saddle. He snarled and used a knife. It was a long, wickedly curved blade as long as my forearm. He swung it in a backhand stroke. He might have killed me easily if it had landed. I raised my left arm. I deflected the blow with my little shield. The knife went downwards. It cut into Bucephalus' hide just behind the saddle.

That horse must have known what had happened. He took off at an even harder pace and the second runner was almost behind us. He urged his horse forwards and tried to strike again. To my intense anger, the horse he was riding turned to its right and bit Bucephalus on the neck close to the shoulder. I used the shield. I struck the rider full in the face, backhand. It unhorsed him. It did not merely unhorse him; it hit him with such force he shot off his saddle. He disappeared from sight into the edge of the dark, gloomy, pine forest.

I was now two horse's lengths from the leader. As luck would have it, we were leaving the forest. We turned left along the river. I had always thought this was the fastest part of the course. My faithful steed did not let me down. He ran his heart out to catch the leader.

We had over a mile to go. I did not want Bucephalus blown. There was the river to my right. To the left was the forest. I could see the leading horse's rump looming ahead like a rising brown sun dawning in front of me. I contented myself with drawing close enough to be a horse's length away and stayed there.

The ice-bound sward beneath us reverberated to the sound of the hooves. We startled a fox running across the path, tail outstretched behind. Neither horse paid any attention. The fox for his part, glanced quickly over his shoulder as he reached the forest, caring nothing for men and their games.

Minutes passed and the last left turn came into view. We were heading north now at last. I knew I could win. Bucephalus was a horse for the Gods to ride, not an escaped slave. The race had tested his mettle and yet he had more to give. I loved him then as a man can love a woman, as a man can love his very life. My horse. My champion. Winged steed, a Valkyr mount. I rode.

The finishing straight.

I could see shiny faces turned towards us. I could hear the

shouts. They were cheering, waving. It was time to go. Bucephalus sensed it. I raised my voice in encouragement. He lengthened his stride. He quickened his pace. He drew level with the rider in front. The man grimaced. He tried to stab at me with a knife. The little shield was useful again, despite its size. I was in the lead at last. It was clear my adversary's horse was tiring. Bucephalus and I forged ahead. It was easy!

As we drew forward the Dacian horse, like the previous one, bit Bucephalus on the rump. It had little effect apart from spurring him on to greater speed.

This time it was my turn to grin. I looked round with a huge, smug smile on my lips. A winners' triumph written all over my face as we reached the finishing point.

In retrospect, it was a stupid thing to do. I failed to see a low hung tavern sign. I turned back. It struck me in the face. I have no recall of subsequent events. Cornelius later told me it catapulted me from the saddle and that landing in a snowdrift was the only thing saving me from a much more serious injury.

I awoke in bed with the grandfather of all headaches and a bruise the size of the Forum Romanum on my forehead.

So much for Dacian horse races.

CHAPTER XVI

"Old things are always in good repute, present things in disfavour."

—Tacitus

The morning after the race, the king summoned me to attend him in the hall. He sent a servant who made it quite plain the king had not invited me; he had commanded my presence.

The king's name was Moscon. He had ruled for almost thirty years and was still far from his dotage. He had no reputation for fairness but his people did not feel he was a cruel man either. Cornelius and I did not quite know what to expect.

It was true I had technically lost the race, although my horse according to Cornelius had won without me. As soon as the hanging tavern sign had liberated me from my saddle, Bucephalus, who probably did not want more bites on his rump, had charged full tilt through to the finish. I had no particular hopes it would let me off the king's hook, but it provided a useful argument if argument became possible.

My head throbbed and ached intolerably as soon as I arose. I felt light-headed at first and had problems focussing my eyes. I seemed to have great difficulty finding all my clothes but managed in the end. Presently, Cornelius and I strode through the doorway of our quarters into the King's

151

Hall.

Gathered around the wooden throne stood the other riders of the recent race with Duras and the king's priest. An audience of nobles sat at the benches on either side of the hall and they stared holes in our backs as we walked past. I still felt dizzy but managed to look up to the king and said, 'My lord king, you summoned me.'

'Yes, Sextus. I want your explanation of how you managed to lose a King's race and to let you know the Royal decision.'

'If I might say a word before your majesty decides?' I mumbled. Speech seemed difficult in the state in which I found myself.

The monarch grinned, showing two rows of blackened stumps. 'No, you may not,' he said, still grinning like a half-wit. We looked each other in the eye. I could see he found the whole business amusing and I detected no real malice.

'Sextus, you may recall the terms upon which I allowed you to stay with us here in Lovosice?'

'Of course, my lord,' I said.

'Then you will realise both the Roman horses and all the torques and arm rings you took are mine.'

'But my lord...' I said.

'Silence, I haven't finished yet.'

The king looked at me, his eyes piercing and bright.

'There may be a way in which you can avoid such a harsh penalty.' He stroked his beard and said, 'You don't have a wife do you?'

'No sir.'

'Perhaps you should have one.'

'I would prefer to wait. I am travelling north and it will be no journey for a woman.'

I caught sight of Cornelius' face in the corner of my eye and realised he was grinning.

'I insist. If you marry the girl I have in mind I will forget about your ignominious failure in the race and we can use your possessions which would otherwise be mine, in lieu of a dowry.'

I saw it then. If I married one of his household, he would use my possessions as a dowry. He lost nothing and avoided the dowry payment which as king, he was bound to pay for any member of his family. He also acquired a warrior, namely me.

'If your majesty wills it, I have no alternative.'

'Don't be so sulky Sextus. She is a beautiful girl. She is my sister's daughter and I have had charge of her since my brother died of a fever years ago. You will meet her at the feast tonight.'

'It will be as you command. I must obey you.'

'Exactly. You may go.'

He turned to one of his councillors and I could have been invisible after that. We left the hall with Cornelius at my side grinning like a drunk on Saturnalia. I stared at the ground; my shoulders sagged. As soon as we were in the open air, Cornelius stopped me with a hand on my shoulder.

'You should listen to the king. There is no value in sulking. He has beaten us.'

'Us? What do you mean us? It's me who's getting married to some woman who could look like a horse's backside for all I know. And anyway, what do we do with a girl in tow travelling north through the German lands?'

'We don't have to go. We can stay here. We have enough wealth to trade in horses. Moscon at least let us keep our goods.'

'I don't belong here Cornelius. We only came for the winter.'

'But we don't even know where we are going. Think about it. We could do well here trading horses and being connected with the king could have many advantages.'

'Such as?'

'Well I must say there is a serving girl in the King's Hall who seems to have taken a shine to me and it's a long time since I had such thoughts as I have now.'

I looked at him in amazement. At first, I could think of nothing to say. He must have been sixty years old if he was a day.

'Cornelius, why don't you get married too? We could both start families. We could live together on a farm and raise toddlers. Your mind is going you raving old goat.'

'Sextus, you should be happy. You have a life, you aren't a slave and you've become a man in such a short time. Marriage will suit you. Trading will make you a man of substance. Yes. Perhaps we don't need to move on.'

'You aren't listening to me. I must go north and find my people. Livia wanted me to and it means a lot to me.'

'She loved you. She would have been content to see you happy and settled anywhere if she couldn't be with you,' Cornelius said.

It was no use arguing, but I thought of her and it was painful. We had too much time on our hands; that was the trouble. My head was banging and I was still dizzy whenever I stood up. Any physical exertion seemed to make my head throb and I was a little forgetful and distrait for weeks afterwards

I lay down on the cot in our shared room. I cannot say what Cornelius was up to, for he did not reappear until afternoon and when he did, he had a woman with him. She was a plump matronly woman whom I remembered had served us at table the previous night. She was all smiles and I noticed dimples in her rosy cheeks as she grinned at me. I understood I was not welcome then, for she asked me by gesture if I would leave the room. I looked askance at Cornelius.

'Sextus, part of sharing accommodation with a friend is to know when a little privacy is indicated,' he said. There was a smile on his face; he spoke kindly and I did not take it amiss. I decided to find Duras, hoping he would not be up to similar activities. As I closed the door, I heard a giggle and Cornelius said something I did not catch. Tempting though it was, I did not linger at the door. I had my pride even then.

I was on edge, waiting for what the evening would bring. The forthcoming introduction to my bride-to-be, in a Barbarian hall filled with feasting people, was not my idea of forming a relationship and as I walked through the courtyard, I wondered what the girl herself was feeling. She must have been frightened. I could turn out to be a wife beater for all she knew.

I bumped into one of the guards on the way out of the compound and I realised I was not very steady on my feet. The blow to my head in the race seemed to have had more of an effect than I had realised. I wanted to sit down but there was nowhere appropriate. Presently, I came to an alehouse and went in more for somewhere to sit than for any alcoholic refreshment. I could not face beer at that time of day so I enquired hopelessly if there was any wine.

'Wine? Well no one ever asks me for wine here. We're so far north the only wine we get is from an occasional travelling trader. That man over there may have a stock. He's fresh in today,' the bartender indicated a tall thin man sitting at a table in the corner.

I walked up to the table and the man looked up as he took a sip from his beer. He had large sad eyes and a long face. His features seemed more suited to mourning than selling, for the corners of his mouth turned down and a less affable salesman could hardly be imagined. If the barman had not pointed me in that direction, I would never have considered buying anything from him.

'What?' he said, with a Roman accent.

'I heard you may have some wine.'

'Wine? Why would a Dacian peasant want wine? Do you even know what it is?'

'My dear fellow,' I said in Latin, 'there is no need to express scorn. It could cost you dearly and then I would be dry. I'll say it again. Do you have any wine for sale?'

I stood above the seated man and rested my hand on my sword to indicate a willingness to use it. I had already forgotten the meekness required of a slave. I heard my own voice as if I was standing next to my body, like in a dream. Perhaps the head injury had made me irritable but I disliked the man's tone of voice. It seemed to indicate disdain and he did not know me at all. He looked at me for a moment and swallowed his mouthful of beer.

'Sorry. I thought you were one of the locals. I'm from Italia and I'm afraid these Dacians get on my nerves.'

'These Dacians you refer to are my hosts and they are staunch fighters who offer very good hospitality to those who treat them with friendliness and politeness. Now, how about answering my question?'

'Oh, the wine. Yes, I have some. Only three skins left. Red stuff from near Ostia. A hint of cherries on the nose. I sold most of it in Noricum. Cost you though.'

'I have money,' I said.

He rose and gestured me to follow as he shouldered his way to the doorway. We walked to a stable five minutes away.

'Any news from Italia?' I said.

'News? About what?'

'Nothing special, just news.'

'Well I hear Verus and his brother don't get on. Verus is going to the East to quell a rebellion in Syria and Marcus Aurelius seems inclined to try to make peace with the Germans. No one thinks he will be successful and there is a likely war brewing.'

'Nothing more local?'

'No nothing really. I met some soldiers in Luvavum who were looking for a runaway slave. Killed a Praetor in Rome and stole horses. Big man like you, with a bald head and a tattoo on his scalp. Never seen such a man myself. Have you?'

'Not around here,' I said, certain no one could recognise me with my thick growth of blonde hair. I still felt dizzy and my headache bothered me. I wondered whether what I had done in Rome had made me famous and was half-inclined to tell this trader who I was. No one could touch me here and I knew it.

'There is a massive reward out for him. The Praetor's son, Marcus Piso is a friend of the Emperor's and has persuaded Marcus Aurelius to offer ten thousand sesterces for the man's shaven head.'

'A handsome reward.'

'I can't imagine he would go north. There are marauding German war bands all over and no one travels the German lands in winter.'

'No, I suppose not.'

'Here, do you want to try it?' he proffered a large wine-skin.

'No, how much?'

'Well to a man who speaks Latin, I could let you have the last three skins for twenty silver coins each.

'What? That's a fortune!'

'Well I have had to drag it all the way from Italia you know. It's the only wine in this Gods-forsaken place, I can tell you.'

'Twenty for the lot,' I said.

'Forty.'

'Twenty five.'

'Done.'

He smiled and I wondered if he had just robbed me. It was a heavy price to pay but as he said, it was the only wine in town.

'Shall I deliver it?'

'Are you serious?' I said, 'I can carry these with no trouble.'

I paid him.

'If you like,' he said and began piling my outstretched arms with the wineskins. They were heavier than I had realised but I was looking forward to drinking the contents. I stood fully laden and turned to the door. My back was to him as I stepped towards the open air when I felt something hard and sharp at my throat.

'You're the one aren't you?'

'What?'

'Since when does a Dacian bastard talk nice Latin. You must have come from Rome. I recognised the accent. What luck. Ten thousand! I can retire now.'

I have learned through long years of violent struggle, if one is going to kill an enemy, however much you hate them, gloating and counting your money is the worst thing you can do.

His right hand held the blade and I held the wineskins. I turned very fast. His blade nicked my throat as I did so, but the bulk of the wine was between us as I turned to my left. It was as if I had thumped him hard with a heavy weight in the chest. He fell. He tried to roll away. I dropped the wine onto his back. I stood on his hand with all my weight. He cried out and the knife lay ownerless on the straw.

I drew my sword.

'You should never attack a man from behind. It's not honourable. Also, never attack a man and then let your greed delay you in killing him.'

He turned over and I imagined I would kill him. I put the tip of my blade to his throat and I saw him swallow with fear. It was enough. I was not very angry, even though the knife cut on my throat was stinging. My head still ached.

'I will accept the wine as a present, in fair recompense for the insult and injury. Do you agree?'

'Yes, yes. Please let me live. I have children.'

'I will not kill you but you should learn we Barbarians, as you call us, have enough honour to treat you fairly. Now pick up the wine and you can have the privilege of delivering it for me. I will follow with drawn sword in case you try to run.'

I let him up and made him carry the wine to the King's Hall. We deposited it outside our room and I could hear squeals this time from beyond the door. It irritated me but I cannot say why. Surely, Cornelius had a right to some levity after all he had suffered since he met me.

The trader left then and I aimed a kick at his departing buttocks as he went out of the door. I never saw him again but I always thought I was magnanimous in allowing him to live. The little nick on the side of my throat healed quickly enough and did me no real harm. I got my money back and had enough wine to drink for a few days. It seemed a useful encounter. My head ached. I learned over the next few hours however, wine does not help headache and in this case, made it worse.

I sat at a bench in the empty hall and poured wine for an hour. I began to think again about the girl who was expecting to marry me. She had no freedom to choose. I could be anyone as far as she knew. It was a cruel way to treat anyone, man or woman. I was after all in a perfect position to see that, having once been a slave. I began to feel sorry for her, but could see no way to change the king's mind. Our German culture treats women with little respect. I know it now. A woman is not property any more than a man enslaved should belong to another. I began to wonder how I would have treated Livia had I been able to marry her as I once wished. The same lack of experience as I suffered from in my fighting skills would have hampered me, I felt sure. My life as a slave had equipped me for little other than waiting at table, and writing Greek.

Livia was not one to bow to a man. She would sooner have put an arrow through me than obey me. Despite that, I had loved her. I had loved the very essence of her and revelled in her strength of character and hard-headedness. Could I, in all honesty, expect my new bride to be like that? It seemed unlikely.

As the wine took hold, I became more and more morose

and finally I became drowsy. Before sleep took me, sitting with my head cradled in my arms at the pine table, a last vision of Livia's face impinged upon my thoughts. I knew then she was still with me in some way. I could feel her presence and I felt like crying.

CHAPTER XVII

"Do not trust the horse, Trojans! Whatever it is, I fear the Greeks, even though they bring gifts."

— Virgil

I hated the Romans at that time of my life. It was the result of having been a slave to them. It was also because I had learned much in my education. I had learned they were cruel and uncompromising. Whole swathes of people put to the sword to subdue provinces; the barbarous killing in the arena and the way they had treated my own people, fuelled my hatred. Despite these feelings, I had to admire them at the same time. The basic concepts of engineering and building and a cultural life with cleanliness and bathing at its heart, seemed worthy of my admiration.

The Dacians by comparison were a rough lot. Hygiene and bathing were not in their cultural repertoire. Despite anything said about them however, they were hospitable. You could land at any Dacian farm, whoever you might be, and they would feed you. There was an unwritten law that guests were sacred. No one would defy such a law for it was based upon honour and trust and had its roots in antiquity.

They accorded this hospitality to Cornelius and me in a measure far beyond our expectations. Every three days or so there would be feasting in the King's Hall. The king provided and paid for the entertainments. Moscon treated us to jugglers, dancing, music and acrobatics. Occasionally when two nobles had a dispute, they fought mortal combats in front of the king's dais. The king awarded all the property of the vanquished to the survivor, including the burden of the dead man's family. Few fights of this type therefore occurred. No one wanted to take on another man's family; the responsibility seldom came cheap.

There was a feast on the night I first met my impending bride. Dacians need little excuse to celebrate and like children they wanted to do so all the time. This particular feast began early and all the Dacian nobles assembled in the King's Hall as darkness began to fall.

Moscon sat on his wooden throne and looked out at the sea of happy, feasting Dacians. He wore a constant and merry smile. His subjects often called him the Laughing King because of that smile but he had a serious side to him too. He made harsh judgment on anyone whom he felt had betrayed his trust and it was a brave man indeed who would cross him.

When sufficient of his subjects had crowded the floor before him, he began the feast by giving one of his formal speeches. Cornelius and I sat at a table listening to Moscon talk about the sanctity of marriage and the penalty for those who strayed. It was a foolish speech for he had one wife, and three mistresses of whom I was aware. How many children he had sired since he became king, was anybody's guess.

The hall was dark and smoky. Flickering torches in brackets lighted the hall and in its centre was a hearth. A massive fire of dry logs blazing and crackling, burned there. Its radiant heat was enough to chase away the winter chill throughout the entire hall. Sparks flew from the conflagration and sitting too close risked being set on fire. Cornelius and I therefore sat at a table where we had enough warmth but we were out of range of the fire's glowing missiles. There was a wooden conduit above the fire to allow the smoke to escape. I had never seen one like it. It was the same size as the hearth but narrowed into a kind of funnel, then, instead of going straight up to the roof, it had a bend in it, stopping the rain descending, but still seeming to create an up-draught drawing the smoke away.

At our feet was a layer of clean straw and down-filled cushions covered the rough wooden benches. All around us were the sounds of happy people, laughing, joking, and smiling. Some adolescents started horseplay so the ushers ejected them but allowed them back in before the food was served. Everyone else seemed to be relaxed and enjoying themselves.

The woman with whom Cornelius had spent the afternoon served us with beer, but when I showed her the wine under the table, she served that to us instead. Cornelius was full of praise for my find.

'A perfect feast. Wine, food and a beautiful young woman, what more could a man want?'

'What?'

He was looking at the woman with whom he had made friends.

'She is a beautiful girl. What she sees in an old man like me beats me. She knows I'm not rich.'

'Who is she?'

'Her name is Roziana. Beautiful name. She was a farmer's wife, but he died in a fire last year. She is all alone and I want to look after her. She's going to teach me a little Dacian. Do you know the word for bed in Dacian?'

'No and I don't want to either. Drink your wine old man.'

'What's eating you? I just said…'

'Look, we have wine and we are warm and comfortable. Do you have to spoil it all with this nonsense? I am about to be married to a complete stranger and all you can do is prattle on about Dacian language.'

'If I didn't know you better I would have thought you were scared. Just an observation but…'

'I really don't want to talk about it,' I interrupted again. 'Is there no way to get out of this?'

'No, like you said, let's drink our wine, and enjoy the place. The Gods will provide the answers. We are only mere mortals on their great playing board. They move us like pieces in a game and we must be patient and let it happen.'

'You've changed your tune.'

Cornelius looked up at his newfound partner. She smiled happily at him and he smiled back too. I was close to hitting him. He didn't understand. At least he had a choice. It now looked as if we would have two women in tow.

'What do you mean?' Cornelius said, turning towards me.

'I've never met a less pious man in my life. What is all this about the Gods?'

'Roziana can only be a gift from the Gods. Can't you see? Beautiful! Beautiful isn't she?'

I said nothing. There was no talking to the man. So this was the natural born killer who taught me the art of death and he was talking like a love-struck teenager. I wanted to tear the hair from my head in frustration. Oh Livia where are you?

Presently, they served the food. There was only one

course but it consisted of many dishes served at the same time. I ate well. There was roast boar and an herb and vegetable mash of which I am particularly fond. It contained some kind of herb I had never tasted before and it had the effect to of making me want more. I never tasted it again until many years later on another journey but that is a different tale. The noise around us was comforting. It rose in volume in an escalating spiral with each passing hour, as if the beer and the laughter made people talk louder.

The wine and the knock on the head seemed to spark off an appetite worthy of Donar. I ate and drank, unlike Cornelius. He hardly ate anything; he drank wine and muttered about his "Roziana" until I wanted to crawl under the table and vomit.

It was then my Nemesis approached. Moscon got up from his throne. The ushers called for silence and as was customary, everyone stood for the loyal toast. We drank the king's health and sat again.

'My people!' said Moscon. 'Since coming to my hall the two foreigners have impressed me.' There was a weak cheer from the back of the hall. 'They have impressed me so much,' he continued, 'that Sextus, the younger of the Barbarians has been chosen for something special!'

Eyes turned to examine me and then back to the king. I felt the icy digits of fear again, prodding, prodding; I know not why. It was a new experience to be singled out in this way. As a slave, one always keeps in the background. At this feast, it seemed as if I was an object of interest. I wanted to run. I had faced Sartorius without running, but now I felt the steely fingers of fear gripping my heart and all I wanted was to be somewhere else.

'Sextus is to marry my niece, Medana.'

166

There were loud cheers and several of the men got up and slapped me on the back, making me spill wine all over the front of my tunic. I did not know what to do next but Cornelius took my elbow and made me stand. Moscon saw me and indicated I should join him on the dais.

I walked down the hall past the blaze in the hearth wishing it would devour me and take me far from this embarrassing moment. The glow of my cheeks must have rivalled the glowing embers in the blaze too. I mounted the dais with a single step and stood feeling discomfited next to the Dacian king. He smiled at me but his eyes were steely and bright. I detected no indication of kindness, only triumph.

He slapped me on the back as the others had done and signalled to an usher on his right. I could do nothing. It felt a little like when the brigands had captured me in the hills above Ariminium. Passive, hopeless.

The usher brought a girl with him. She was an angular girl with a long thin pretty face and a ready smile. She had large, deep, dark, penetrating eyes and she stood before me in a thin gown with a dark-blue woollen cloak around her shoulders. The front of her gown was low cut and I could make out the shape of her breasts beneath.

'Well here she is. Her name is Medana. She is my sister's daughter. It is a great honour I offer to you. It would of course, be wise to accept graciously,' said Moscon looking more serious.

'I thank you most sincerely my lord. I would not be so churlish as to refuse such high honour as you offer me.'

Moscon indicated a low bench for me to sit on.

I gestured to the girl. She looked at the floor. Taking her gently by the hand, I guided her to sit beside me. There was no communication between us. She stared at the ground in

167

front of us. I stared straight ahead. Neither of us spoke. I wanted to drink. It was a nervous reaction but in the end I stood to get my cup.

Poor Medana misunderstood and followed me to the table where Cornelius sat trying to talk to his newfound lady-friend. Roziana exchanged a few words with my betrothed and she smiled to the girl. Medana looked sad and anxious. It was as I had expected. It seemed obvious to me she was an unwilling participant in the whole charade, but there was nothing either of us could do. The King had spoken.

Medana took my hand then in her cold bony fingers and led me out of the hall. I remember feeling relief at being out of the stifling atmosphere of the celebrating Dacians. No one seemed to notice and no one followed us. We walked to the barn where they kept the horses. There was a hayloft and we climbed the ladder as if it was the most natural thing in the world.

I thought then of Livia and could not shake the memories from my head. Medana just stood there looking at me then she looked down at the hay beneath us and she sat down on a bale of straw.

She stood presently; she let her gown drop from her shoulders to the dry hay at our feet, revealing her warm, thin body. She wrapped the cloak loosely around her to keep out the cold. She reached for me. She seemed to think this was expected but I knelt down and pulling up her gown, I covered her. I had no more intention of making love to her than I had of running away naked.

She looked up and all I could detect in her eyes was gratitude. It was as if she was going through the motions of everyone else's expectations. Within moments, we were both sitting side by side and I think neither of us knew how to react.

I patted her hand. She looked up and smiled for the first time since our introduction. She squeezed my hand and I smiled back at her. We lay in the hay. I had no wish to return to the feast and seemingly nor did she. Moments passed. There was little verbal communication for she spoke no more Latin than I spoke Dacian.

Eventually, she did speak. Her voice was clear and strong and easy on the ear.

'You great killer.'

I think she meant to say warrior but I supposed killer would do.

'Yes' I said.

She understood that one and she laughed. It was a delightful sound hanging in the air in the hayloft for it was sheer girlish pleasure. We lay down and both drifted off to sleep, still holding hands.

The night passed and we awoke both still much as we were the night before. I was holding her hand and she did not withdraw it. We sat up and she touched my cheek gently with a soft, warm hand. She stood and held her hand up to me indicating I should stay. She climbed down the ladder.

I waited wondering what I should do now. I hoped no one would realise how nothing passed between us in the night. The Dacian warriors might have thought it was unmanly but I had not the heart to touch her. It would have been a violation; she was young and pretty but I knew she was an unwilling partner pushed forward by Moscon in the hope of saving himself some dowry money.

I don't know whether she knew about the arrangements. Gods know I was in ignorance myself. I had no idea what the timescale for the wedding would be.

169

I pondered my predicament. I supposed I was stuck with her. Cornelius and I were due to move on in the spring. I hardly knew what I could do with a young woman in tow. I began to realise the king had tried to trap me and wanted me for a Dacian warrior. He must have been sure I would not leave with a wife.

She returned with two cups of buttermilk. I descended the ladder for she could not come up carrying both the cups. We sat on a bale of hay and studied one another, sipping the fresh buttermilk. I could feel we both had a kind of attraction to each other but for me it was as if Livia stood between us and I found it hard to see through her shade.

Medana said in Latin, 'You good man.'

I smiled and said in my limited Dacian, 'You nice girl.'

She pointed to things around us and named them for me. I repeated the words but knew I did not need to learn the language. I could see with my own eyes what was going on in her head. It was a friendship she sought, not a sexual encounter. I did my best to be friendly but the language barrier made it hopeless. I was unsure whether to teach her Latin or continue with what I thought was a pointless lesson. After we had tried to converse for half an hour or so, we gave up and Medana left to go back to the royal quarters where she no doubt had her accommodation.

I could see no way out, but destiny has a way of forcing itself upon us as the Gods sit watching. They must laugh at us mortals, for we always struggle so hard with our ignorance. Yet the Norns weave our future according to the Gods' dictates and we move with them. My future however turned out to be very different from my expectations at the time.

CHAPTER XVIII

"Cui bono?"
(To whose profit?)

— Cicero

Cornelius was slow to arise next morning. I waited for him in the King's Hall, for by the time he got up, slaves had cleared the place and removed most of the sleeping drunks who had not already awakened and left of their own accord. He approached me with a smile I had not seen before. He looked younger than ever and he had clearly either slept well or been up all night, I could not decide which.

'Well Sextus, my boy, how have you passed the night? I hope the king's niece treated you well.'

'I spent the night with a girl called Medana. She was nice but I was troubled because I wished it was Livia all the time,' I said.

A frown clouded his face and I realised it had been a stupid thing to say, reminding him of Livia at a time when the fates had given him some kind of solace.

'I can understand,' he said. 'You have to let go you know. She waits for us both in Hades and we will see her again. I think she would not expect you to be celibate for the rest of your life. It would mean your love for her is destructive and not a treasured memory to last all your days. Each time you see a girl and like her, doesn't mean you have been unfaithful to Livia's memory.'

'I suppose not, maybe it was just a bit soon. You seemed to have an enjoyable night.'

'Oh yes! There is life in the old dog yet.'

'The habit of sleeping with dogs is not one I am fond of, but if it's what you want to call your new companion that's up to you I suppose!'

Cornelius threw a gentle cuff at my head but I ducked and we both laughed. It was the shared laughter of true companionship and I realised then how close we had become. We had fought, grieved, and travelled together, but there was much more to it. He had taught me much of what I had needed to stay alive in a tough, cruel world and I loved him for it. It seemed to me, he was now the only person in my life for whom I had real feelings.

I went to the stables and saddled Bucephalus. I rode him out of the King's compound across the snow towards the wood. The day was overcast and there was no birdsong or other sound in the air. The silence lent an eerie atmosphere to the ride, but I was insensitive to it and rode on. The memories of Livia began to subside as the cool morning air rushed past my face and hair.

To my disquiet, I noticed a flicker of light from the forest edge. It was the tiniest fraction of a reflection, but my eyes had been my strongest sense for a long time and I knew I had seen something. I chose to ride past. It was half an hour's ride back to the town and there was no point in causing alarm if all I had seen was a peasant cutting wood. I rode past for a few minutes and then approached the edge of the forest and tethered my horse. There was undisturbed snow all the way up to the tree line and I entered the dark shadow of the forest. I crept as best I could, through the pine trees, avoiding any sticks which might snap and give my position away. I took off my Roman sandals for I wore them still despite the cold; having grown up in such footwear, anything else feels uncomfortable.

I moved with enough stealth to be almost silent. After sneaking along thus for about fifteen minutes an unexpected sight rewarded my caution. Squinting through the shadows, I saw row upon row of armed men on foot with swords, spears, and shields as they walked slowly and as quietly as they could in the direction of the town. The thickness of the pine trees made it impossible to tell how many warriors there were but the dense forest teemed with soldiers. I thought this must be a very large war band or worse, an invading army.

I knew it was vital for me to get back to Lovosice without the war band detecting me. I could not move very fast in the forest so I cut to my left and gained the tree line. I ran in the snow as quietly as I could and found Bucephalus where I had left him. I stroked his face with my hand and whispered soft words of gentle encouragement. He started and it made me look over my shoulder just in time. Three men were running at me with swords drawn. They were large blonde men and there was no mistaking their German origins.

Their approach left me no time to mount and worse still, my only weapon was the knife I used for eating. I turned towards them and then turned again keeping Bucephalus between us; I drew my knife and sprinted as fast as I could towards the forest. As I entered, I turned and ducked to one side behind a tree. The first man came a little ahead of the others and I turned very fast. In the rather cramped space I was able to put the blade square into his left eye. He screamed and I grabbed his sword-hand using his body to shield myself from the two men who were both striking at me with their weapons.

I wrenched the sword from my first adversary's hand and was able to parry one of the blows. The others landed on their comrade's back. I backed away holding the sword in front of me. They clambered over their dying companion. I stepped forward and struck two double-handed blows, one to each attacker. Neither blow did any damage, but it made one of them overbalance. His companion struck at me again. I parried. I came back with a backhand swing, striking him in the face, laying it open to the bone. The impact stunned him and I brought my blade down fast at the last man. He parried and regained his balance. We looked at each other for a moment. He said something in a Germanic language that sounded vaguely familiar but I understood none of it.

He did not move as I feinted to the right. He was clearly a swordsman. His companion had recovered enough despite his wound to swing his blade at me. I sidestepped with ease. In that instant the uninjured man made his move. He stepped forward fast. He feinted to his right, and then deftly changed direction with a stab at my stomach. I turned sideways to avoid the blade. It passed in front of me. I used the hilt of my sword and caught him on the side of the head. It was a very quick move, but as so often happens in retrospect seemed in my memory to have been in almost slow motion. He dropped unconscious to the forest floor. The wounded man stabbed at me again. It was a clumsy blow. It never landed. I stepped aside. I pushed the point of my sword into his chest. The blade went downwards between his head and shoulder. There was a squeal of pain. He was down, wheezing his life away as blood welled up into his throat.

I did not stop to finish off the third man but sprinted to

174

Bucephalus and rode like a Fury towards Lovosice. There was no pursuit. I presumed either the three men were stragglers catching up with the main force, or a rear-guard left to deal with anyone foolish enough to do what I had done.

Bucephalus sped me back as if he understood the urgency and we reached the gates at breathless speed. The guard at the gate looked down and asked if I had a good ride. I shouted the news we were under attack and told him to alert the rest of the guard. I rode through the gate. The guard slammed it shut behind me and I galloped up the main street to the king's compound. Behind me, I could hear the sound of the bell at the gate ringing its frantic summons, calling the king's soldiers to the walls.

The King and his men greeted my news with surprising calm.

'There is no great hurry to do anything,' Moscon's voice boomed across the assembled nobles and soldiers. 'Let them come. These German pigs do not understand siege-craft. They have not the patience for it. They have poor supply lines and I have no worries about holding them off in this weather. The river protects our flank and the wooden wall is strong. They will appear and hope we will come out to them and we will simply watch them starve.'

I looked at the men around me and all were nodding their agreement. Some who had rushed to the Great Hall were still donning their war gear. Their leather armour and bearskins smelt of animal fat and they were arming themselves with swords and spears. They carried the round shields with central metal bosses typical of the Dacians.

Duras spoke first from the front row. 'Father, let me take out a war band and bring back their heads. It cannot be a very large band of Germans or we would have had news of their coming long ago. The worst that can happen is we discover their strength. The best would be we drive them away.'

'Your brain must be no bigger than an apple,' smiled the king. 'Duras, you have no common sense. We do not need to fight these foolish Germans. We can sit here and wait without a fight. When they retreat we can avenge the insult of their presence and harry them until they reach the border.'

'I think this is no small war band, I saw hundreds of them in the forest. I think Duras is partly right in that we need to discover their numbers and then decide what to do. For all we know they have brought plenty of supplies or they may have raided locally to obtain them.'

'And since when does a king listen to a boy who is just a guest?' said Moscon. 'Do you have much experience of these matters? Which wars have you fought in boy?'

His words forced me to silence and I realised my comments were out of place, for it was quite true, I had no experience of warfare. I was after all, not even a member of the king's family, at least not until I yielded to his plan for me to marry his niece.

'I have experience of warfare,' Cornelius said, 'I have been in many wars when I was a young man. I think Sextus is right. It is no use finding out you face an army instead of just a raiding party after they have laid siege to your walls. You need to send out scouts and gather intelligence.'

'It is kind of you to volunteer. Why don't you take Sextus and Duras and do some scouting. Meanwhile we will stay here and see to the fortifications,' the king said smiling broadly, for he was after all, not using any of his less expendable troops.

'You do us great honour,' Cornelius said.

Cornelius, Duras, and I left the Great Hall to find our mounts. What three men could do against a huge war band was beyond my wildest imaginings.

'What do we do now?' I said.

'Exactly what the king suggested,' Cornelius replied. 'We reconnoitre. We should be able to keep our distance and still learn what we need to know. Don't worry. What do you think Duras?'

Duras said, 'We ride fast and look, then we ride back. Nothing simpler.'

CHAPTER XIX

"Each man is the smith of his own fortune"

— Appius Claudius

Riding south, parallel to the edge of the forest, we remained out of bowshot. Our horses' hooves threw up snow in clouds around and behind us, as they thudded on the hard ground. There was no difficulty locating the enemy. They were not a war band; they were an army. There were five groups of infantrymen with spears and each group consisted of about two hundred soldiers. They appeared, from a distance, to be well armed and organised, marching in ranks, which was unusual for German raiders. Cornelius said they usually marched in long columns with their supply wagons behind.

We pulled to a halt before them. In front of this German army rode two leaders on horseback, both of them large men carrying spears and shields.

'That one with the black beard is the king of the Marcomannii,' Duras said. 'He is a fearsome warrior. The man next to him is a Chatti king, I recognise him from a tribal council I attended with my father a few years back.'

'If they have brought two kings with them then this is an invasion and not just a raid. We must get back and warn the town,' Cornelius said. 'We have no guarantee this is the whole force either.'

Turning our horses to ride back to the town we saw a vast

force of cavalry emerge from the wood, level with us. As soon as they appeared, about twenty of them formed up in a tight formation and charged. We spurred our horses on as fast as we could. Bucephalus was not tired and as we rode, I stroked his mane and encouraged him, in a way that only I knew how. He was a strong horse and I had no fears they might catch us. I glanced over my shoulder as we rode. Cornelius on his roan mare was ahead of me and Duras on the other Roman horse came level.

The German cavalry rode for all they were worth, but they were unable to close the gap and after a mile or so, they gave up and turned around. We slowed to a stop and looked across the snow plain at the advancing army.

'Do you think there are many more?' Duras asked Cornelius.

'There could easily be the same number still in the forest and we saw at least five hundred horsemen. The defences on the wall will have to be strong. If I were the Germans I would certainly attack and quickly, before their supplies begin to run short.'

'Exactly what I was thinking,' Duras said. 'We had best be getting back.'

'They can't get over the walls though, can they?' I asked.

'Of course they can,' Cornelius said. 'They only have to have a few ladders and then get over in a couple of places and it will all be over. There are no trenches dug and there are no ballistae. As far as I am aware the Dacians don't even have a lot of archers.'

'We have some archers but they're mainly hunters and not fighting men. We have light javelins, not like you Romans, but short throwing spears and they're very effective at the short range on the walls.'

'All the Barbarians, sorry Sextus, I mean Germans, will need is a few men over that wall and their numbers will tell.'

We rode harder then. I did not know how many men there were in Lovosice but we could be facing as many as two thousand Germans, from the combined forces of the Marcomannii and the Chatti tribes. The cold wind bit our faces and a little snow began to fall. The sun shone through the weather adding a strange golden hue to the sky. There was a yellow tinge to the clouds in the south heralding more and heavier snow. I wished I were elsewhere preferably in Italia where it was warm and there was not the constant danger of battle and death. Despite my misgivings, I knew deep inside me, it was not my destiny to die in this place. I had a simple conviction this was so, but no real reason for the thought.

As we neared the town wall I could make out soldier's heads lined up on the wall-walk. They waved to us and shouted encouragement. When they opened the gates the king was in the courtyard behind waiting for news, surrounded by his nobles. When Duras told him what we had seen, he scowled.

'How can they have two thousand men, so far from their borders in winter? They cannot supply so many men so far from home!'

'They have supplies with them and I am sure the reason we have had no news of their coming is they have killed all in their path and probably have accumulated vast supplies by now,' Cornelius said.

'Listen, old man. We have only half their number of armed men, but all the same they will have a hard time crossing the walls. They are not Romans and they do not have the patience to maintain a siege, it has always been so

180

in this part of the world.'

'With their numbers, they don't need to wait; they can storm the walls and overrun the town with ease.'

'I have sent word to all the rest of my kingdom. Ten thousand warriors could be here in a week. We only have to hold out.'

The king turned around with that and walked to his hall.

We looked at each other. All three of us knew the number of defenders was small. It was an unexpected attack but a good military organisation would have had advance warning. I wondered why there had been no intelligence. Duras went to the King's Hall and began to organise the defence. Men with javelins and bows defended the walls and infantry waited below ready to join in the fray at any point where the walls looked like being scaled.

There were three gates in the outer wall so the prospect of the enemy attacking all three gates at the same time seemed unlikely. The king felt that if one gate remained clear then a cavalry charge would surprise the attackers. Cornelius and I were better fighters on foot so we stayed at the wall and waited for the Marcomannii and Chatti infantry to attack. We waited but nothing happened at first. Time dragged. High above us a stir of black crows circled, dark and raucous as if they signalled someone's fate. I shuddered, feeling like a man who waits for some unpleasant meeting, unwilling to wait, yet knowing the tryst is inevitable.

Then they came. A black speck on the distant snowscape at first; their shapes became recognisable as men then as hoards of men. The army had come and relief came to me too. It seemed to me their presence cut the tension for I knew now we would fight and that certainty seemed reassuring.

181

The attackers camped outside, beyond our missile range and appeared to make themselves comfortable. They had tents and within an hour, their baggage train arrived with their womenfolk and supplies. They lit campfires all around and it was a strange feeling to have so many fires dotting the snow-covered plain around us. Cornelius and I stood on the wall and looked out at the army settling outside the defences.

'They seem to be enjoying a little holiday,' Cornelius said.

'What are they waiting for?' I asked.

'I don't know,' Cornelius said. 'Maybe they have more men arriving, or maybe they really do intend to lay siege to the town. It seems unlikely. Last time I was in this situation in Germany, they just attacked and kept coming until enough of them had died and then they melted away.'

'We have visitors,' I said.

Medana and Roziana climbed the ladder to the platform behind the wall. The women had brought some broth with them and we drank it together. Medana was shivering so I slipped my arm around her as we watched the army encamped before us.

Medana said, 'Many soldiers,' in a quiet voice.

'Yes,' I replied, 'we will fight them soon.'

We remained thus for a long while for there was nothing to do now but wait. There was little else to say either. The light began to fade early. In the dusk, the enemy's fires surrounding the town glowed with a threatening brightness. No one I spoke to seemed optimistic. There were only seven hundred defenders and of those, only two hundred could fight on horseback, for all Duras' boasts about the Dacians being great horsemen. I felt the only real hope was the arrival of reinforcements but no one seemed to know how long it would take the surrounding Dacian towns to send help.

Cornelius retired to bed with Roziana leaving the two of us looking out at the sea of campfires before us. It would have been romantic had it not been for the obvious threat those fires posed. After half-an-hour or so we tired of watching the invaders and Medana led me back to the hayloft.

'Perhaps death tomorrow,' said Medana. She looked at me with wide sad eyes.

'No, tomorrow we kill,' I said.

She stared into my eyes again and stood closer. She put her arms around my neck and I could resist no longer. Our lips met in a careful searching kiss, both of us sampling something new and pleasurable. I slid her gown from her shoulders under her cloak and she began to unhitch my sword belt. We undressed and came together in exploratory pleasure, touching, caressing. We made love gently and slowly in the hayloft. Perhaps she felt I might die the next day and I suppose I must have sensed those feelings. Afterwards, we lay in each other's arms, our cloaks keeping out the numbing cold that reached for any exposed part of us as we lay together until morning. I kissed her when I awoke but she slept on. I dressed in haste and wondered how I felt about her. Cornelius was right; it was not a betrayal of Livia. I did not love Medana as I had loved Livia but it had been a wonderful night for me and I sincerely hoped it had been for her too.

Livia had been different from any woman to my mind. I gave myself to her in my entirety and that may be why she had pervaded every part of me. I wondered as I walked back to the wall whether my affection for Medana had attenuated those feelings in some way. I felt like a man on a long hard road; its twists and turns taking me to new places, but the places left behind still fresh and potent in my mind. I dismissed the thought as soon as it arose in me. I had loved Livia but she was no longer alive. She was a thought now in my head, a desire; a past love I could never retrieve. I knew then that both Livia and Medana would be with me in my memories forever whatever the future might bring.

I returned to the walls while Medana slept on and continued the monotonous vigil. At mid-morning, the reason for the delay became plain. In the distance we could see more men on the horizon. As the approaching forces came into view I realised they were a third group or tribe. They had a triangular cloth banner. It was red with a snake embroidered on it. When Duras came to see who had arrived he frowned.

'Franks,' he said, 'they come from the north, on the east bank of the Rhenus River. They are fearsome fighters and men with honour.'

'What do you mean?' I asked.

'It means they fight as men should, with swords and shields and they give no quarter. They do not go in for meaningless slaughter and they don't kill women, they enslave them.'

I warmed myself at a brazier. The ramparts were dotted with them and although they kept the soldiers warm, their purpose was to light fire arrows and melt pitch, which the defenders could throw down on attackers and their siege equipment. No more than a third of the defenders were on the wall at any one time, another third were in readiness behind the wall and all along the wall, piles of arrows and javelins stood ready for the attack.

There was a sense of tension in the air. We knew the wait

was over and action would come whether we were ready for it or not. The first casualty was a soldier standing only yards away from me. An arrow fired into the air soared up and away from the Chatti camp long before any attack, landing on the wall. It skewered the man's foot. He had to have the shaft broken and the arrow pulled through for it had passed clean through and anchored him to the wood beneath.

The fickleness of fate came home to me then; how there exists a narrow line between being the lucky one and the one who meets his end. I still wonder what strange fortune decides who, in a line of soldiers, will go first to Wuotan. Is it someone the Allfather singles out, or do the Fates merely choose at random? I have no answers even now, but I do know that the one who survives is not always the lucky one. I hoped the Dacians would be lucky, but the numbers seemed to justify no optimism and the king's assertion that we could hold them seemed to make little sense.

I felt icy fingers on my spine as I watched the enemy draw up their battle lines. To us watchers it all seemed to be happening with an unbearable sluggishness. I know now this is a common tactical ploy. Taking your time makes the enemy nervous and nervous men run from battles. That is not to say over-confidence reaps rewards either. Too much confidence in battle leads to recklessness and results in far more blood spilled even when you outnumber your foe. I could feel my heart beating, my mouth arid, and I was breathing like a runner.

When they came, they came at us fast; one mass of howling anger. They kept no reserves. First their archers fired their missiles at the wall to keep our heads down. Then the ladders appeared. The Dacians had built the wall well, out of thick timber from the pine forest and there were narrow gaps in the wall at ground level and on the platform to allow our men to fire missiles back at the Germans.

Crouching behind the wall, Cornelius explained we could be sure the Germans were climbing up the ladders as soon as the hail of arrows ceased. They would stop as soon as their men were on the wall to avoid hitting them. We waited. I found this the most difficult time. I had alternating feelings of wanting to flee and wanting to fight.

The clatter of the arrows gradually ceased and we knew it was time. Time to fight, time to die. I peered over the edge of the wall and saw the top of a ladder, propped up against the opposite side. Time seemed to slow and I can recall how the first German warrior appeared head first with sword in hand. He was a brave man that.

As soon as his head appeared, an arrow flew from behind me. It took him in the face. In silence, he disappeared from view. My fear seemed to dissipate. It left a feeling akin to rage. I did not understand; it was as if I resented the fear I had experienced only moments before. The only other reaction left to me was a red, flaming anger. It drew my limbs into it and threw me towards the climbing enemy.

The next man I saw leapt from the ladder. Cornelius on my left, much to my frustration, killed him outright with a sword cut on the throat. It was almost before I knew what was happening. The man was crouching. About to stand. Then the old man struck. Blood flowed as the German gasped. He fell from the wall to the courtyard below. I had all that fury and fight inside me and had not even wetted my blade. My pulse raced, my head throbbed; I was losing control.

Another man crossed the rampart on my right and this time he was on my side. He was a tall blonde German wearing chain mail and a round pointed helmet. He swung an axe at my head. It was a slow move on his part. I had no difficulty in avoiding his blade. I swung my sword downward and took his right hand clean off at the wrist. He screamed. I silenced him with a stab to the chest. I had no time to savour my victory. Two others replaced him almost at once.

The German furthest from me went down with a javelin in his chest. The second proved easy to kill with my sword. A third came at me. I hit him with my shield. He fell from the wall. No doubt, the soldiers below killed him. The sounds of battle were all around, men screaming, battle cries, death screams, weapons ringing and shields clashing. You could smell the blood.

The entire wall and platform convulsed with fighting, screaming men, killing and thrusting. I saw a man with only a bow leap from a ladder. He fell with a javelin in his throat. I saw our men hard pressed to my right as more and more of our assailants crossed the wall. It all seemed slow. Indeed, in the thick of battle a strange slowing of all around you seems to descend. All I felt was anger, akin to the feeling when I killed Piso all that time ago in Rome. Have I not said I could have killed a hundred magistrates at that moment? It was the same feeling, but now there really were hundreds to kill.

I charged into the fray. I swung my blade to left and right. I pushed with my shield. I kicked with my sandaled feet. I cannot recall how many lives I took. My fury flowed through my veins like a liquid fire. No one came close in the end. It became hard to distinguish who was enemy and who was friend. I just wanted to kill. A frenzy of bloody battle-lust.

Tyr was smiling down upon me then I think. I was tireless. I wielded my sword with ease. My left arm felt as if the shield upon it had no weight, no heaviness. I heard myself scream a battle cry with no human tones. It was a sheer animal cry of fury. I was ten feet above the wall, looking down upon my own body, as it swung my sword, parrying blows, and killing, over and over again.

How long the fight lasted, I cannot tell; it could have been many hours or only minutes. It was all a continuum to me. A single battle-rage carried me upon its shoulders. The smell of blood tingled in my nostrils. I felt more alive that day than ever before in my life.

CHAPTER XX

"What you would not have done to yourselves,
never do unto others"

— Severus

The first attack was over after about two hours. It was a hard fight but we all knew we had the better of it. Our casualties were light, compared to the attackers, whose bodies littered both sides of the wall. We cheered and shouted insults as they withdrew. We knew it was a tactical withdrawal and they had only been testing our defences with a short assault.

I was unscathed. It is hard to believe it, but I had fought for almost two hours and not sustained even a scratch. Cornelius was also unharmed. The platform on which we stood was awash with blood and bodies. We threw the German bodies over the wall once we had stripped them of anything useful.

Looking out at the Germans below, I wondered how long it would be before they came again. They must have lost a hundred men but showed no signs of discouragement. They looked back at us, pulled fierce faces, and shouted battle cries. It seemed to me the whole world waited in that moment. It was mid-afternoon and I knew that even if they attacked now it would be a short fray since storming the walls would be more difficult at night. Arrows find it difficult to find their targets in the dark.

The battle lust had left me as suddenly as it had come and although I was tired, I felt a great relief and elation. In that first battle I learned a little about myself and realised I loved what I was becoming.

When I had left Rome, it was as a murderer and an escaped slave. I was still a killer, but deep inside I knew battle-killing is honourable. Rugio, Sartorius and the others had shaped me but not for this. This was what Cornelius had trained me for and I knew I had not disappointed him. Pride, I suppose you might call it, but it was well earned and even deserved.

We had not long to wait. The arrows announced the on-coming soldiers. We again kept our heads low and waited for the ascending men, who climbed and died. It was much the same the second time. Neither side gave way nor did either side gave quarter. I killed attackers until my arm began to tire. The battle fever did not come again that day, which I found curious. This time it was a calm fight and consisted of a series of hand-to-hand combats. They all went my way except with one small, grey-bearded German who had vaulted over the wall armed with a sword and shield, his helm bore a red and black, winding snake design. I saw him stab one of the Dacians, who fell to his knees, blood pouring from a wound in his chest. I cried out and rushed at the man. He looked at me curiously and parried my blade. He did not strike at me. He smiled and said something I could not understand. I felt it was a strange time to try to make conversation and swiped at him again with the sword. Again, he parried and this time said something like, 'Galdar.'

There were other words but I did not understand. We looked at each other and he suddenly nodded to me and was gone, turning into the fray behind without another blow or slash at me. I stood still and pondered. It must have lasted two or three seconds only but maybe in the moment of action, such time seems much longer. In the throes of battle, it is not safe or sensible to remain in one place for more than a second and this came home to me with emphasis. A huge man swung a battle-axe at my head. I raised my shield a fraction of a second too late and although it took most of the force and saved my life, I felt the very tip of the axe hit my right shoulder.

It was a superficial enough cut, but it made me drop my sword. There was pain and my arm felt weak. His axe had swung past me in its stroke. He leaned forward. I caught him with the edge of my shield. It hit him under the chin. His head whipped back and with amazing speed, he was down. I raised the shield and brought the edge down hard on his neck. I kicked him over the edge of the platform.

I turned, but with no sword could only defend myself. I tried to get back to where I had dropped my weapon, but it was impossible in that mangled mess of fighting men. I headed for the steps leading down to the courtyard. I had to batter defender and foe alike to get there, but I made it and went down.

Looking up from below I could see the Germans were gradually getting more men onto the platform. Although our men were fighting like heroes and we had archers below firing arrows into any groups of our foes, it was clear the enemy had all but taken the wall in one or two places. I could see Cornelius. I had to smile. He stabbed and hewed with his sword. So fast was he, his blade seemed to have a life of its own. A fallen German crawled on the ground close to my feet, sword in hand. I hit him hard with my shield and took his sword, weighing it in my hand. The balance was good and the blood-groove long enough, so I thought I could use it.

I climbed the steps and joined my mentor. We fought side by side now, killing all who came at us. We began to advance towards where a group of enemy gathered. There must have been five or six of them. We attacked them with a fury that made them give way and step back. We became a killing machine and advanced as we killed them and stepped through their blood.

Despite anything Moscon might have said to the contrary, it became a hopeless fight. There were just too many of them and after reinforcements came from the King's compound, we were able to descend the steps safely. More and more attackers crossed the wall, hacking, snarling, and whooping. The defenders formed a line four men thick. We began to back away from the German attackers who formed up in the courtyard and started to rush our lines. They pressed so hard Cornelius and I on the left flank were pushed to our left, as the line gave way and finally split. The Germans poured through the gap in our lines and turned, killing many of our men who they could now attack on more than one side.

We fought as well as we could and no man turned and ran, but we continued to give ground. The men with us fell in a bloody mess and soon we were isolated in a small street with four attackers confronting us. I felt torn and bloodied. Cornelius was soaked in a mixture of his own sweat and his victims' blood but he again seemed unscathed. They advanced upon us and all four had spears and shields. Our position was untenable and we knew it. I swallowed. My spit tasted sour as it dried in my mouth. My heart beat fast, thinking I had reached my end.

A sound drew me back to reality. We heard the clatter of hooves approaching behind our enemies and I saw Duras, mounted on one of our horses, swinging a long-handled battle-axe from the saddle. He took the head of one of our opponents clean off and Cornelius finished two of the others in the space of time it takes to say so. I swung my blade at the man opposite me but he turned and fled back toward the courtyard and his own men.

'Well met I think!' exclaimed Duras panting, with a smile on his bearded face.

'Well met indeed,' I said smiling back.

'Are you hurt?' asked Duras indicating my shoulder.

'Not badly, but we have lost the walls and soon they will be at the King's compound. Should we go there and fight?' I said.

'Have your wits become addled?' Cornelius said. 'No sense in dying to-day and besides, if Moscon dies, Duras here will be the next Dacian monarch. He is more precious than you might think. What say you Duras?'

'You are right, we will have to flee. Follow me.'

We followed him as fast as we could considering we were on foot and he was riding. He led us around a corner and the sound of the battle seemed to fade as we found ourselves in a small lane, at the end of which stood the East Gate.

'Wait here,' he said.

We had no choice but to do as he ordered. In what felt like an endless time to us, he returned with two horses. They were sturdy Dacian mounts but Duras stayed on the Roman racing horse. We mounted and headed for the gate. The gates were ajar and we squeezed through and rode straight to the river. It was too wide to ford so we had to dismount and lead our horses into the swift, icy current. We held onto their manes and they swam across but the speed of the torrent carried us a long way downstream. The cold of the river numbed us to the very bones and we shivered violently when we were able to get out onto the icy bank. In the cold snow, we took off our clothes and wrung them out so they were as dry as we could get them. We dressed and mounted again and with nerveless, numb fingers and feet, we rode east into the pine forest. It took a good half-hour of hard riding before we reached a clearing in the woods and were able to light a fire to warm ourselves. My shoulder bled freely but it was not painful, for there was too much to think about and I think there was still a heat and fervour in my soul after the battle.

'They won't be looking for stragglers yet on this side of the river but we can't stay here long,' Duras said.

'Where can we go now?' I asked.

'We may have to cut around to the east then head north. The Romans have built many forts with huge trenches between them further west, and the Marcomannii will not follow us close to the fortifications.' Duras said.

'Yes you are right,' Cornelius said. 'The fortifications are called the Limes, they were started by Julius Caesar and there are a lot of Roman troops there. It will be safer on the west side of the Rhenus, the east side will be crawling with Germans. We might be able to cross the Limes from east to west, at night if there is no moon. The problem is the trenches have wooden spikes and the only crossing places are close enough to the forts to make us easily visible. Pray for a dark night.'

'The Limes it is then,' I said as we mounted.

'We will have to travel through Noricum and Germania Superior and avoid both Roman and German soldiers. It won't be easy.'

Our limbs were still very cold, but as our clothes dried out, we became a little warmer. Townspeople fleeing from the Germans crossed our path here and there, but we did not stop. We rode until it was night and we tried to find some shelter. We had no cloaks and no money to purchase any. A small farm in a sheltered valley came into view as night began to throw its shadows around us. We dismounted and walked towards the door. A sturdy farmer and two others, who we assumed to be his sons, came out with swords and axes but when they saw Duras they all knelt with bowed heads.

'Please get up my friends,' Duras said smiling for the first time since our escape from Lovosice, 'We just need feeding and some cloaks would help us enormously.'

Of course he said all this in Dacian, but Cornelius and I understood quite well what was going on. The farmer ushered us into the little farmhouse and directed us to places by the fire. The farmer's wife poured portions of rabbit stew for us from a pot hanging on the fire and soon produced a rough hard rye bread to accompany it. Soon we all felt much better. My shoulder ached now and I pulled down my tunic to look at the wound. It was of course bigger and more painful than I had at first thought. Battle wounds are like that; they do not hurt much at the time but the pain comes on once you relax.

The farmer's wife had some skills with a needle and thread, having often sewn up wounds on her animals, so she sewed up the skin with a surprising dexterity considering the bone needle she used. She put a clean bandage on my arm and said something with a smile. The wound healed well and left me only with a dull ache that pains me now when the

195

weather is cold so it was lucky we reached the farm.

We took a night's rest for we did not expect pursuit that night. I thought the Germans would be too busy getting drunk and raping the women in Lovosice. That made me think of Medana and I realised the thought was painful. I was to think of her often after this and wished we could have taken her with us. It saddened me we would never lie together again; never know each other and never live as we had planned. My brief time with her had been the first real affection I had expressed since I lost Livia. Now I had lost her too. I went to sleep wondering why the Fates had done this to me again. It was as if they wanted me to be alone; as if whenever I came close to love they took it all away. I felt like a man who stoops to pick up a bright and shiny object at his feet, hoping for gold, but discovers it is only ice melting away in his eager hands.

CHAPTER XXI

"All pain is either severe or slight, if slight, it is easily endured; if severe, it will without doubt be brief."

— Cicero

I awoke in the morning having slept badly because of the pain in my shoulder. I could only lie on my left side and the wound had begun to swell and ache. To add to my problems my muscles ached from the exertions of the fight on the walls. I had been dreaming of that tall tattooed warrior on a horse fighting Romans again. The dream always ended the same way. I had supposed I was that warrior but this time I knew deep inside, it was not me. I told no one, for the dream made no sense to me and besides, it was only a dream.

I arose at dawn and walked out into the farmyard. The farmer was already up and the farmer's wife was boiling eggs on the fire in the hearth.

The farm was small, with a few cattle and small fields which in season, grew wheat. Thick snow covered the yard, for there had been a fresh snowfall overnight. Despite the early dawn light, the snow reflected off it brightening up the yard.

I went to see if the horses were feeling better than I was. I talked gently to them and checked their hooves and backs.

One had a small saddle sore, which I tended to with a dressing of moss and spittle. I fed them some hay, which the farmer provided and walked back to the farmhouse. It was a small building with three rooms. There was a large room opening onto the yard, in which the family cooked, ate, and rested. There were two adjacent rooms opening onto the living area. We had occupied one overnight on palettes of straw and the rest of the farmer's family occupied the other smaller room.

Cornelius was the first to join me.

'Sextus, we will have problems travelling in this weather, but we have to distance ourselves from the Germans. If they discover Duras is still alive they will send men to look for him. He is well known and easy for them to recognise.'

'He could come with us,' I said.

'Where are we going? I thought you wanted to go north to try to find your tribe. We can hardly travel with an enemy king in tow can we?'

'We can't leave him here. He did rescue us you know.'

'I know that. He will have to come and anyway he is the only one who speaks any of the languages.'

'There was an odd thing that happened to me during the fight on the wall,' I said and told Cornelius about the warrior on the wall and how he had tried to talk to me and mentioned the name "Galdar".

'Do you think he was from your tribe?'

'I don't know but he was smaller than the rest and wouldn't fight me.'

'Was he a Marcomannii or a Chatti?'

'I have no idea. He looked different from most of the men we fought. He had a chain mail vest and his helmet had a snake design on it.'

198

'Perhaps he is a Frank, and thought you looked like one of them?' suggested Cornelius.

'Maybe I am a Frank, I don't know.'

Duras, who emerged from his room looking glum, interrupted us. We ate, saying little, for Duras was unlike his normal self, cheerless and down.

'Duras, we want to go north from here, after crossing the Limes. Sextus wants to find out if he is a Frank,' Cornelius said.

'We can do that if you wish. My only other alternative would be to raise an army to take back Lovosice but I think it will be very hard at this time of year. No one will want to leave their farms now and I think the Germans will reinforce anyway. I do not understand why there were Franks with the other two tribes. The only relations we have had with them have been friendly. Maybe there is a big confederation now and it is not merely the Franks, but all the other tribes who are planning to take over land from the Romans as well as the Dacians.'

'It sounds like there is going to be war, and we seem to be caught right in the middle of it,' Cornelius said.

'Should we head for the Frankish lands then? If I have come from there then I may have relatives who would shelter us,' I said.

'Sextus, my friend I have no option but to go with you for the time being, but I will have to return in the spring and try to throw out the invaders, or die trying,' Duras said.

We planned then to travel north-west through Raetia and Noricum and cross the Limes into Germania Superior and then turn north again but it was a long journey and I had no money. We had to stay in Roman provinces for the time being; otherwise, we would have to pass through the lands of both the Chatti and the Marcomannii. The farmer gladly supplied us with feed for the horses and cloaks even though it left them short themselves. The Dacians were not mean people and were glad to help Duras who they realised might become their king one day.

We rode away from the farm as the sun was coming up, throwing long shadows behind us, across the snow. It was a clear day and there were few clouds above. It was bitterly cold and the cloaks we had been given were threadbare and thin. The horses struggled in places because of the depth of snow and they would start to limp if we rode them too much in deeper places. The cold affects them like that and it is usually wise to find the shallowest areas through which to ride.

We crossed Raetia in four weeks. The going was slow and we had delays finding new fodder for the horses. They did well enough during the trip and by the time we reached the Limes, the weather was starting to get a little warmer. Much of the snow had melted although it left small areas where it persisted, but the rest was a mud mire.

Our first sight of the Roman fortifications was in the afternoon of a cold spring day. There was a mist hanging low across the plain as we left the forest. We could see the forts rising above it in places. They were stone-built towers high enough to allow a view of the ground in between each. We could see across the distance that there were men, presumably Roman soldiers, high up in the towers and we caught an occasional glint of light as the afternoon sunshine reflected off metal, flashing across to us.

We dismounted and decided to wait until dark before attempting to pass the fortifications. There were long trenches cutting a deep scar into the ground in front of the towers on the eastern side. Between the towers, we could see staggered crossing points positioned so that archers could aim from both towers simultaneously.

For the Germans to attack across the trenches would have been suicide and I could understand how strong these defences were and why they had succeeded in keeping the German tribes out of Germania Superior. Say what you like about the Romans, they certainly knew how to defend their frontiers.

We ate some bread and cheese and drank some beer with it. It was still cold and as the day ended we began to feel the drop in temperature even more. We did not dare light a fire for warmth so we tried to keep warm with our threadbare cloaks as best we could. The sky became overcast and it was thus a conveniently cloudy night. The watchers in the towers were likely to be looking out for people crossing from west to east in any case and that, coupled with the darkness, served to protect us from Roman eyes.

When the night was at its darkest, we set out. We passed through between the two towers without the watchers on the towers spotting us thanks to a mist hanging in the air, which enveloped us like a pale grey blanket. The problem was seeing where the Romans had dug their trenches. They contained spikes of wood so a fall into any of them could easily be fatal. Our luck held for we negotiated the tortuous track leading our horses between the trenches.

We had reached the halfway mark between the towers and the pine forests when Cornelius signalled us to silence.

'We are not alone,' he whispered.

'Where?' I asked.

'Between us and the forest. I heard a cough and there seem to be horses trotting in the mud.'

I looked at Duras and he returned my gaze. Neither of us heard anything but we both knew Cornelius was not a man to imagine danger. We took our horses and walked them towards some tall pines with as much caution as we could intent upon hiding. We entered the wood and tethered our mounts. Turning, we hid ourselves in a thicket and watched. There would be only Marcomannii in those woods and I doubted we would be welcomed with open arms.

We saw them pass like ghosts in the mist. Visibility was limited but I could make out at least twenty riders moving in single file. The final rider had a string of five horses in tow behind him and I saw Duras move quickly forward. I reached forward to grab him and pull him back but missed by a hand's breadth. Cornelius drew his sword and we followed the Dacian to the edge of the thicket. The last man had drawn abreast when I saw Duras draw a knife. I saw Duras change his knife from right to left hand as he approached. My heart was in my throat as I watched the big man run out of the thicket and reach up with his blade towards the rider.

It is hard to imagine what risk Duras was taking. If there was any sound, the other riders would have turned and however well-armed we were, they would have slaughtered us. A man on foot has almost no chance of defending himself from a mounted soldier.

As it happened, Duras was so tall he managed to grab his quarry by placing his right hand over the man's mouth and stabbing, quick as a flash of lightening at the man's back with his left. It was no mean feat, for it was a long way to reach even allowing for the small German horse's stature. The whole process took seconds and created no more noise than dust falling in a burial mound.

The rider fell towards Duras who, with speed and complete silence, dragged him to the ground. I saw him crouch there for a moment as the next rider disappeared into the mist. Duras led the string of six horses towards us. I have no knowledge of what the other riders noticed. We never saw them again. We did hear someone calling minutes later but there was no pursuit and no search party.

Duras led his prize into the wood. All remained quiet and we walked the string of horses along with our own to the far side of the trees. There we rested and took stock.

I said, 'That was dishonourable.'

'What?' Duras said.

'Dishonourable, it was hardly a fair fight.'

'Honour doesn't come into it. We are at war,' Duras said.

'But it wasn't fair.'

'Look, they have taken everything from me. I have no kingdom now with my father dead. They all owe me for that. They spilled my father's blood in Lovosice. Do you expect me to forget it? Everyone I ever knew died in that town alongside my father.'

'You don't know they killed them. Maybe they are just captives.'

Cornelius said, 'Sextus, do you know what the Germans do to their prisoners?'

'Well, no,' I replied.

'You don't want to know. They torture them to death. Duras is right, he has a lot to pay back.'

I turned to him still feeling irritated.

'Either way you've captured a lot of horses, Duras,' Cornelius said.

'Yes we will not starve. We can sell them on our journey north.'

'Has it occurred to you,' I said, 'we have to feed the beasts?'

'What?'

'We have hardly enough for the horses we are riding,' I said. 'What do we do with six more in the middle of winter in this Gods forsaken place? Romans on one side, who want us dead and Marcomannii warriors looking for their missing friend on the other?'

'Don't be so hard on the King of the Dacians,' Cornelius said with a smile on his old face, 'We can find a farm on the way and I have money for feed for the horses.'

'Money?' I said.

'You mean you didn't bring anything of our goods with you?'

'Of course I didn't,' I said.

'Unwise, my friend,' Cornelius said, with a grin.

'I am sure the horses will come in useful for trading if we get to the north. I speak good German and I think they are very fond of horses, even if it is only to cook them.'

'Cook them?' I said.

'If they can't ride them they cook them. Germans are a strange people,' Duras said, shaking his head.

'Look, we can trade them but not to anyone who might eat them. Is that clear?' I said.

'I will pay for the feed for the horses and we can share the profit when we reach our destination, wherever that is,' Cornelius said, looking sideways at me. 'I must say I would have been happy to stay in Lovosice. I found a good woman and I had prospects, which is more than I can say for my arrival in Germany.'

'I don't want to talk about it. Medana was a lovely girl and I too would have stayed or at least wanted to take her with us,' I said.

'Sweet on her were you?'

'What of it?'

'Well it's just you only fucked her for two days,' Duras said and sniggered.

I said, 'She was nice and maybe we could have made a good match.'

'She's probably being raped by some bastard of a Marcomanni right now. Makes my blood boil. I want them all dead,' Duras said.

'I need a rest,' Cornelius said. 'I'm in agony from my foot. I picked up a splinter from the floor boards in our room and it's caused a bit of pain.'

'Well at your age I suppose a rest is important,' I said.

Cornelius aimed a gentle punch at my head and I ducked. We stopped for the night. We did not think the Marcomannii warriors would find us. We camped in a gully on the far side of the Limes. We were confident the Romans could not see us and we were all tired.

I wondered what the future would bring. Where was my destiny taking us? I knew I had to get home and everything now pointed to the Franks. Some of their warriors seemed to think I was like them. Why else would a man stop in the middle of a battle to talk? The experience reminded me of the look in the dying German's face when we rescued the Dacian girl. I could have sworn he knew me. That of course was impossible. Perhaps, I thought, it meant I bore a resemblance to someone in the Frankish lands, but who could fathom such thing? I was too tired to think about it and sleep came before I could analyse the consequences of looking like somebody else.

CHAPTER XXII

"In hoc signo vinces"
(In this sign shalt thou conquer)

—Emperor Constantine

The mist had still not cleared in the morning. We knew it was morning because of the birdsong but the heavy fog remained disorientating and oppressive. I felt cold. My leggings were not keeping me as warm as I had expected them to and my cloak felt heavy with moisture. Once you become wet when travelling you remain so, but only a village idiot would light a fire so close to the Roman fortifications.

I got up and washed my mouth out with water wondering whether we had enough provisions for the journey north. It was a foolish thought and shows how I had no concept of distance. What slave could be expected to know how long it takes to travel anywhere? I puzzled over that as I bashed the end of a stick with my knife-hilt against a stone and used the squashed end to clean my teeth.

The forest edge was scattered with low shrubs and thicket and we found it hard going leading the string of horses. We split them up in the end and each of us led three.

'Are you all right?' I asked Cornelius, for he was limping.

'No, my foot seems to be getting more painful; I will be pleased to ride once we get into open country.'

'Let me look at it,' Duras said.

'What, are you a physician as well as a linguist?' Cornelius said.

Duras laughed at that, one of his deep thunderous roars. We stopped then and Cornelius took off his sandal and then unwrapped the cloth surrounding his foot. The sandal straps had cut into his lower leg because of the swelling and his toes were a dark shade of purple.

'You need to bathe it in hot water,' Duras said, knowing he made a useless comment. We could not light a fire here so close to the Roman lines and hot water was not available.

'Oil and wine might help,' he said eventually.

'Duras, you are a great warrior, but your suggestions on wound care leave a lot to be desired,' Cornelius said.

'Sorry, it's just we need to do something with it.'

'I know. I don't think I can walk on it now I've taken off my sandal. Where are we?'

Duras said, 'Don't know exactly. Maybe three or four miles east of the Limes. We could risk riding now as I think the ground opens out soon.'

We lifted Cornelius into the saddle. It seemed to cause him terrible pain but he said nothing. I could tell he was suffering by the look on his face. It was only an infected splinter and with all the swelling in the foot, we had not been able to find it. There was nothing we could do. We rode.

We progressed parallel to the line of fortresses making up the Limes. The Romans had built them to keep people out and they had easy observation of the land in which travelled. Most of the time, we used woods for shelter, keeping the tall pines between us and the towers. It was not hard to escape detection. Perhaps they did see us, but there was no reason for them to attack us since we would have looked like simple travellers and nothing more. By mid-morning, we came to a road. It passed north-west from where we joined it and we guessed it would take us eventually to the far north, which seemed to be the place we were going. We made our way slowly along this road. It was a long straight wall built into the surface of the ground, like all Roman roads.

By midday, we came to a farm. Had it not been for Cornelius, we would have given it a wide berth unless we could steal fodder for the horses. As it was, we had to stop. Cornelius had begun to mutter to himself and he shivered frequently. I guessed the infection in his foot was spreading.

There was a thin spiral of smoke rising to the dull grey sky half a mile from the road, and a small track led towards it. We assumed there would be a farmhouse. We approached slowly so as not to alarm the occupants.

There was a low wall around the brick-built house. It occurred to me this was exactly the type of building Cornelius had hoped to build near Ariminium. It seemed so unfair to me how the fates had denied him that comfort in the closing years of his life, as he had planned. Had I not come along, Sartorius would never have had the chance to take Livia's life and the world would have been very different for my friend. All of it was my fault; had I not killed my Master and escaped Rome, the world as Cornelius and I experienced it would have been very different.

I found these thoughts disturbing but I knew that a man of quality will rise through such adversity and I was determined to weather the emotional storm welling up within me. One cannot alter the pattern spun by the Norns, they weave our future, and we cannot influence them.

We crossed the small courtyard. Duras dismounted and I

sat on my horse looking round. I could see no sign of life and wondered who would light a fire and leave home. He knocked on the door and moments later, a woman opened it.

She peeped cautiously around the doorjamb and asked what we wanted.

'We are travellers, horse traders, and we are on our way north,' Duras said.

'Best get on your way then,' she said.

'We stopped because one of us is sick. He needs help.'

'Sick?'

'Yes, he got a splinter in his foot and it has turned septic. Can you help us?'

'There are rumours of a great plague spreading from the east. Are you sure it isn't something like that?' said the woman.

'Quite sure,' I said.

'Well my husband is not here and I don't think he would like it if I admitted three armed men to the house.'

Duras said, 'I understand, but our need is great and if we wanted to harm you, you could not stop us. We are warriors as well as traders.'

The door opened a fraction more and we could see the farmer's wife now. She was only a young woman, perhaps my age. She seemed nervous and kept looking beyond us, presumably for her husband.

'Please, my friend is really sick.'

I could see the indecision written all over her face and it only took Duras a moment to convince her.

'We are honourable men and would never force an entry into your home, although it must be clear to you that we could. If you refuse us hospitality it would be contrary to the laws we all observe towards travellers.'

The barb went home and she opened the door. Duras and I managed to help Cornelius down from his horse. He almost collapsed as we supported him. He was feverish and constantly moved his head from side to side, muttering.

Cornelius' horse stood still in the courtyard. She wagged her head from side to side as if she knew it was serious. That mare loved Cornelius and knew when he was not well I think.

We manhandled our friend into the farmhouse. He was unable to stand and could put no weight on his left foot. It still looked bad. It had swollen even more and the purple colour had spread from the toes to the ankle.

The farmhouse was of a different design to a Roman house but had a large central room, ventilated by square holes high up in the eaves and hung with drapes all along the walls. There were sleeping quarters off the main room and I wondered if the design was not a little like the King's Hall in Lovosice but on a miniaturised scale.

We laid Cornelius on a cot in one of the small rooms opening out into the main area. There was hardly room for the four of us in the sleeping-room. The farmer's wife pushed Duras out but allowed me to stay. Her Latin was rustic but understandable. She brushed past me and returned with hot water, placed some herbs in it, and began to bathe Cornelius' foot. He was restless and I had to hold him down.

I looked at his face. It was thin and drawn, his wispy grey hair hanging limp in the sweat from his fever. He looked his age for the first time since I had met him. He voiced incoherent mutterings and moved his head from side to side, oblivious to his surroundings. I became distraught. How could a splinter of wood cause such a rapid decline?

When she had finished, she wrapped a clean linen bandage over the foot and I noticed she did it starting at the toes, winding the cloth carefully up the leg, to avoid making the swelling worse.

'You seem to know what you are doing,' I said.

'Yes, I was a camp follower when my husband was in the wars. I have tended many wounds in my time.'

She smiled and I could see beneath the creased brows, she was quite pretty.

'How is he?'

'Your friend has infection in the foot. It seems to be advancing rapidly. My husband will know what to do. It looks bad though.'

Cornelius was sleeping now so she took us into the main room and sat us down at the table.

Duras said, 'We are travelling north to the Frankish lands, to sell our horses. We will need to buy fodder for them. Is that possible?'

'Of course, but you will have to talk to my husband about that. I have a feeling you won't be able to move on for some time. Your friend is not fit to travel.'

'No,' I said.

I was worried now. At the start of the day, Cornelius had been well with just pain but now he was seriously ill. I still did not understand how it could happen. To me he had always been so resilient. We had been in fights, and now battles, yet he had remained unscathed. A simple spicule of wood seemed to have had more effect upon him than whole armies had. It made no sense to me. I wondered what Gods would do such a thing, or was this some kind of retribution by the divine beings for some transgression he had committed unbeknownst to me?

With the passage of time I had become more dependent on the old man. I feared for his life now. I felt alone too, for the first time since I had met him. I felt restless and after the farmer's wife, whose name was Fulvia, had given us soup I went and sat by my mentor's side. My youth seemed to creep back into my mind and I felt like weeping. So the day progressed. The three of us took turns at sitting by my friend's sickbed. The smell of the rotting foot began to permeate the still, cold air.

The farmer returned in the late afternoon. I glanced at Fulvia and she seemed close to panic when she heard him outside.

'He won't like me letting you in. He doesn't like strangers.'

'We will pay him for our keep. We only need shelter until Cornelius can travel.'

'It may be some time.'

'You think so?'

The arrival of the farmer interrupted us. He entered and looked at us with irritation. He must have been in his fifties, small and dark. He seemed to be a humourless fellow who never smiled. How a young woman like Fulvia could live with such a man puzzled me.

'Who are you?' he demanded.

I explained what we were doing in his home.

'We really just need to stay long enough for my friend's foot to heal enough for us to travel,' I said.

'I want you all out of here by the morning,' he said.

'But we can't travel now. Don't you understand my friend is very ill?'

'Looks all right to me,' he said.

Duras looked at the man with mounting irritation.

'Not me you idiot,' he said, 'he's lying in that room.'

'Oh,' said the farmer. He walked to the threshold of Cornelius' sick-room and wrinkled his nose.

'Smells like he's dying,' he said.

'It's his foot. He picked up a splinter a few days ago and it seems to be festering.'

'I'll have a look,' the farmer said with ill grace.

He unwrapped the foot, none too gently. Cornelius stirred in his sleep.

'His leg will have to come off.'

'What?' I said.

'That smell and the colour. Don't you realise it's turned to gangrene? If his leg isn't removed it will spread up his leg and he'll die as sure as spring will come,' the farmer said.

Close to panic, I refused to believe it. I knew Cornelius would never accept life with one leg. If only I could talk to him. He was not awake and I had no way of knowing whether I could rouse him.

'Can we wait and see if he wakes? I need to know he will allow his leg to be cut off.'

'You can wait all you like. The longer you do, the more likely it is to spread. It's up to you of course. I won't throw you out. The laws of hospitality demand you stay. I didn't realise how sick your friend was that's all.'

'Sextus, we need to talk.'

It was Duras, his tall frame filling the doorway. I got up and we went into the stable and tended the horses. The farmer left us to it.

'He's dying, you know that?' Duras said.

'Only if we let him. The farmer says we have to cut off his leg.'

'Have you done that before? I haven't.'

'Of course I haven't. What do we do?'

'Maybe the farmer knows what to do. He's used to looking after animals. Maybe he…'

Faint sounds of shouting drifted across to us from the farmhouse.

'Sounds like he isn't too happy about us being here. Hope he isn't considering telling the Romans. If he is, we may have to kill him.'

'No. I won't have it. He has let us stay and he acknowledges the Laws of Hospitality. Even if he did turn us in, I would not kill an unarmed farmer.'

'Maybe you're right, but I don't want to be here if a troop of Romans come.'

'No. What do we do about Cornelius, Duras?'

'We'll have to take the farmer's advice I guess. What was his name?'

'Don't know. Didn't ask did we?'

'Maybe if we get him on our side he won't mind us being here so much. We can pay him.'

We walked up to the farmhouse without any expectations. Then we heard a scream. It spurred us both into action and we ran.

The scene confronting us was a complete surprise. Fulvia stood, wide-eyed and blood-spattered in the doorway of the room adjoining Cornelius' room. A bruise the size of a hen's egg stood out from her forehead. In her hand, she gripped a knife. Blood dripped to the floor from its blade. She was immobile and I could see shock on her face.

'I killed him, killed him,' she said.

'Who?' I said, running the few steps into Cornelius' room.

He lay still, his face contorted in a grimace, the skin a

bluish hue. He was not breathing and I turned in a rage.

'You killed my friend, you bitch.'

I raised my hand to hit her.

'No, he did it,' she said quietly.

'Your husband?' Duras said.

I muttered 'He's dead Duras, dead.'

Duras said, 'What? She stabbed him?'

'No,' she said again, eyes staring.

I looked at my friend's body, my legs felt weak. There was no blood and the dripping knife made no sense.

'What did you do?' I said. 'What did you do?' snatching the knife from her hand. She looked at me wide-eyed and in silence.

'Sextus, look here,' Duras said.

I threw the knife into the corner of the room, pushing her out of my way; I looked past Duras into the other room. The farmer sat sprawled over a chair in the far corner. In our haste, we had overlooked him. There was a pool of blood on the earth floor accumulating from a slit throat.

I realised then whose blood it was on the knife and knew I had misjudged the situation. I ran into Cornelius' room and stood wondering what to do. He was stone dead. There was nothing to be done. Tears came.

CHAPTER XXIII

"Habits change into character."

— Ovid

'Sextus, you have to get over it,' Duras said. I had sat weeping over Cornelius' body for hours. I had no one else apart my big Dacian friend. The day was wearing on and I could see the light was beginning to fade. I was aware through my wet eyes that Duras looked tired and care-worn. The smell was unpleasant in the room but I had no inclination to leave. At one time, while I sat saying my farewells, I wondered if his death had been a simple mercy.

For a stranger to smother you in this pit of a place was not what I would have wished for this warrior. He had taught me so much and he had been patient and sometimes kind, at least as far as one could expect kindness from a man who had led the sort of life he had. At the end of his life the fates had cheated him. He had lost Livia and his farm. The future with me must have held few moments to which he could look forward. He had taken it all without complaint and I never understood how he did that. I never had seen him give up hope and it was one thing I was determined to absorb from him.

'I can't help it, he was like a father to me for two years,' I said.

'That's what I mean, it was only two years, and that isn't

a long time you know. You have to let go. I lost my real father in Lovosice. I don't shed tears. Revenge drives me. After I have taken back what is mine by right, I shall grieve.'

'This isn't about you. I have never had a father. Cornelius was something special.'

'Special was he? He was a special killer. He taught you to kill. Did he actually teach you anything else? Honour? Or how to treat others?'

'I don't recall you expressing strong feelings about how you treat others.'

'What?'

'I've never met anyone who consistently puts himself before others quite so much as you do.'

'Thanks.'

'Welcome.'

There was silence then, interrupted only by an owl hooting outside. Duras put a hand on my shoulder.

'Sextus, we have to move on. We have time to burn Cornelius but then we have to go. The Romans may come and then you will be in real trouble.'

'Can't we wait? I need time,' I said.

'Time, my friend is one thing we don't have. What about the woman? She can't come with us can she?'

'We can't leave her here. She murdered her husband. I dread to think what the people around here do to women who do that.'

'They would never know,' said Duras.

'Of course they'll know. People around here must know him for a wife beater. We can't risk it, for her sake.'

'I suppose we can drop her off somewhere on the way, but she isn't coming all the way north with us. It will be risky and I don't relish the idea of having a woman in tow.

217

It's hard enough defending myself, but with a woman to think about, it could be too dangerous.'

'Look Duras, she killed him because he suffocated Cornelius. We owe her some help'

'That wasn't what I heard her say. She killed him because he was beating her again.'

'Yes, but she was trying to stop him.'

'She didn't do a very good job did she?'

'Look, all I'm saying is she did what she did over the murder and he turned on her. I want to help her.'

'Have it your way, but as soon as we find her a place to stay we leave.'

'All right,' I said wiping my face clear of the tears.

'I still need time to adjust. I don't know what to do. Cornelius always seemed so certain of what to do next and I have no such certainties in my head. Whenever I am fond of someone they seem to die.'

'Good job you aren't fond of me then,' he smiled at that and I looked him in the eye.

'We only have each other now to rely upon. We can't quarrel.'

'We aren't quarrelling, we're arguing, it isn't the same thing. In Dacia we have an expression…'

'No, please,' I said, holding up a hand. 'If you come up with any more of your homespun Dacian philosophy nonsense I will go mad.'

'All right. We'd better talk to Flavia or whatever her name is.'

'Fulvia. And be nice.'

'All right.'

We walked into the main room and Fulvia was not there. I called her name. No answer came and I began to wonder if she had gone to the Roman authorities. She could have told them we murdered her husband and she was innocent.

I should not have misjudged her in that way. I went to the room in which she and her husband slept. There was no answer to my knock. The wooden door was hard to open on its leather hinges, so I pushed with my shoulder. I stopped in the doorway. I was unprepared for what I saw. There was a hook in one of the rafters and hanging from it, suspended by a rough Hessian rope was the farmer's wife. Her face was purple, her tongue protruded from her mouth in a grotesque caricature of her living expression. I wondered if someone had put a curse on me—cursed to carry death with me wherever I went.

'Duras, help me,' I said as I tried to lift her off the hook. He came and seemed less surprised than I was.

'Well she couldn't have had much of a future. She married the man and he gave her a bad life it seems. It's as if she wanted to follow him. I suppose there wouldn't have been much for her to look forward to.'

'I don't understand. Maybe she heard us talking.'

'Perhaps, but that doesn't mean it's our fault. It's tempting to burn down the whole place. It would be a fitting funeral pyre for Cornelius.'

'No, the smoke would be seen for miles and I don't want anyone to know we've been here, Roman soldiers might want to investigate and we are not people they would treat well. They might even discover I'm an escaped slave.'

Duras said, 'We'll make a pyre for all three bodies and scatter the ashes after. Then we get enough feed for the horses and we go, whatever time of day it is. This place makes me feel very uncomfortable. It's as if there are evil spirits here.'

'I don't feel that; it feels restful in some way. I know we could look at it the way you say but I don't get that feeling here. Let's get the job done.'

We built a pyre out of wood that we stripped from the structure of the stable and we built it high. There was an amphora of olive oil in a corner and we soaked the wood in it then carried the bodies out, laying them on the woodpile.

It lit easily with the oil flaring at first then a column of smoke rose high above us into the afternoon sky. I stood looking at the flames. A deep sadness came into my heart. I remembered how Cornelius and I once wept over Livia and how we had both suffered when we burned her body. There is something sacred about disposing of a body in such a way. It leaves a kind of cleanliness as if driving off the spirit from the body thus leaves the world renewed. I had placed a coin in Cornelius' mouth, not that he was pious, it was just I wanted to be sure.

I watched as the bodies curled and their backs arched. Cornelius' right arm extended as if reaching out to me. I knew it was just a fancy but it was as if he was pointing. It struck me his arm was pointing north.

CHAPTER XXIV

"Accept the things to which fate binds you, and love the people with whom fate brings you together, but do so with all your heart."

— Marcus Aurelius

We rode north, always north. I was too benumbed by the death of my friend and mentor to take much notice. Stabbing my mind all the time were thoughts of 'why me? what if?' I could not escape a feeling that with a little prescience I could have changed what had happened to Cornelius. Had we travelled slower and sought proper attention for his infected foot he might have lived. I missed him so badly. Was there not some bard who wrote, "how are the mighty fallen"?

I knew it was useless to think like that, for none of us have control of our lives in that way. It happens as the Gods wish it though leaving all choice to the Gods is a passive way to lead one's life. I suppose that even if they do decide everything, at least they preserve for us the illusion of choice and perhaps that is what allows us to progress. It was hard not to become bitter. I thought of Livia often in those days of travelling. The two people I valued most in my new life of freedom were gone and it was all through following my selfish destiny. There had to be some purpose to it all. If there was, I could not see it.

Duras did his best to teach me German. He had mastered Latin, German and Dacian and it helped to pass the time as we rode. We rode all night until the bright, clear, frosty dawn made us realise how much distance we had put between us and that terrible death-farm.

In the cold dawn light we changed horses with our feet crunching the frost beneath us. We let our tired mounts rest as they trotted alongside. We ate and I consumed the food in a mechanical way. Nuts, dried fruit and stale bread; it seemed an anti-climax after the feasting in the King's Hall in Lovosice.

By midday, we needed to rest, water and feed the horses. Happily, we had plenty of fodder. We attached the feedbags to the mounts without difficulty. We needed rest too but dared not stop more than a few hours. I rested first and then Duras. His snoring was so loud I began to worry someone might hear him but nothing happened and there was no pursuit.

The landscape changed as we rode north, although it remained cold. We rode at night and slept during the day with one of us keeping watch while the other rested. We continued like this for about twenty days. I say 'about' because we lost track of time. My grief over Cornelius and the hard weather combined to make me unthinking and vague as if exhaustion and grief had taken the upper hand. We had taken enough money from the bags of our dead comrade to buy food and fodder at farms on our way. The farmers were not suspicious and some offered us accommodation in their barns out of simple friendliness, but we always declined, not knowing whether they might betray us to the Romans.

We came to a flat watery land. There were many bogs and swamps and the meadows and grassy places were wet

222

and smelt of rotting vegetation. Frozen pools reflected the light with a supernatural radiance as if some strange secret lurked beneath their icy surface.

When we came to the River Rhenus we realised the only way across was by boat or ferry. It was huge; we could see lumps of ice formed around driftwood gliding by at speed. It took us days to find a crossing point. There was one three days on from where we struck the river. A bridge spanned the river to a small island and beyond was a ferry operating between the island and the east bank.

'It'll cost you,' the ferryman said.

'How much?' I enquired.

'Twenty pieces of Roman silver, not the German stuff, it's half lead.'

'That is almost as much as we have,' I objected.

'Can't help that, everyone has to pay.'

'How about,' Duras said, 'if I kill you and we use your boat?'

He was scowling and fiddling with his sword.

'You couldn't get across without me. I know where every rocky outcrop and every shoal is. Do you? I know how to avoid the floating ice. Do you? Now be sensible. You need my help to cross and I want the money. It's a service. I'm not robbing you. My friend Sigvelt a mile down, charges more than I do.'

'It's just a lot of money, that's all,' I said putting my hand on Duras' wrist.

'Well? Last chance,' the man said. He was a small, plump, cheerful man who smelt of sweat to such an extent it choked me and I am not over-sensitive.

'It will take all our money, is there no compromise?' I said.

'I'll take two of the horses instead if you like. I can sell them for the same money I guess,'

'We're being robbed, Sextus,' Duras said.

In the end, we parted with two of the German horses. We had no option. The man led us to the riverside. He had a flat-bottomed barge. It looked stout and reliable but I discovered on that crossing a profound and lasting dislike of boats. Ice floes hit the boat on two occasions and although the ferryman was nonchalant, it scared me. My relief when we disembarked was sufficient for me to utter a silent prayer to Wuotan.

We made camp on the other side of the river and passed a freezing uncomfortable night. Duras seemed unaffected but I regretted camping near the river; it was bitter and cold. Moving water always seems to drop the temperature on a riverbank. This river seemed to conjure up an icy, biting wind that entered my clothing anywhere it could to chill me to the bone. Next morning we rode again, eastwards this time, but the red, rising sun held no warmth.

We came to a large town. By now I could converse in simple terms in the common German tongue, thanks to Duras who could speak good Latin (for a Dacian) and reasonable German. We rode to the outer wall, which was little more than a palisade. There was a flimsy wooden gate and a gatekeeper enquired whether we had business within.

'We are just travellers with some horses to sell,' I replied.

He let us in and the place seemed like any other German town I supposed. It seemed to be as wet and cold as any we had passed on our journey. An alehouse stood on the tiny main street and we went in to find out who the local people might be. If they were Marcomannii or Chatti then we would move on. We had no desire to mix with them after our experiences in Lovosice and the fact that Dacia was at war with them. The inhabitants of the town turned out to be Franks.

We had seven horses so we looked like traders despite the arms we carried. We stayed for a few cups of beer and then took our horses down to the stables where we hoped to spend the night.

I drifted off to sleep wondering if I had come to the end of my journey or whether this was just another potential battleground. Perhaps time would tell. I hoped the death-curse stalking me so far would relent in its pursuit of every-one with whom I came into contact. I had more strange dreams of tall blond warriors around a fire in the snow. Each had a spear and they wore bearskins. Another man, separate from them emerged from a hut bearing a tiny bundle. He was tall and fair and a thick blonde moustache that hung down in a luxuriant journey to his throat adorned his face. He was bald and his head bore a tattoo like mine. I realised it was a baby he carried in his immense hands and as the baby raised a mewling cry seeking some maternal warmth the men stood around and sang a chant in guttural tones. The dream was vivid and colourful and I awoke in a sweat. Sleep came again but there was no repetition of my dream.

I awoke refreshed next day to a beautiful dry winter's morning. Birds sang a greeting to the day as the sun was expressed its bleak attempt at sunshine outside. It took me a few moments before I realised where I was. I thought at first I was at Cornelius' farm near Ariminium. Perhaps I was dreaming of those days, which now seemed so long ago. When realisation came to me, it filled me with sorrow but the mood only lasted a moment; I was young then, after all.

Duras surfaced almost immediately too. He groaned and

broke wind, which seemed to be the usual way drinking beer affected him. Happily, I had controlled my intake, having learned a thick head was an unpleasant way to greet the day.

We had a little food left from the journey and we ate some dried fruit and drank water from our water skins. I felt as if I wanted to go no further and for some inexplicable reason felt I had arrived, but knew of no concrete evidence that I belonged with the Franks. Even if I was of their blood, there was no reason why they should shelter me. I was after all a Roman by culture and only a German by birth. It occurred to me I might hate being amongst these people whom the Romans had taught me were Barbarians.

I looked back at the two years in which so much had happened. It was as if killing my Master had given birth to me. It was as if I had never lived until that moment. I had thieved and killed, won and lost and never stayed in any place for more than a few months. It would almost be out of character for me to stay more than a few weeks even if these people were my kin.

Duras went outside and left me to see to the horses. We had seven, most of them taken from the Marcomannii in the forest and although it had been a struggle to feed them on our journey north, we hoped to sell five of them and make enough money to stay in one place and take stock of our situation.

Duras returned with the stableman. He was a fair-haired young man of similar stature to me and he had a full beard like Duras. The thin wispy growth I had acquired since leaving Lovosice palled into insignificance by comparison.

'Greetings, my name is Pippin, I am the horse-master.'

'Who was the man last night?' I said. Duras helped me by correcting my rough German language.

'That was my stable-hand. Who are you?'

'My name is Sextus,' I said smiling. As we shook hands, I looked at his grey eyes, and decided I liked this man. He explained how his father had tended the horses before him and he had taken over the task when the old man died of a fever.

'Fever is common here because of the damp.' Pippin said. 'Your friend tells me you want to sell some horses.'

'Yes, we have five for sale but we will need to keep two for ourselves. Where can we get a good price around here?' asked Duras.

'There is an animal market once a week. The next one is in two days' time. Before that, if you are in a hurry, you might consider selling them to me, but I think you would get a better price if you wait until the market, as I don't trade horses much. I don't mind if you pay me for the stabling once you raise the money. I'm about to go to see the village elders. It would be a good idea if you came and introduced yourselves. We are suspicious of strangers these days, since most of our men have left to join the war against Rome and the village is mainly in the hands of women and old men.'

'War against Rome?'

'Yes,' Pippin said. 'All of Germania is rising against the oppressors. Marcomannii, Chatti and even the Franks are allied against Rome. The fighting hasn't started but it is coming.'

'You weren't tempted to join them?' Duras said.

'No, people here consider my position to be an honourable one. Without expert care, the horses we depend upon so much won't thrive, so they consider me to be of value. In any case, I'm not much of a fighter,'

Pippin smiled at me and I felt an odd kinship. I could see

he was a pleasant man with a disarming manner, like most horse lovers. Duras and I looked at each other and we realised we had either to lie or declare ourselves. I decided I could trust this man with his soft words and disarming smile.

'Pippin, I need to tell you who we are before we go with you, because we may not be so welcome when you hear our story.'

'I hope it is a short one, I am late already for the elder's meeting.'

I told him much of our story including my escape from Rome. He looked at me, surprised.

'I think you will be well received here; you may be a Dacian,' he said, indicating Duras, 'but this far north we have no real quarrel with your people. The Franks who attacked your town, are led by Guntramm. He is a powerful lord in the south of our land, but he does not always follow the will of the nation. His uncle is the Warlord of all the Franks. I do not think there is an official war between us yet, Dacian.'

'So they may receive me well, you think?' Duras said.

'Perhaps. I think they may want to discuss also whether Sextus came from our nation. He has a Roman name but he looks like one of us. I almost feel his face is familiar but I do not understand why.'

We followed Pippin through the narrow streets, avoiding the dung and mud as best we could. The ripe smell of the middens and the more appetising smell of food cooking mixed in the air, confusing the senses. The little town was awakening in the winter sunshine and people were beginning the business of their day. Children ran across the street and some played in groups as children do anywhere in the world. It seemed a peaceful town and we noticed no intimation of any threat or danger. Many of the people came across to us and expressed pleasant smiles to Pippin. It seemed they held him in high esteem. I gleaned from this that to be in his position as the carer of horses, was a place of honour.

We reached a low hut, larger than the others in the centre of the town. There was smoke from a fire spiralling up from a hole in the thatched roof and as we entered, it took a little time for our eyes to become accustomed to the dim half-light within. Seated around the fire were nine or ten elderly people. There were both men and women. It became clear to me that women had respect here and their opinions were valued in sharp contrast to the Romans or the Dacians for that matter.

As we entered a tall thin man with grey hair in long braids, stood up and greeted Pippin. Duras translated their words as best he could.

'We greet you and honour you, Horse Master,' he said. 'I see you have strangers with you. Will you tell us who they are or can they speak for themselves?'

'They can speak for themselves, Lothar,' said Pippin with a smile. 'You may not understand all they say, for their language is a little strange and the younger one speaks only a little of our language. They have travelled far and wish to trade horses. They took them from a Marcomannii war band. They are not simple horse traders I think.'

Lothar, the headman looked us up and down for a moment and asked us by gesture to sit.

'You have a tale to tell. We would hear of your journey and Pippin will help you to give us your story if your language should falter.'

Duras and I sat and the circle of elders shifted to a semi-circle to accommodate us. I told the tale of my life as best I

229

could in my limited German and Pippin and Duras filled in those parts where my language was inadequate. There was a hushed silence when I had finished. I had left out a good deal and I had not touched upon Duras' position in all of it.

'So your friend and teacher, the old Roman, died and yet you still came here knowing the Marcomannii from whom you fled, are allies of the Franks?' enquired Lothar.

'I had little choice. I felt drawn here but I don't really understand why. All my life I have wondered where I might belong. The Romans taught me much, but I have longed for the place I was born. Perhaps some spirit deep within me has brought me here searching for who I am. I have a tattoo on my head, which seems to be something your people have as well. It was one of the reasons why I came here.'

'You have a tattoo mark on you head?'

'Yes, it is like a long snake eating its tail.'

There was a hushed silence around the fire. I could distinguish the sound of children playing outside. Presently, an ancient woman seated cross-legged at the back, shifted in the quiet of the smoky hut. She looked very old and had to roll onto one side and then onto all fours in order to stand. A young girl of maybe ten years, who sat with her, helped her to her feet. I had never seen such an old woman in my life. Her clothes were ragged and her face such a mass of intertwining wrinkles she looked as old as the pine forests we had ridden through on our journey north.

She approached me on unsteady legs, supported by the girl. She spoke to me in a high pitched and cracked voice. I had a strange feeling the voice was familiar. I fancied that cracked voice was the one in my mind when I killed Piso.

I could imagine it repeating 'Coward, coward,' in my ear. I shivered as I looked upon her. It was as if I faced my past, present and future enshrined within this withered woman who approached me now.

In the gloom of the hut, her face looked shrivelled and dark but even that seemed unthreatening to me, as if I could trust her. Her eyes were dark and serious and the firelight reflected from them and gave them a ghostly look.

'I know you young man,' she said, pointing at me with a bony, wrinkled finger. 'I am Chlotsuintha, I am a witch. I serve Wuotan. I held you in my arms when you were fresh from your mother's womb and I gave you to your father. It was I who put the mark of the Midgaard Serpent on your head. It is Wuotan's mark and it tells the world you are destined by prophecy to rule and lead our nation to a better place.'

The old face cracked into a toothless smile. 'Wuotan has spared me all these years for this purpose. I had no other reason for living this long, long time and it has always puzzled me why I did. I see now how the Norns have engineered this moment.'

To my immense embarrassment, the old woman knelt, slowly and with difficulty, in front of me placing her forehead on my hand. I did not know what to do next. I bade her get up and I looked around the hut. All the faces regarded me in silence as if they expected me to do something. I had no idea what to do.

Presently, Chlotsuintha spoke. 'We must shave your head so the mark can be seen. Your uncle, Odomir will not wish anyone to know who you are, for he is the Warlord now. The High Council has chosen his nephew, Guntramm, who is your cousin, to succeed him. If you are worthy then you must take the title from them both. It is your destiny, but you cannot fulfil it with a stupid name like Sextus,' she smiled and then emitted a high-pitched cackle. She calmed and began to cough. She spat on the fire and said, 'That name is the name of Roman slavery and not fit for a Warlord of the Franks. You know Galdir? Galdir? You know this word?'

'No. I don't know much German.'

'Galdir is the song of rage and anger men feel on the battle field. It is the spell of Tyr, God of war. It fills men's souls and drives them to the madness that brings death and destruction to our enemies. Your father was Galdar and you were Galdir. You must take your name back and rule our people in the times of war approaching—like a storm cloud from the south.'

'I… I am no leader, I'm just a boy... I know nothing of such things. I...I don't even know your language properly or any of your customs.'

I confess I panicked. I got up and ran from the hut. I heard Duras speaking to the elders in low tones as I pushed the leather flap aside. There was laughter and the thought occurred to me I had made a fool of myself but I could not prevent myself from running. I ran all the way to the stables and sat on a bale of straw, my head in my hands. I had no idea what to do.

I knew I had brought this upon myself but I was not the only one responsible. If Livia had not encouraged me to go north and find my people, I might perhaps not have come this far. I was not the man I had once imagined I was. It was worse than anything I had envisaged. People here expected something of me, which I did not have. I was no leader and I knew it.

I waited for Duras. He would understand. We could leave and go elsewhere, but where? South were Romans and west there were more Romans. North was only a wide sea and I did not think my chances would be very good with the eastern Germanic tribes. I felt alone, and like a child wanted to cry.

CHAPTER XXV

"To have command is to have all the power you will ever need. To have all the power you will ever need, is to have the world in the palm of you hand."

— Emperor Tiberius Caesar

I sat with my head in my hands on that bale of straw for what seemed like hours. Thoughts flooded my head. I had found out who I was but the biggest question in my now tired brain was not who but what I was.

The horses around me seemed restless and as a way of distracting myself, I began grooming the one I had ridden the most. I talked to the horse in gentle tones and his restlessness dissipated. My own feelings also found some calm from contact with the horse. Even now I still groom my own horse for I find it a restful way to solve problems in my head and to examine issues in the calmness it brings.

The thought I was son to a Frankish Warlord and some seemed to have expectations of me seemed absurd. I was an escaped slave and although Cornelius had taught me to wield weapons, he had not prepared me for anything like this.

My thoughts soon drifted to Livia. My Livia, whom I missed with such avid desperation. She had pushed me unwilling to seek this very place and these people. I pictured her in my mind riding with me back to the farm. My mind reverberated to the memory of her voice as she suggested I should seek my origins. I wished I could tell her what had happened since those days that seemed so long ago.

What if there was civil war because some faction wanted me and another wished to maintain the status quo. I smiled to myself. Who would want to follow me? I felt as if I was nobody and I could not imagine anyone wanting me to be a Warlord or king, whether I was a rightful heir or not.

What would this uncle of mine think? Perhaps he would only see me as a threat and would want my blood rather than welcome me into his open arms as some kind of kin.

These thoughts spun around in my head so fast I flitted from one thought to another with exhausting rapidity. I was glad in the end to be interrupted in my thinking by the arrival of Duras and Pippin who had walked back to look for me.

'Well my friend, it turns out we are both dispossessed princes! I always thought there was more to you than meets the eye! I have had a long talk with the council of elders and they understand your worries.'

'Duras, if you explained to them, we can guarantee it will all go wrong! What on earth did you say?'

'I told them who I am and I am here to help you, that's all. They agreed you could keep your hair for the time being so you can learn the ways of your people before you declare yourself to the High Council. Chlotsuintha has offered to teach you of the German Gods and her girl will teach you the language and customs. You are to present yourself to this little village council in three months' time for examination. At least all they want is your hair and not your head!' Duras laughed in his typical booming way and he even conjured up a smile from me too.

*

I spent the next few weeks with the little girl who had been helping Chlotsuintha. She wore a cloak of falcon feathers made by Chlotsuintha to remind her of the power of her namesake. Her name was Frija. She taught me to speak her language but it was not difficult. I think some of the words were buried deep in my head since the Romans first took me, but there had been no way to release them until now. In two months, I became almost fluent, with daily coaching. Duras learned the language too. I had thought he was not a particularly intelligent man, but he was shrewd and languages seemed to come easily for him.

Frija was a strange girl. She had intense blue eyes and a wistful smile that seemed to suggest she knew much more than she was telling. She always looked at me as if she knew what I was thinking and often when we talked, she would answer a question before I had asked it. There was something frightening about her for that reason, but she taught me well.

My main difficulty was the religion. Chlotsuintha spent hours telling me about the German religion and it was she, who first stimulated my interest in the true Gods. I learned the stories of Wuotan the Allfather, how he had traded an eye in exchange for all knowledge at the foot of the tree of all knowledge and even the story Cornelius had once alluded to of the two ravens sitting at the Allfather's side who bring him news of events in the world of men.

She told me of her rune-stones and how she read them. She told me of the prophesy cast when I was born, describing how I would be a great warrior and leader and would take the people away to a warm dry place where there were fertile lands and good weather. One thing I did learn from her was how my parents had died fighting the Romans who enslaved me. She described how Galdar my father, had led his men in a hopeless battle against a huge Roman army and I learned how he had died bravely, sword in hand.

'That's odd,' I said. 'I had a dream of a big man who looked like me, fighting Romans.'

'Yes, it was your father reaching out for you from Valhalla. In my world, I hear him often. Your mother too.'

'My mother?'

'Yes, a good woman. The Romans killed her as she tried to protect you.'

'You knew her?'

'Of course. Her name was Gertrud. She was tall and strong with a beauty many envied.'

'I wish I could have known her.'

'You would have, had your father not been betrayed.'

'Betrayed?'

'Your uncle should have come to his brother's aid, but he didn't. No one knows for sure, but I have my suspicions. The rune stones told me.'

She told me how my father had died trapped by a huge Roman force in his town. His brother Odomir had claimed to be fighting elsewhere and failed to come to his aid, yet benefited by becoming Warlord in my father's place.

'Do you think he refused to help so he could become Warlord?' I asked Chlotsuintha on one of the days when she was teaching me.

'Some say there was no reason for his absence, others say he had his hands full fighting elsewhere, but you know, I never believed it because there was only one Roman army and if he wasn't fighting them, then who was he fighting?'

'Then it is unlikely he will be pleased I have come home?'

'Of course he will not be pleased. He would stop at nothing to prevent you claiming your birthright as the Warlord. The High Council have chosen his nephew Guntramm to be next in line and he will succeed Odomir. For you to become Warlord you must defeat your uncle in a fair fight and he is a formidable warrior—believe me. Even if his age has begun to rob him of his power he can appoint a champion to fight in his name.'

'I have no worries in that respect. Cornelius taught me well in both hand to hand fighting and battle craft.'

'You talk often of this man. He was a Roman but it sounds as if he cared for you.'

'I saved his life once and he spent the rest of his life protecting me and teaching me. He took on the responsibilities of a father.'

'The fates have spun an interesting web around you. I pray they will continue to favour you. I cast the runes last night and they confirmed the prophecy and more.'

'What more?'

'They foretold our nation will one day be defeated but will rise again from the ashes and Master huge lands for all eternity.'

'Then it doesn't sound as if I will be a very good Warlord if I lead the nation into defeat.'

'It will not be your doing but the Romans; for they are prophesied to take over the whole world for a long time, but our nation's time will come after theirs and last much longer.'

'How do you know all this, Chlotsuintha?' I asked.

'I am one with Wuotan and he tells me things through the rune stones. Like all rune stones, I made them by moon-

238

light and smeared them in my menstrual blood. The ones I use have not only my blood but also the blood of witches for six generations. They have a power many times greater than any others.'

I paid little attention to her ramblings; I was convinced she was mad. It seemed to escape me that no one else in the town thought this. Everyone held Chlotsuintha in high esteem. She had lived longer than anyone could remember and had been a royal soothsayer for many years, as far back as my grandfather. It all ended when Odomir, my uncle, had become the Warlord. The Warlord never summoned her and another had taken her place. She was forgotten for all those years I was away, but she had kept her faith and always believed I would come back to lead the Franks to glory.

And the prophesy? Well, I had my doubts.

BOOK II: WARLORD

CHAPTER 1

"The friendship that can cease has never been real."

— St Jerome

I leaned forward and patted my horse's neck. The tree line in front of me was dark and sombre, a sharp contrast to the long yellow grass upon which I dismounted. There were gorse bushes at the edge of the forest and white meadow asphodel gave off a fresh scent intermingling with the smell of the pine trees. The sun was shining from a blue summer sky, interrupted from time to time by small, white, fluffy clouds. Finches warbled in the background. The heat seemed to rise from the ground making me sweat. It was a beautiful day though I cannot now recall why I was alone or where I was heading. Crossing the meadow behind me was a cart-track and beyond that, to the south, were those seemingly endless, rolling, green hills that make Raetia the wonderful place it is.

'You're a good horse, Valknir.' I said.

He shook his head gently to acknowledge me. I have never had a horse like him. He was a gift from my uncle Odomir. Despite that, I loved him.

'You may be a Dacian horse, my friend,' I said to him, 'but you have straight legs unlike most of those cow-hocked Dacian mounts.'

Duras always argued to the contrary, but I think most of the Dacian horses are cow-hocked. Not this one. He was perfect. His broad chest showed stamina and his legs were thick, muscular and strong. I looked at him with a fondness many would reserve for a woman. He was a responsive mount. He answered every little direction I gave him with my feet. He listened to me and knew my voice.

I tethered him, stroked and scratched his mane behind his ears, and he shook his head.

'Feisty aren't you? Fancy you biting that Roman in the skirmish, and kicking that other one! No horse could be as good as you are in a battle. By Wuotan I swear it!'

His name was Valknir—a flying steed. It was an apt name, for when I rode him in battle it was like flying with Wuotan's Valkyr maidens.

I remember entering the wood after dismounting. I needed to pass water and although I had no reason to suspect there would be enemies about, I made to enter the forest out of sight to relieve myself.

I had only taken a few steps into the bushes, when the first arrow flew past my left ear with a buzz like a wasp. It caused a slight air movement I could feel, as if someone had waved a hand at the side of my head. The arrow buried itself in the nearest tree. It vibrated noisily for a second. I looked at it in stupid surprise as it dawned on me I was under attack.

They aimed the second arrow badly too. It hit my left leg from behind and it passed through my thigh on the outside of the bone. Half of it projected through those muscles that straighten your knee. My leg refused to support me and I was down. I cursed and crawled into the thicket in which I was hoping to pass water. Happily, it happened before I had relieved myself.

As I lay in the bush I managed to draw my knife. I notched the arrow in no time, and then broke it behind my leg. I pulled it through fast. There was some bleeding. I had no time to study the damage. I heard footsteps and cracking twigs to one side. They were hunting me.

I had a sword, but anyone who has been in such a predicament will realise the difficulties of drawing a long German sword fast and in silence, when you are lying down. I crawled painfully around the trunk of a pine tree, and hauled myself upright.

There were at least three men. I could hear them communicating as they searched for me. Turning, I drew my sword. Almost immediately, I heard a noise behind me. I felt a blow struck on my right shoulder. I was wearing a vest of chain mail and it prevented serious damage. Clearly my assailant was an amateur. He should have used the point of his sword.

For me, it would have been a reflex. Cornelius drilled it into me years before.

'Use the point and stab! Against chain mail you can't make cutting strokes tell with a sword!' he used to say.

I turned fast to my left. The blow to my shoulder had made me drop my sword. I still gripped my long knife in my left hand. I slashed at the man who was attacking me, before he could raise his weapon again. He stepped back. As he did so, one of my attackers struck me again from behind. This time it was on the back of the head. I pitched forward, losing my helmet.

In that moment, all became a dizzy, flying, rotating mess. The man with the sword stood over me. Through the swirling images I realised he raised it two handed. He was finishing what he had begun.

Events then took on a surreal quality. Time slowed down. Although my head was still swimming, I am sure I saw it with clarity; the point of an arrow emerged from his mouth. He pitched forward. As I pushed his bleeding head away, another arrow came whistling through the air straight into the chest of the second man. I managed to get to one elbow. My head cleared. I saw a third man running away, then a horseman whose likeness I had never seen before chased the running man.

This mounted warrior and his horse wore chain mail. The warrior wore a brightly polished helmet. The whole scene unfolded before my surprised eyes with extraordinary speed. The horseman drew his sword. He threw it into the air. He caught it so it pointed downwards. He reached down, and stabbed. It descended into the soft part between the running man's head and shoulder.

It was a mortal blow. The victim collapsed in a heap. The mounted soldier turned his horse with incredible speed considering the armour encumbering his mount and he rode towards where I lay. I looked up at his face, squinting because of the bright afternoon sun behind him. It made him look like a god.

'Neatly done,' I said, my surprise getting the better of me. The blow to my head had clearly not improved my powers of conversation.

'Not a challenge really, they weren't expecting me to be there. Who were they?' my rescuer said, in thickly accented German.

'I have no idea. They certainly weren't Romans, that's for sure. If you didn't know them, why did you help me?'

'Three to one is not my idea of a fair fight. To leave them

to kill you would have been dishonourable. I took a chance.'

I managed to get to my feet and leaning against the tree, I peeled up my mail shirt and cutting a strip from my tunic with my knife, I staunched the blood oozing down my thigh. I looked at my two assailants.

'Which tribe were they?' said the warrior.

'This one's a Chatti, you can tell from the armour. This other one is a Marcomanni. That's a surprise. I was riding with a war band of theirs only two months ago. We attacked a large contingent of Romans and destroyed them. We had quite a celebration afterwards and there was no feeling of tension or dissent from any of them.'

'It was lucky my wife and I were passing. They would have killed you. Are you usually this bad at fighting? I've travelled a long way to forge an alliance with the German people but if this is the best you can do, then maybe we aren't suited to be fighting together.'

I must have scowled at that, for he smiled and dismount-ed.

'Please don't take offence; it is only my foreign sense of humour! I am from Sarmatia. I have travelled far for many months. Do you know where can I find a place to rest overnight?'

'I am Galdir of the Franks and I welcome you. You saved my life and I will never forget it. I will be delighted to take you to our camp and will see you are comfortable,' I said.

A covered wagon appeared on the little path traversing the field. Seated on the front seat was a woman. I had never seen her like before either. She also had chain mail and wore a short throwing axe and a short sword at her waist. Next to her on the seat was a quiver of arrows and a curved compo-site bow. The small child in her arms added a bizarre quality to the whole scene, for who would expect a mother to dress and arm herself in this fashion? Of course, I had heard of warrior maidens who lived in Sarmatia, but this was my first experience of one.

'You must indeed have travelled a long way to get here, we see few Sarmatians,' I said, feeling surprised and taken aback.

'Indeed my friend, all the way from my country north and east of Pannonia. We are seeking the court of either the Franks or the Marcomannii as I have an embassy to impart.'

'I am a relative of the Frankish Warlord Odomir. I'm his nephew and will be pleased to introduce you to him.'

So saying, I managed to mount my horse with help from the Sarmatian and I indicated west to the young woman who sat stony faced and unreachable in the wagon.

Her husband's name was Lazygis and he was a short stocky man with a long thin face and a nose with a slight hook to it. He had braided black hair, a drooping black moustache, and dark searching eyes. He wore red badges with golden trim sewn on the front of his mail shirt. In his hand, he carried a spear, but he disdained a shield. His horse was huge and broad and clearly quite used to wearing a mail kirtle for the stallion showed no signs of tiring.

'Do you need to travel in the wagon?' asked the woman, in a clear but accented German.

'Thank you but no. It would be unbecoming for the nephew of the Warlord to arrive back at our military camp in a wagon.'

Her voice was affable enough and as I glanced at her, I noticed she had the same long face as her husband but her features were delicate and her long black hair hung untied in straggles upon her shoulders. Her child was perhaps two

248

years old and she held him with one arm as he slept peacefully with his head in the crook of her arm, despite the undulating and sometimes violent rocking of the wagon.

'Thank you for what you did for me at the forest,' I said as we rode without haste to the Frankish camp .'I was careless to get trapped in that way. There was no reason to expect an attack this close to our camp and certainly not from fellow Germans. I would usually have been able to take care of myself.'

'If you couldn't, then you wouldn't be here would you? You would have died long before I came on the scene! These are dangerous times after all!'

I smiled at my companion. Lazygis smiled back and I could see his wife smirk as she negotiated a bump in the track we were following. He had an easy smile and I warmed to him

'We have come to seek an alliance and have brought gifts for both the Frankish king and for the Marcomannii leader. How is the war going?' Lazygis said.

'It goes well. In fact, it goes surprisingly well considering we are fighting Romans. The thing about the Romans is the discipline of their soldiers makes them hard to kill. They have large shields making an impenetrable wall punctuated with stabbing short swords. As soon as we get close in battle, they wait until there is a dense press of our men and they advance through our blood. Our men find it hard to wield long swords or axes in such confined spaces. We have started carrying shorter swords as well as our long swords just for such a situation,' I said.

'There is no infantry alive who can stand against a full speed charge of heavy Sarmatian cavalry. We are horse archers as well. We are hoping to move all our people south and west if we can, so the thinking is, we could all join forces and crush the Romans.'

'We have no heavy cavalry or horse archers, so I imagine my uncle will be very pleased to have an alliance. Tell me, why is your wife wearing chain mail? Do all your women dress like this?'

'Yes, it is our belief that women are stronger than men in many ways. They learn early to fight and ride. I hear your women are treated like cattle and do little fighting.'

'Indeed, we are happy for them to be beautiful and stay at home when we fight. They take charge of the home when we are away. Some women in Gaul even learn to fight and to shoot a bow.' I could feel the sadness welling up inside when I said this, for I thought of Livia now lost to me, whom I had still loved more than life.

'We are very different I think.'

We rode slowly, a combination of my injuries and the wagon's sluggish pace. The journey was short, for the attack had happened only a few miles from where our troops were camped.

The camp itself was huge. We had thirty thousand men. There were camp followers and horse tenders and smiths all following our Frankish army. The Marcomannii and Chatti were in an adjacent camp but they each numbered by almost twice as many men as us Franks. Their accompanying followers numbered almost as many as our whole army. Relations between us were good. We had fought alongside one another for almost four years and had spread our influence from the Rhine to eastern Dacia and south as far as the Danubus River. The Roman opposition was weak and although they showed no signs of folding, we had won most of the battles. We were moving south now in a push to take northern Italia.

The joint Roman Emperors, Verus and Aurelius were rumoured to be gathering their men to fight us near the Limes, but it was four years since I had been there and I could not recall the layout of the defences.

I led my new Sarmatian friends to the centre of the camp where the Warlord, my uncle Odomir had his tent.

It was a grand affair. It rose fifteen feet high and had a huge tent pole in the centre with numerous poles at the sides. The round area of ground, thus enclosed, was enormous. In that tent he ate, he entertained and he treated it much like a kingly hall. He was in truth king of the Franks in all but name. They had many kings in those days, but all paid homage to the Warlord for it was his duty to lead the armies and protect the people.

Lazygis helped me dismount. My wound was becoming painful now although it was no longer bleeding. As I limped towards the tent, Duras appeared from within.

'What in the name of Tyr happened to you,' he said supporting me by taking my arm over his shoulder. It felt like he was hoisting me into a tree since he was a head taller than I was.

'You wouldn't believe it,' I said. 'I was attacked by two Marcomannii and a Chatti armed with bows and swords. They were trying to kill me when this Sarmatian turned up and killed all three. I was very lucky; they were on the verge of completing their task. It was some of the best horse archery I've ever seen. Gods my head hurts!'

'You were lucky indeed then,' said my enormous companion. He was still trying to get back his land and kingship from the Marcomannii by diplomacy but he had sworn an oath that if that did not work he would raise an army and take back what was his. We were all killing Romans at that time so we had shelved most of our internal struggles.

'I don't understand why they were trying to kill me,' I said.

'Have you quarrelled with anyone?' asked Duras.

'No, no one at all. But it's clear someone wants rid of me. I expect it was my uncle but I have no proof and I could be wrong.'

'We had better get those wounds tended or they'll fester,' Duras said. He turned to the two Sarmatians and introduced himself.

'I will show you where you can make camp and when you are ready, Galdir can introduce you to Odomir the Warlord of the Franks,' he said. He raised his eyebrows when he said this and made his opinion of my uncle clear, to me at least.

When I approached my uncle's tent, the guard outside told me he could not receive visitors. He told us to return in the morning. I hoped my guests did not feel offended but Odomir was the Warlord after all.

We wound our way through the vast camp. The Sarmatians would not have a tent and the wife, whose name was Ayma meaning 'life of Ma', their chief deity, refused to even enter a tent and insisted on camping in the wagon. They put up an awning and seemed comfortable enough. Duras took me to the surgeon's tent where one of our medicine men treated my wound with oil and myrrh and bound it with a clean cloth. It only festered a little and healed quickly but left me with a slight limp.

CHAPTER II

"Learn now of the treachery of the Greeks, and from one example the character of the nation may be known."

— Virgil

I fetched my Sarmatian friends in the morning. The sun was shining and there was not a cloud in the sky as we threaded our way through the camp. Dew reflected the early morning sunlight as we picked our way between tents and the materials of war littering the place. I had to apologise once as I stumbled over a man's shield lying across my path, for my leg was painful and made me limp.

'What's your uncle like?' asked Lazygis.

'In what sense?'

'As a man, of course.'

'He's a big man. He's like me in build, but that's where the family resemblance ends. The man has no sense of humour. He was a fierce fighter in his youth and if you asked his men, they would tell you one of his best attributes is he leads from the front.'

'A warrior king then?'

'Sort of, at least he used to be. He rewards his men well from time to time and it ensures their loyalty. Can't say I trust him much though.'

'He's your uncle. You must trust him surely?' Ayma said.

253

'Can't see why I should. He trusts no one except maybe my cousin Guntramm. He surrounds himself with guards and he even has a food taster. Apparently he thinks someone might want to poison him.'

'Surely you wouldn't do that, would you?'

'Me? No, certainly not. I'm one of his dependants. It wouldn't help me if he did die, since Guntramm is ahead of me in the line of succession. Anyway, I have about as much desire to be a Warlord as I have to become a Roman emperor.'

'Has he always been the Warlord?'

I looked sideways at Lazygis and wondered if he knew more than he was admitting to but the suspicion passed, for he bore a disarming smile and his eyes betrayed no guile.

'No, if you must know, my father was Warlord before him. When my father died, he took over. It was when I was only a child.'

'And he took you in?'

'No, not exactly. The Romans captured and enslaved me. I spent fifteen years as a slave of theirs. It's a long story. I'll tell you about it sometime.'

'The Romans killed your father then?'

'Yes and my mother. My father died fighting. Odomir and he had quarrelled over the future of our people. Odomir always wanted to join the Marcomannii in a war against Rome but my father wanted peace. He wanted to relocate our people to a better terrain across the Rhenus. I learned all this from a witch called Chlotsuintha after I returned home. She did say she thought Odomir delayed coming to my father's aid because he wanted to be Warlord. I still don't know the truth of it.'

'And since then your people have been fighting alongside

the Marcomannii and Chatti against the Romans?'

'Yes, it seems to be going well. The alliance has taken back all the land north of the Danubus, and we are now threatening Raetia, Noricum and Pannonia. I don't know why he wants to expand his dominions though. We've hardly enough people to populate the lands we have. Maybe he's being incautious and it will come out against us in the end, as my father thought. Ah, here's Duras.'

My friend approached smiling. He stepped lightly of step for such a big man.

'Well here you are. Galdir, thank you for letting me sleep a bit longer! I needed it after last night!'

To my intense irritation, he slapped me on the back. I could have hit him in return, since my shoulder was still very painful.

'They were asking me about Odomir,' I said through clenched teeth.

'Him, humourless fellow. Not my sort of man, but I'm hoping he can persuade the Marcomannii to give me back my kingdom which they stole from me,'

'Stole?' Ayma said.

'Oh, I'll tell you all about it later. We'll go visit the old fart and you can see for yourself.'

'It seems there are many stories to hear.'

'Don't worry, Lazygis,' I said, 'they are intertwined.'

Lazygis, Ayma, Duras and I entered my uncle's grand tent together after a mail-clad guard announced us. Odomir sat on a carved wooden chair at the far end of the huge tent, surrounded by his bodyguard.

Our Warlord frowned as we entered. He had a fiercely scarred face from many battles and I would describe his facial expression as pinched. I am not sure such a description exactly captures his troubled, grey, cod-cold eyes. He usually had a look on his face as if someone had squeezed an unripe fruit in his mouth and he always fiddled with his thinning grey-blonde beard.

I was limping as I approached but I thought I looked in reasonable shape until Odomir showed a look of real concern or maybe surprise.

'You're limping. Have you been in a fight?' he asked frowning again.

'No my lord, I was attacked by three men at the edge of the forest yesterday afternoon. Had it not been for this brave Sarmatian warrior they would have killed me. Lazygis here killed all three.'

'Indeed it was fortunate for you he was there. Did the attackers say anything before they died?'

'No my lord, it is difficult to talk with an arrow driven through your throat!' I smiled as I spoke. Odomir who, as I have intimated, had no sense of humour at all, ignored my joke and turned to regard the Sarmatian couple.

'I am most grateful to you for helping my nephew, whom I value above all others, save only Guntramm, my other nephew.'

My uncle glanced sideways at me as he spoke then turned back to the Sarmatians. 'I hear you have come with a message from your king and I would be pleased to hear what you have to say.'

'I am Lord Panogras Lazygis, Prince of the Royal court of Sarmatia and I have a gift for the leader of the Franks from my king.'

Lazygis gestured to his wife and she unwrapped the bundle she carried. The wrapping was a red silk cloth an outstanding and unusual colour. It fell away and revealed a sword of beautiful workmanship. This sword was short in length but the blade itself was shiny as a reflected moon on a still lake. Etched into the blade were a number of symbols, which I later learned were representations of luck and Deities from the Sarmatian culture. Red and green gemstones adorned the hilt and it had a rounded finger guard. It was a wonderful weapon and probably quite useful in close quarters because of its short blade. The scabbard bore decorations equally grand, for it sported a gem-encrusted belt accompanying the sword. It was indeed a treasure and a gift worthy of a king.

Ayma stepped forward to hand the weapon to Odomir, but two bodyguards immediately stepped forward and blocked her path. One of them reached forward, took the blade from her hands, and gave it to my uncle who said, 'In these times of war I have learned to be cautious of strangers with such gifts. I am sure you can understand.'

I was ashamed at his rudeness even though it was as close to an apology as he ever gave for insulting his guests. It was as if the Sarmatians were merely common people who had walked in from the road outside. I looked down in embarrassment and avoided Lazygis' gaze. This was not the way I would have received such a fine gift.

Lazygis smiled but I could see it was a cold smile and it held none of the warmth he had expressed in his humour on the road.

'Lord Odomir, I come as an emissary of my people to offer you some men for the battle ahead against the Roman oppressors. Even as we speak, a thousand of my compatriots are on their way to join with you and your army. They are proud, strong men. When they charge in battle, no infantry can stand against them. We hope to serve you well and fight alongside your men.'

'It is with great pleasure I welcome your men and their ambassador. I will be very pleased to have you join us in our coming victories against Marcus Aurelius and his brother Verus. I would be pleased if you and your companion,' he paused, looking Ayma up and down with distain, 'would join me in a small feast to celebrate the end of your journey and its successful conclusion.'

'We would be most honoured to dine with you Lord,' Lazygis said, and bowed before my uncle.

I walked with my Sarmatian friends back to the wagon. I could think of nothing to say to excuse my uncle's behaviour and we walked in silence.

We returned in the late afternoon for the promised feast. We had again to put up with the strict security of my uncle's tent. The guards searched us thoroughly. I could see the look of anger on Ayma's face as the guards ran their hands over her. It betrayed her contained anger. I could only admire her self-control.

Servants brought seats and set up a table in the middle of the tent. Odomir did provide good food and sometimes entertainment. Lazygis sat at his right hand with Ayma and my aunt Clotildis sat to his left. She had been married to my uncle for only two years and it was the first wife he had lived with who was generally and unreservedly acknowledged to be pretty. She was more my age than his and she came as a bright spark of light into the gloom of the Frankish noble court.

I always felt most of the Frankish women were unattractive but I never quite understood why. It may be because I had spent most of my youth in Roman lands, albeit as a slave. I was used to seeing and admiring women of strength and bearing. The Frankish women with a few notable exceptions were plain and plump. In our society being plump is a sign of fertility, health and therefore wealth. If you had a fat daughter you would have to fight off her suitors by the time she reached the age of twelve.

Clotildis was young, beautiful, and pleasant company. I can only guess how she felt about being married to my uncle as she was never willing to say. In sharp contrast to her husband, she had a good sense of humour and she and I had spent many pleasant afternoons just talking and laughing. I do not know if my uncle disapproved but there was no impropriety; perhaps he was glad someone in the army could entertain her. All he wanted her for was his bed and judging by the way he spoke to her, he had little other use for her. My uncle did not allow her in the tent when there was any business of war to discuss, but at banquets she had to dance for any distinguished visitors even when they were only kings of the Marcomannii, who are among the most brutish of people.

She was tall in stature and slim in the body. Despite her waif-like figure, she had a naturally regal bearing only someone of good birth could demonstrate. Her facial appearance was kind. She had the freckled fair skin with which we Germans are almost universally afflicted. Her freckles were however, a beautiful adornment to her blue eyes and light brown hair, the whole in summation portraying a woman of rare beauty. If she had not been my uncle's third wife, I think I could easily have fallen for her myself the first time I laid eyes upon her.

The thing preventing me from seeking a physical relationship with Clotildis was not loyalty but self-preservation. The penalty for playing fast and loose with a monarch's wife does not bear description. As I already had doubts about his intentions towards me, I did not intend to give Odomir an opening he could use to remove me from the tribal scene.

We drank the usual beer. If there is one German tradition that will become defunct in the future, it will be beer drinking. It is a flatulent, bitter drink and leaves me always with a thick head. Duras and I sat far away from the royal table, as was our wont. Duras was a pig. I loved him as a brother but he was, even if I put it politely, a pig. He still drank ale until it literally swamped him and he never seemed to get enough. It may have been a function of his great size but I think now it was because he was a Dacian and they are scarcely human when it comes to having a stomach for beer, as I had learned in the court of his father Moscon. The food was good as ever. We had roast wild boar stuffed with apples and that vegetable mash flavoured with herbs to which I am particularly partial.

The smell took me back to the times when I was with Livia. I thought about those strange days, spent with her and Cornelius. What I still missed the most was that she had not only been beautiful but she loved me as I had loved her. I still loved the fact she had been a huntress and a fighter, despite which, she was the most wonderful sweet woman I have ever met. My love for her still dwarfs all other feelings for women I have experienced since, bar only one. Perhaps it is always so for men. Their first love remains in the mind and builds into something more wonderful with the passing years. Only Medana had come close in my mind, but I had known her for such a short time before the fall of Lovosice. I often thought of her too but it was always with regret, as anyone would over a lost opportunity.

Towards the end of the meal, the entertainment began.

260

Unfortunately for everyone except my uncle, it was a group of jugglers. Odomir loved jugglers. This great big man, clumsy in many respects, loved jugglers to the exclusion of most other forms of entertainment. It exasperated me. Having been the guest of Duras' father for all those months and experienced a wonderful table and excellent entertainment ranging from singing, dancing, acrobatics, and mortal combat the comparison palled. Although I had no love for Duras' father, I have to concede he entertained his guests well. Not so, my uncle, he loved jugglers so much they occupied three quarters of the entertainment all year round.

I was not the only one afflicted by such boredom. Guntramm, my cousin, shared my dislike. He never turned up for a meal until the juggling had finished.

I often wonder if my dislike of jugglers has offended the Fire God, Loge, the trickster of the deities. It seems to me, he played pranks on every aspect of my life then and even now. How else in the end, could I have become so entangled with my uncle's wife?

That night, the entertainment ended and we all bade each other goodnight by drinking a toast to the Gods and to each other and my uncle was drunk enough to swear an oath of friendship with the Sarmatian people. Duras left with us, though he needed support from me as I escorted my Sarmatian guests to their wagon. I bade them goodnight and I found I was drunk enough to ask Ayma to forgive the insult paid her by my uncle in refusing a gift from her hand.

'It is not for you to forgive the behaviour of your uncle. Not only are you not responsible, you show politeness and hospitality and we are both most grateful to you for your reception of us.'

'I hope all the same, you will not be offended.'

'One day I will spit in his split skull. We Sarmatians never forget an insult. The stupid man was a fool to think he could treat us, his honoured guests, in such a way. For the time being however, we are allies and must fight side by side and such things must wait their turn with the passage of time. All will be as Ma makes it,' said Ayma referring to the Sarmatian mother god. Her eyes showed cold, glinting in the light of the flaming torch in her hand.

I looked at her quizzically for I was not certain whether she was joking. I saw no sign of humour in her face however and it was only when Lazygis broke the uncomfortable silence, I was able to relax.

'My wife means nothing by this, let me assure you. We are allies and we will fight side by side. In the morning if you wish, I will show you the skills for which we Sarmatians are famous. I will show you how to shoot a bow from a horse.'

'You are most kind,' I said, 'but I have no bow and it is a while since I have shot one.'

'Don't worry, my friend, I have many spare bows and plenty of arrows for you to practise with.'

'Until the morning then,' I said. As Duras and I staggered to our tent, I wondered what skills the Sarmatian was talking about. The morning however left me in no doubt.

CHAPTER III

"A horse is a thing of beauty... none will tire of looking at him as long as he displays himself in his splendor."

— Xenophon

We breakfasted outside our brown leather tent. Duras looked bleary eyed. He spoke little. He was clearly not enjoying the summer sunshine which reflected off my helmet. It was the only part of me reflecting anything, for my chain mail was black. I had taken it from a dead Marcomanni warrior in a forest after we joined my uncle's army. Neither of us liked the Marcomannii for they were a cruel and barbarous community. We had heard what they had done when they had overrun Lovosice, Duras' home city. They had raped the women and killed all the men. I suppose the way the Romans took men from conquered nations and made them into Roman soldiers was better, but I hated them both anyway.

The day was warm and sunny; high above us black crows circled, soaring high in the air currents. Our camp was in a field adjacent to a pine forest which loomed dark and forbidding on the mountain slopes. It was easily defensible because of the slope but we had no particular fears the Romans would attack, even if they knew we were there.

Many of our men feared the forest. They had various religious reasons for it and often ventured to the edge to put offerings to the Gods at the base of a large tree, or even to nail food or other sacrifices to the tough bark. They steered clear of the trees at night for it was rumoured the spirits of the dead wandered lonely and malevolent through the dense undergrowth and waited for their prey. Even Chlotsuintha the witch did not believe it and dismissed it as childish nonsense, and I must admit I had no real faith in such stories either.

I went to the picket line to see to Valknir and ensure he had hay. When I returned, I found our Sarmatian visitors were at the tent. Ayma held her little boy's hand and he looked around with large dark eyes framed by lashes the length of which any young woman would have been envious. He was dressed as any other of our children would be, in leggings and tunic. The bulge of the cloths in his leggings was a tell-tale of his developing continence. He smiled when he saw me arrive for I smiled at him and knelt down to say a few words. He understood none of it of course, but realised I was not a source of danger.

'His name is Panogaris. He likes you,' said Ayma with the first broad smile on her lips I had seen.

'He is a handsome young man,' I said. 'He will be a prince and a warrior, like his father.'

'How is your leg?' asked Lazygis.

'About the same. I don't know if I can ride with you this morning.'

'Oh but you must. I am sure the exercise will be good for you. I promise not to tax you too much.'

'With such a gracious invitation how could I decline?' I said but I did not feel like learning bow-craft that morning; my head and shoulder still ached and my leg pained me.

Notwithstanding my initial complaints, we went to the picket line and I saddled Valknir. Lazygis had already saddled his horse and it still surprised me how well his horse could move wearing heavy chain mail.

We rode out of the camp to a field where our horses were sometimes tethered. There were horse posts dotted at intervals of about ten feet from each other around the field. Lazygis remained mounted and showed me his bow. At each end it was curved and was made of a combination of horn and wood. The horn tips produced hardness and the wood gave a springiness lending the bow considerable power compared to the conventional instrument that I had learned to use in Italia. Since Livia taught me how to use a bow I had stopped using one because it always reminded me of her. I could not refuse this time however, out of politeness.

'Now to show you what can be done from horseback with a weapon like this,' Lazygis said.

He rode the horse to the far end of the field and began to ride back fast. As he passed the first post, he turned to his left and I realised he had nocked an arrow without my even seeing it, so fast was his movement. As he swivelled, the arrow flew away and embedded itself in the post. He turned his horse and this time did the same from the other side. With no difficulty at all, he skewered the horse post from the opposite side. He turned a third time and did the same once more. He rode to where I was standing.

'Now it's your turn,' he said with a broad grin.

'If you can teach me to do that, then you could teach Donar to make louder thunder,' I said.

'Who is Donar?' he said.

'Never mind,' I said, as I took the bow and quiver from his outstretched hand. I mounted Valknir and we rode to the far end of the field as Lazygis had done moments before. I coaxed my steed onwards and tried to imitate Lazygis. It was much less smooth and as I turned to release the arrow I fell off my horse. With my current injuries I was lucky not to sustain any serious damage. I lay on the soft grass looking up as Lazygis approached. I was cursing.

'Well, that was an interesting exhibition. Why exactly did you dismount in such a hurry, were you planning to stab the post with the arrow by hand?'

'I don't think there is any reason to laugh at me. It is difficult to stay mounted when you are twisted to one side, you lose the support of the high front and back in the saddle,' I explained.

'Of course, I understand, it is because you have no stirrups,' Lazygis said.

'Stirrups? What are stirrups?' I asked, feeling puzzled and sore.

Lazygis indicated two triangular pieces of metal at his feet, hanging from the saddle of his horse.

'Are they stirrups?' I asked.

'Yes, my people never mount a horse without them. You can get up into the saddle with ease and when you ride they allow you to stand in the saddle, steadying yourself to do the fighting or shoot arrows without falling off. It is why the Roman cavalry is so weak. They charge with their lances and there is every chance they will fall off even if they hit their targets. It is simple: they don't use stirrups.'

'So with these things you can remain stable in the saddle?'

'Yes, of course, we are not the only ones to use stirrups. There is a tribe called the Vandals to the east of my home country who also use them.'

'Can I try them?'

'Of course,' he said and dismounted. His horse was taller than Valknir and it took me a while to learn how to command him. After several minutes, I began to understand him, and he responded to my voice quite well. I made a second attempt at the archery. This time, although I did not fall, I missed the post twice and hit it with my third arrow. I looked at my Sarmatian friend.

'Well, it's a start I suppose,' he said.

I spent the rest of the morning practising and found my skills improved although I could not match Lazygis for speed or accuracy.

'It is a matter of practise. You must understand I have been doing this since I was old enough to sit on a horse, so it is not an easy skill to learn as an adult. Some have managed it though.'

As we rode back to the camp, I decided to make some stirrups. They would be easy to make and I could get our saddler to mount them on my saddle. It occurred to me also it was out of character for the Romans to be so mistaken. Cavalry had always been their weakness because of the instability of the rider, even in a Roman saddle which had a high front and back. As Lazygis said, the riders often fell off during battle. I remembered knocking Marcus Piso out of the saddle when I stole his chariot horses with Cornelius. It was a typical example. To be able to stand in the stirrups would have made the Roman cavalry invincible. No wonder the Sarmatians were so fearsome, they could fight as well in the saddle as when they stood on the ground.

On our return to the camp we set about fashioning the new gear and it was easy to find a saddler who fitted them to straps on our saddles. After the midday meal, I visited Clo-

267

tildis and sat in her tent, as I often did when I had time, and we talked of politics and other matters.

'Tell me about Rome,' she said.

'Rome is a big place; there would be much to tell you had it not been for the fact I was a slave most of the time I was there. Slaves do not see much of the place unless their owners send them on errands. Most of my errands were in the Subura, a foul place full of criminals and poor people. The rich people live on the hills called the Quirinal and Esquiline where there are huge stone built houses with courtyards and gardens and they all have large numbers of slaves to do the work.'

'Do you miss Rome?'

'No not all. I miss wine. I acquired quite a taste for it when I was in the Subura and afterwards. It is much more palatable than beer.'

'And women? What are the Roman women like?'

'They are haughty and aloof. They spend a lot of time on their appearance and some have slaves just to do their hair, with no other duties.'

Clotildis lay back on her couch and looked beautiful. My attraction to her, however unwise, was beginning to get the upper hand. She gestured to me to sit with her. I got up from my low stool with a grimace, for my leg wound was troubling me.

'How did you get that wound?' asked Clotildis.

'I was attacked by three Germans at the edge of the forest yesterday. Lazygis the Sarmatian killed all three in a display of archery and horsemanship that was quite splendid.'

'Here let me see it, perhaps there is something I can do to help.'

'No, really, it's all right,' I said in obvious embarrassment.

268

She sat me down on her couch. She began to undo the leggings by the thongs fastening them at the side of my leg. I took her hand gently in mine and we looked at each other. Face to face and eye to eye, we both seemed to realise we desired each other. Still holding her hand, I pulled her towards me and our lips met in a moist, slow kiss seeming to last forever. We looked at each other in slight surprise I thought, for neither of us had seemed to have planned such a moment. It just appeared to happen and neither of us now wanted to control ourselves.

'We can't do this you know,' I said. The warmth, proximity and smell of her, stimulated me as only a beautiful woman can. My control over the situation was slender to say the least and my desire for her gripped me with an unrelenting pressure.

'No, you're right, we shouldn't but I don't seem to be able to control it,' Clotildis said. She half smiled and parted her lips in a way I was finding irresistible. She sat down next to me and we kissed again. There followed a flurry of clothes and passionate fondling I hesitate to detail. Suffice to say, we made love in a hasty, desperate and passionate moment that spices my recollection every time I bring it to mind. She called my name as she reached her climax and stroked my face with gentle hands afterwards. It was an act seasoned by the desperate risk, and overwhelming in satisfaction for us both. Afterwards, we had little time to lie with each other or caress one another as lovers do, for we both knew anyone could enter and find us. We ended sitting opposite each other smiling and enjoying the strange moment.

'You know what you have done, don't you?' she said with a faint glimmer of a smile. There was a subtle glint in her eyes, which seemed for a fraction of a second to belie her passion in the moments before.

'Yes I think I do. I have betrayed my uncle and my principles and risked my life. You know, I don't really care. You are the most beautiful woman I have met in Germania, without qualification, and I want you desperately.'

'I know,' she said. 'If you were to challenge your uncle, you could become Warlord yourself; after all you have that right by birth. We really could be together then.'

'Yes but I don't want to be Warlord. I just want to make love to you. Anyway, there would be Guntramm to consider. He's going to succeed Odomir and so far, he has been backed by the High Council.'

'The Warlord has to prove he is worthy in order to lead. If the council considers someone else is more worthy, they will change their allegiance quickly enough. I can help you with that.'

'I thought you had nothing to do with politics. Odomir doesn't even let you sit in on the council meetings.'

'No, but I have friends who do.'

'Friends?'

'Yes, you don't think you are the only one who shows an interest in me do you?'

'Do you mean you make love to the whole council?' I was beginning to feel irritated, perhaps jealous, but I knew deep down I had no right to be. Clotildis was after all someone else's wife.

'Of course not, silly! I do lead them on a bit but I have never let anyone touch me until today.'

I believed her, but I had been through enough in my life to know not to trust blindly, whether it was a lovely young woman or anyone else.

'Clotildis, you are a beautiful, passionate young woman,

but I still have no ambitions to be Warlord. I don't have the qualities needed to lead a nation. I spent most of my life as a slave in Rome and although I know the Romans and have seen their plots and machinations at close quarters it does not mean I picked up any of the political skill I witnessed.'

'You can do it! You lead men every day in battle. Trust me.'

'No, I can't do it, please don't ask me again.'

The look on her face told all. I wondered if she was using me, but I was still consumed by desire for this beautiful young woman. As I made to go, she called me back and said, 'We must meet again soon but somewhere more private. I will find a place.'

I smiled and kissed her then left. I walked back to the tent wondering what I had gotten myself into. Was she playing me? Would she risk discovery just for the pleasure of a sexual encounter with her husband's nephew?

I doubted it and I knew she was doing this for political gain; there was after all much at stake. I still had the smell of her on my hands and I could almost taste her flesh pressed against my lips. I could not escape the feeling of lust sprouting in my brain like a ripe seed. I could not believe she had planned it all but I realised I did not really care.

'Me a Warlord? Impossible!' I thought.

This is the way a beautiful woman can achieve everything in politics: by using men's desire. I recalled how Lazygis had said that in his land they considered women to be stronger than men and I wondered if this was what he meant.

When I reached our tent Duras was sitting by the tent opening, sharpening his sword. He had a smile on his face when I approached.

'Well, where have you been?'

'I was visiting Clotildis, she was lonely. There isn't much for a young woman to do in the day in a military camp.'

'I am sure you can keep her busy,' he smirked.

'What on earth do you mean? We are only friends. You surely don't think I would try anything with her. She's the Warlord's wife.'

'How long have I known you? Five years? Six? Do you really think walking back from Clotildis' company with that look on your face doesn't tell a tale?' Duras was grinning from ear to ear now.

'You're mad,' I said.

'No Galdir it is you who is mad. No one but a crazy fool would put himself into such a position. You may have to kill your uncle at this rate. Anyway it's only a question of whether he kills you first.'

'I know, but I have no proof he sent the killers yesterday do I? Even if I did, what good would it do me? He is the most powerful man in our nation and he could swat me like a gnat if he wanted to. It doesn't make sense he hasn't killed me already.'

'Yes it does, when you think about it. There was all this doubt about your father's death and there must be quite a few in the ranks of the Frankish nation who would support you if you chose to fight. Chlotsuintha hinted as much on that first day after we arrived in the Frankish village.'

'Look I'm too tired to talk about all this now. It makes my head hurt.'

'That is not the only part of your anatomy that will be in pain if you become indiscreet, I can promise you,' Duras smiled at his attempt at humour and I crawled into the leather tent and lay down.

272

CHAPTER IV

"It never troubles the wolf how many the sheep may be"

— Virgil

A week had passed since I made love to my uncle's wife. Despite my frequent attempts to repeat the adventure with Clotildis, I had not managed to find an opportunity to be alone. My lust and desire burned in me and I thought of little else, even when learning arrow-craft from my new friend Lazygis. It devoured me. We practised every day and I was showing signs of mastering the technique. In return, I showed him some techniques with a sword and we found the arrangement mutually profitable, but every moment I thought about Clotildis.

Guntramm returned from a foraging party he had led into Roman lands. He had returned with wagonloads of corn and wine. The wine I felt was out of character but I was quite pleased to see it. I had not drunk wine for a long time and was looking forward to sampling it.

Guntramm and I looked alike. This was of course because we were cousins. He always acted as if he was my senior and since he was five years older, this caused me no offence.

He would taunt me over the manner of my father's death and made comments to the effect that Galdar was an incompetent. My cousin was not a stupid man but he was most unwise to cause trouble between us. I fought with myself to control my rage and not challenge him to a fight, because I knew my uncle would forbid it and likely send me away or worse: it might give him the excuse to have me executed. Try as I might however, I was unable to stop Guntramm from goading me. I had nothing else against him. He was a sound battle leader and popular with his men.

On his face, he bore a long scar running down the left side of his forehead onto the cheek. Men said he obtained it in battle but there were also rumours it was in a knife fight over a woman. He was a drinker like Duras but what concerned me most was that the two of them hated each other. Guntramm often insulted Duras, which was another reason for me to dislike him.

Duras and I had been through much together in a short time. So much so, we felt like brothers. We had sworn an oath of friendship when I returned to my people. Chlotsuintha the old witch had taken the rune reading and muttered incantations and it was a ceremony my people took seriously.

Guntramm had been part of the army that attacked Lovosice and I heard he had killed Moscon, his men and most of the inhabitants. I had lost Medana there too and although I later enquired about her I learned nothing. I cannot say in truth that I loved her. I was certainly fond of her and would have done almost anything to protect her but I was unable to when it came to the sacking of the town. Naturally, Duras did say he needed to take revenge one day against those who had killed his father and we often speculated why Guntramm tolerated our presence. Both Odomir and Guntramm had good reason to want us both dead.

When I met Guntramm for the first time, we were fighting the Romans. The battle had gone well. We had defeated an army of two legions. I should point out that when I look back at our military efforts I feel embarrassed. A Roman legion only numbers about seven thousand men. They also used auxiliaries as they like to call them. Such troops were soldiers from conquered nations whom the Romans transported to the other side of the Roman Empire and forced them to fight for Rome. It was very effective because there was no escape for an auxiliary and they always had people at home who might suffer if they revolted or mutinied. The army in question had twenty thousand auxiliaries to complement their legions, but we still vastly outnumbered them. We hit them with our infantry first and the Roman lines buckled. We sent in our cavalry and they caused a rout. I rode with the right flank of our cavalry.

I was busy slaughtering fleeing Romans when I saw Guntramm. He was unhorsed and defending himself from three legionaries. They were approaching him with swords drawn and his death in their eyes. They fanned out and were closing in on my cousin when I approached. I dismounted behind them and killed one before he even knew I was there. The second thrust at me with a gladius. Since the Romans were routed, there was no battle-line and there was plenty of space to wield my long German sword. I parried his blade and followed through in a circular fashion to my right. The momentum of the blade carried it upwards and I brought it down hard, two handed, between my adversary's shoulder and neck. The force of the blow was considerable and my blade cut well into the man's chest. The secret is to draw the sword towards you as you strike for it makes the blade cut, as Cornelius often said.

I put my foot on his chest and withdrew my blade. Guntramm had dispatched his opponent and looked at me smiling. He laughed then and said, 'Thank you boy. When you grow up I will show you how we grown men do it.'

He turned and mounted Valknir and rode away leaving me in the middle of the fleeing Romans. I never forgave him for he scorned my help and took my horse into the bargain. That episode coupled with the taunting he engaged in over my family, meant there was little love lost between us from that time onwards.

On the day in question, Duras and I attended the council meeting in the Warlord's tent. The huge leather dwelling rose from the centre of the camp like some massive boulder on a pebble beach, dwarfing the structures around it. Its floor of hard trampled earth acquired the firmness of rock in dry weather. There were rough wooden boards put down in places but that did not prevent the inevitable mud or dust tainting every visitor, even in summer. Torches flared around the tent, hanging from brackets in the uprights supporting the roof. They were ingenious for German workmanship for they did not fall down and started no fires as far as I can recall. That monstrous leather tent was the very hub of the Frankish war-camp.

Odomir sat on his throne at the apex of the semicircle of leaders drinking beer from a cup made out of the skull of some enemy or other. I cannot help but think it must have spoiled the taste of the beer but Odomir seemed happy enough with it. In any case, he did not provide any refreshments for the council. He was, as ever, a mean man and perhaps he did not have enough cups; he certainly had enough enemies.

The council consisted of older Warrior-kings from many

different towns in the Frankish kingdom. Theuderic was a minor King from the south of our land. He was the first to stand up and speak. He was tall and spoke with a lisp, an affliction cursing him from birth.

'Warlord, we have come far from the land of our fathers in this fight with Rome. Now is the time to decide the future. We have fought many battles and we can go south or we can go home. Whichever we do is a path to honour, for we have fulfilled our duties in the alliance with the Marcomannii, Chatti and the Cherusci. My men wish to go home, their families need them, and their lands need tending. To go south to the Roman lands holds no pull for my people,' he said.

There was a hushed silence then and the kings who sat around the tent in a circle looked at each other, shifting in discomfort. They were mostly big men, and the bearskins they wore enlarged their outlines to monstrous proportions. No one in the council had weapons, for my uncle in his paranoia saw to it they left their spears and swords outside. His bodyguard stood at intervals around the tent to ensure his safety. Theuderic was voicing something no one else in the council would have dared. There had been four years of constant fighting; the only break from the battles had been in the winters, and far from home as we were, it brought little respite for anyone in the army.

Odomir stood then. He was a big man too and by the depth and strength of his voice, he commanded respect. All eyes turned to him as he spoke.

'Are we cowards? Do we run before the cursed Roman dogs who seek to overrun our lands and those of our noble allies? No! We are Franks and that means we hold true to the faiths of our people and we honour the oaths given with so much Frankish blood dripping from the corpses of our dead. I will hear no talk of leaving this place to return home, like whipped curs, with our tails between our legs and the hoots and insults of our allies at our back.'

Chilperic, another of the Frankish kings, stood up next; he was a small man for a German, with dark hair and a frowning face, furrowed and scarred from long years of a hard life.

'Odomir speaks truly. It would be dishonourable to leave this army now, when we are on the verge of a great victory. We can cross the Danubus and there are few men left to stop us. A pestilence has struck the Romans in the east and the war they wage with the Parthians has weakened them. Now is the time, in the very equinox of their fortunes for us to strike. Now is the time for victory, riches, and an extension of the German lands to a place that is always warm and crops grow.'

He sat down among murmurs from the older kings in the tent. Guntramm stood up then. He waited for silence before he spoke and he glared at the kings assembled before him.

'You all know me,' he said. Although I follow my uncle, I have always had my own views. We can end this war. We only have to stand firm this one time and the defeat of Rome is certain. If we abandon our allies to go home, we will always be the small nation who backed away when the real men fought against the Roman oppressors. We have a real chance of huge plunder in northern Italia and we would be foolish to lose our nerve. We are warriors. We are Wuotan's chosen men and we must stand firm!'

He ended his little speech by raising his voice slightly and it boomed across the tent-space to a cry of agreement from almost all of the gathering.

There was one man however, who stood out from the rest by his silence and a sombre look on his face. That man was Eudes. He was an old man now but he had fought alongside my father many years before. He had commanded armies and all but a few of the council respected him. He was a small man but shrunken by age and not parsimonious nature. Despite his small size, he had a voice men listened to and the respect in which the council held him was obvious.

'Hear me, brothers in blood! I am here because my Warlord has commanded me. It has always been so, since the beginning of our nation. A man called Francius came to some of our people when he deserted from the army of Marcus Antonius a hundred and fifty years ago. He drew together a number of tribes and gave us a name; that name was not built in blood then, but we have always been able to maintain our sense of belonging since those times by fighting to protect our lands. This war is not a war to protect our womenfolk and children. It is a war to make our nation own more land and take great plunder. This is the war Odomir planned many years ago, a war his brother Galdar opposed in council repeatedly as a few of you will remember. And why did Galdar oppose this war?' he looked around the tent at the bearded lords who held his gaze.

He frowned. 'It was because it will not benefit our nation in the end,' he went on. 'We have barely enough people for the land we have in the north. How do we manage to settle a land so far south? Why should a man thirst for more land than he can reasonably maintain? That is what the Romans have done and it will do them little good in years to come. You should not try to take more from the pot than you put into it. Better to move our people in a migration without fighting Rome and settle west of the Rhenus.'

279

Again, there was a murmur of agreement from the no-bles. Their opinion seemed to swing like a hangman's victim. Odomir stood and looked at Eudes. He smiled a cold smile.

'I am the Warlord. Whatever my brother and I might have disagreed upon all those years ago is like water flowing to the sea from the mouth of a river. It is gone forever into the past. We must look forward to new times and greater glory!'

As he sat down again Eudes stood up.

'Odomir has led us for long enough. We need a new leader who does not want constant war. The son of Galdar sits here with us now and by the tattoo marking him as our Warlord, I think he should lead us. He is young and needs guidance but I say he is the rightful leader for our people.'

I was amazed. I had done nothing to deserve such re-spect. Almost everyone else in that tent had done more than I had in war and in politics. Eudes was risking his life and I think he knew it. Several others stood and spoke in a similar vein. There was uproar until Guntramm stood again and called for silence.

'Council hear me! I am the nephew of Odomir. You chose me, only a few short years ago, to be the rightful successor to the title of Warlord. No one can tell me that an upstart, escaped slave, and son of a fool who betrayed his people, can take on the role promised to me. He is a mon-grel cur like his father and he has no courage.'

The entire assembled company turned to me then. I real-ise now Clotildis must have had something to do with the unfolding events despite her absence from the council. She had a way of manipulating men; making them blind to her purposes until it was too late. Hindsight is a wondrous thing.

The insult to my father was more than I could bear and I cursed under my breath. A red heat rose in my brain. I could do nothing to prevent it and my temper got the better of me. I flew at Guntramm. All I could see was a taunting laughing tormentor and although neither of us was armed, I wanted to kill him there and then. He sat to my left and I launched myself at him with a speed that surprised even me. I grabbed him by the throat and we both rolled on the straw and dust covering the floor of the tent. My hands tightened; his hands punched. To the sound of his rasping breath flashes of light flared in my visual fields as each blow struck home. It took only a few moments for Duras to break up the fight by restraining me. Odomir helped Guntramm to his feet. They both regarded me with self-righteous indignation as if I had committed a crime in the sanctity of the Warlord's presence. It was nonsense of course for fights among the council members were commonplace.

Guntramm was rubbing his throat and looking aggrieved; I was almost snarling.

'Guntramm, you have been insulting my father for a long time now and I can tolerate it no more. Either you take back what you have said or I will kill you in a fair fight as honour demands, as Wuotan is my witness.'

With sudden and uncharacteristic clarity, I realised I had just played into Odomir's hands, and wondered if it was he, not Clotildis who had engineered all this to get rid of me. A word spoken is like a sword cut, once delivered, you can never take it back. I had issued a challenge and the council expected me to finish what I had started. To my right I noticed Duras was staring at the top of the tent pole as if to say he thought I had finally gone mad.

'I swear by all the Gods we will fight tomorrow and I will

take your head!' Guntramm said, barely concealing his glee. 'Believe me, you will not be holding a sword when you go. I'm going to take you apart limb from limb. The manner of the fight I leave to the Warlord for it is his honour for which we fight.'

It was quite a clever way to put it. He was suggesting that he was defending his uncle's honour and I realised I had let the pair of them pull me into this forthcoming fight. Guntramm, I knew, was a much-respected fighter and his battle prowess was a legend among the younger soldiers in our army. I wondered what form the fight would take until Odomir stood and faced the assembled kings.

'In all my years as your Warlord I have only sought to serve my people faithfully. I now see this young man, whom I have taken in and treated like a son has poison in his veins, and in his treachery, he wishes me deposed. It is right Guntramm should fight for my honour for he is to be my successor appointed by council. I declare that the Gods will decide this in the morning and the two of them will fight on horseback with lances and sword, but no shields. Until then, the council is adjourned.'

He sat down with a smirk and as my temper cooled, I began to realise I had been played yet again. Played by Odomir and Clotildis alike. Guntramm wanted to fight me and it was clear now he had my uncle's approval. If he killed me in a fair fight all would be satisfied for it would be an honourable death and the council would then accept Odomir was the only rightful Warlord, but it would mean a lengthy and protracted war against Rome.

As the council broke up Duras slapped me on the back and smiled broadly saying, 'Well you really have a way of making an impression on people, don't you?'

'What's so funny?' I said. 'The swine was begging me to kill him. Wait and see what happens tomorrow. I'll nail him to the ground.'

'You realise that you have interfered with my blood oath to avenge my father don't you? Are you now taking on my enemies? Am I a child or a maiden that I have to have others exact my revenge for me?'

'No Duras, but I had a girl in Lovosice and I lost her. Don't you remember Medana? Maybe I just want revenge for that but it is mainly because Guntramm insults me and my parents and this fight is a point of honour.'

'You watch your step; I hear Guntramm has killed many in combat on and off the battle field. He is the most feared of all the cavalry chiefs. Rumour has it he fought three men single-handed and killed them all with about as much difficulty as if they were children.'

'I'm well enough trained, Cornelius saw to that.'

Duras looked at me with a wild, grim flash of his eyes. He was not pleased I was denying him his revenge.

We reached our tent and found Lazygis sitting outside warming himself at the fire. We told him of the forthcoming fight. He shook his head and muttered something about 'Too young, too young.'

He too slapped me on the back and said he would sacrifice to his God, Pan for a successful outcome.

With such confidence instilled in me by my friends I slept in fits and starts and dreamt of Cornelius as he lay suffocating in that farmhouse. He had always taught me to keep my guard up and it was exactly what I intended to do.

CHAPTER V

"The scars of others should teach us caution."

— St Jerome

I awoke early. I felt worn to a ravelling and my right shoulder ached intolerably. My leg wound had still not healed and I had a slight limp. To cap it all I began to worry in case I had over-reached myself in taking on one of the most feared warriors in the Frankish army. I wished Cornelius was with me. He always said reassuring things and pointed out weaknesses in our adversaries, bringing me comfort when I needed it most.

I walked over to the picket lines where I had tethered Valknir. He looked fit and healthy. He pricked his ears up and he whinnied with impatience and restlessness. He was a true warhorse and I found a degree of confidence again after brushing him down. I did not feed him. He needed to be keen and alert for the fight. I checked my saddle with the stirrups and wondered if they would confer any real advantage in the fight to come. We were not to use shields. If I had no shield, I might lose the advantage of the stirrups, as I might be unable unbalance my opponent using them. This meant the fight would be short. If neither combatant were able to shield himself the initial clash would depend upon who was the best spearman. It could mean instant death if either struck well with the spear. I had never seen Gun-

284

tramm fight before except on the battlefield and I remained uncertain whether he was better with a spear or with a sword. I could hold my own with either, but favoured the sword.

I trudged back to the tent. It was clear a summer's morning, dawn had broken and the early rays of sunshine raked the camp like spikes and spears. There was birdsong too and the smell of campfires taunted my nostrils as I meandered between the leather tents. The sound of that multitude stirring thrust itself on my consciousness yet my thoughts and anxiety served to keep all at arm's length. I noticed I was sweating and my breathing was a little too fast. As I re-entered the tent where Duras was still snoring, I found I was biting my lip and it bled a little. I had never felt like this before a fight.

Duras awoke. He rolled onto one elbow and looked up with sleepy eyes.

'When is the fight?' he said, yawning.

'I don't know. I suppose it will be when Odomir feels like starting it. There is no one up yet.'

'Can't sleep eh?'

'No I slept badly and woke early,'

'Don't worry. Do you think the Gods would let you survive all the shit we have been through in the last few years and then let a miserable turd like Guntramm end it all for you?'

'I have no idea, but I know I am more scared of this fight than any other I have had.'

'I think you will do what you always do. You will lose that violent temper of yours and use all the skill Cornelius gave you, and you will win. Relax my friend. Anyway, worrying won't help, it will only sap your energy. I can promise you one thing though.'

'What's that?'

'I'll kill him if he kills you. By all the Gods I swear it.'

'Hardly a comfort to me, since I won't be there to witness it. It won't turn out like that. I'm going to kill him,' I said with no small measure of uncertainty, perhaps trying to convince myself.

I made some food but could hardly eat any and sat, still feeling jumpy and miserable.

'Galdir, you look uncomfortable.'

It was a female voice. I looked up and smiled as I saw Clotildis approaching us. She was wearing a red robe of thick wool and a belt of gold around her waist reflecting the sunlight. I must admit the vision of it convinced me a goddess had descended to the camp and was spreading light and beauty around her.

'Duras,' I said, turning to my companion, 'could we have a few moments?'

'All right, I know when I'm not wanted,' he said, 'I'm going for a shit anyway. Don't get seen!'

'Duras is at his most charming at this time of day,' I said, smiling, 'do you want to go into the tent?'

'Don't be so silly Galdir! I do not go into soldier's tents! I am the wife of the leader of your people. I do need to talk to you though.'

'All right,' I said, 'we can walk.'

'You will win this combat to-day. When you do, the next fight you have will be with my husband and if you kill him, the rewards will be very pleasant for you.'

She squeezed my hand gently and quickly and let hers fall to her side. She looked into my eyes and I knew there was more to her promise than just her body. There was guile and coldness there; I saw just the faintest flash of seriousness making me feel despite my intense lust that I should be careful. On that morning, I had other thoughts to distract me than a sexual relationship with this beautiful woman and so I took my leave on the pretext of getting ready for the fight. I knew neither Guntramm nor I would ask for quarter. I also thought it could have been equally true of Clotildis although her battle was of a different nature.

The time spun by the Norns passes by whether we are willing participants or not, and so after what seemed to me to be an eternity, a mailed soldier approached my tent and summoned me to the horse-field. I was reassured, for I knew every pothole and every molehill in that field. It was where I had practised almost daily with Lazygis since he had arrived.

The atmosphere was like a massive battle about to erupt, not one small fight between two men. I led Valknir through the massing crowd and the number of watchers clearly did not put him off. I stroked and scratched his mane slowly and spoke as gently as the background noise allowed. He knew my voice and remained calm. I wished I too felt calm, but I was ill at ease. There was a cramp-like feeling in my stomach and my mouth was dry; I could feel my heart racing, thrumming its rapid beat against my ribs.

Odomir was in the centre of the field with two mounted soldiers. He sat upon a beautiful black stallion. My jaw almost dropped when I saw it. It was Bucephalus one of the mounts Cornelius and I had stolen five years before from the Piso estate. I recalled how Duras' father had taken him from me and I even recalled his name.

Guntramm was also there. He sat astride his Dacian war-horse, smiling and waving to the crowd. I felt more like running away than smiling and waving for I had a feeling of dread deep within me. We none of us know what the Gods have planned for us, so in truth, we should not worry when we do have some kind of chance. I was just scared I suppose. It shames me to say so but I suspect people do better in almost anything if they are nervous than if they are too relaxed and I was certainly not relaxed now.

Odomir did not delay what he hoped would be a short entertainment and he gestured me to the other end of the field. Guntramm rode to the opposite end. Odomir leaned forward in the saddle and raised his arm. The crowded soldiers quietened as if the Warlord had removed their tongues. Silence, thick and turgid hung around us as the crowd waited, breath baited.

The Warlord dropped his hand and rode off the field. The fight had started.

At that precise moment my fear left me. It was as if a cloud lifted from my mind and I saw with such clarity I could read exactly what Guntramm would do. We walked our horses toward each other at first then at a slightly increased pace until we were cantering towards each other. The trick is not to charge, for then you have no time to parry and strike.

I stood in the stirrups and pointed my spear at where I expected Guntramm's head to be when we met. He did much the same. As we were about to clash, he lowered his lance. He swerved his horse to his right, as if turning away. It is a common trick. I thought it was not worthy of him. He thought I would turn my horse towards him. By moving his horse sideways, he could then unbalance me. I turned the opposite way. We circled and came to a stop facing each other. We looked at one another. His scarred face was smiling. He stared me in the eye. We sat thus for a full minute before either of us spoke.

'Your mother was a whore. She probably enjoyed the rape by those filthy Roman pigs. Your father was a fool too,' snarled my opponent, 'Odomir planned it all. He knew the Romans would trap the foolish Galdar and we watched as he rode from the village and they cut him down. I laughed at his death and pissed on his headless body, although I was only a lad.'

I knew he was trying to goad me into losing my temper. He wanted me to make a rash move. That is not the way my temper works though. It is a much more intelligent beast than that. It rises quickly; once kindled, it merely drives me into action and speed. I admit I was angry. It was battle anger and not the vengeful, unseeing beast, which afflicts many men. I remained cautious. I looked at Guntramm and smiled back. It must have been intensely irritating for I think he became angry himself.

With startling suddenness, he drove his horse straight at me. I was ready. I was still quite stable on my mount. His first stab with the spear was straight at my chest. I was so stable I was able to twist in the saddle in time. The spear tip went past me. I struck with the side of my spear. Its length prevented me from drawing it back to stab. I struck him on the left shoulder. A glancing blow, it did little harm. It was enough to warn him I was no novice.

He turned and came straight back at me. This time he feinted to one side. Then he changed direction. He had his spear held short. He wanted me closer. No doubt he still wanted to unbalance me. I made a slight mistake. I tried to do the same as before. I realised too late the first stab was a feint. He changed direction quickly. He caught the right side of my twisted abdomen. My mail protected me. The point of the spear penetrated and drove through skin and muscle passing clean through without damage to my internal organs. I knew what had happened. He tried to withdraw the spear but it snagged on the chain mail. He had to let go of it or fall from his horse.

The wound was painful but I had no time to examine it. I was panting and in some pain. With difficulty, I straightened up. I managed because I had to. I reached down and pulled the loose spear from my mail.

Guntramm drew his sword. Charging straight at me to take advantage of my incapacity he had the sword point held straight out from the shoulder. He was a big man with a reach long enough to almost equal my spear. I parried with the point of the spear and his sword snapped the spear's shaft in a deft movement.

I rode away from him buying time, as I drew my sword. I felt I had to attack. I had already sustained a wound. I was well aware that all I had done so far was to defend myself. Besides, I was getting irritated.

My mind conjured up the insults and the sneers from this man. I was nowhere near losing my temper, but I could feel an anger rising. My fear and trepidation became things of the past. I rode to meet my cousin.

Our swords clashed with a ring audible all over the field. As we passed one another he tried to hit me backhand. It was a fraction late. I threw my shoulder towards my opponent. Had it not been for the stirrups there would have been as great a chance of my overbalancing as my opponent. I sat steady as a rock as our shoulders met. I could feel the impact transmitted to my left leg in the stirrup. I knocked him clean off his horse.

I had no desire to allow him to remount. I slapped his

mount on the rump with the flat of my sword. It reared and chased off to the opposite end of the field.

Guntramm lay on his back, spread-eagled and winded. I dismounted fast. I placed my foot on his outstretched hand, which still held his sword. I placed the point of my blade at his throat and pressed gently. He came to within seconds and realised all was lost. His blue eyes stared up at me with a rage sculpting the hate he felt with intense clarity.

'I won't kill you if you swear to apologise to me in front of the council and you stop goading me. I can kill you easily on horseback or on foot. I have no wish to spill the blood of my own kin and would rather you live, but it is up to you.'

'I swear,' Guntramm said. 'I will not goad you after to-day and if we are both stood before the council later, I will apologise to you,' Guntramm said with a look as if the very words were a sour taste to him.

I sheathed my sword and stepped back. I felt wildly elated. I was unable to stop myself smiling despite the pain in my side. I had defeated him and I would put him to shame before the council. I could almost feel Clotildis in my arms.

With my left foot in the stirrup I heard the blow before it landed. A sword can sing as you wield it. It only happens with a good blade and a hard swing. With German swords which are long and relatively blunt compared to a curved Thracian sword, it takes great force to make the blade sing. I heard this one and knew what to expect. I had fast reflexes in those days. I dropped to the ground. I rolled under Valknir. A horse will always hesitate to step on a recumbent man. Since he had no rider urging him on, Valknir obeyed his instincts. He allowed me to roll beneath him. It happened very fast. It was almost with one movement. I rose and stood on the far side of my horse.

Guntramm swore and swung his sword again. It was a high, two-handed blow aimed at my head. To my intense anger, he struck my horse. Valknir whinnied. He turned his head very fast to defend himself. He reached down and bit Guntramm on the left side of his face. It was a horrible injury. A horse has teeth, but uses them for munching not cutting and the damage from a hard horse bite is terrible; it crushes and rips in a jagged and untidy manner.

Valknir took off half of Guntramm's left cheek and mouth. My cousin stepped backwards howling with pain. Valknir reared and one of his metal shod hooves struck my cousin on the right shoulder. I always said he was feisty. It was a crippling and painful blow. It landed with a sickening crunch. I heard it and winced. It must have broken the collarbone and most of the upper ribs on that side. He dropped his sword and fell to the ground. He lay still this time, his breath coming in rasps. Perhaps the hoof had struck his head too. Blood ran red into the grass and a small artery on his face spurted in a little red fountain, onto his chain mail.

I went to Valknir first. There was a terrible cut on his withers, a deep incision, just next to the saddle but luckily the saddle had taken much of the force otherwise the blow might have broken his back. He calmed as soon as he heard my voice, and allowed me to stroke his neck and examine his wound. It bled freely. I staunched the bleeding with a strip of the tunic from beneath my chain mail. I walked him over to where my adversary lay bleeding, grunting and wheezing. I shook my head and gestured to the crowd the fight had ended by drawing my open hand, palm-down from right to left. With confident and exultant steps, I walked Valknir away towards the tent. My side was hurting and the accumulated injuries of the last ten days were beginning to take their toll. I did not look back, but I heard the tumult of the crowd.

CHAPTER VI

"The secret of all victory lies in the organization of the non-obvious."

— Marcus Aurelius

The council met again next day. They voted with Odomir to continue the alliance with the other German tribes for the time being. This meant we were marching south to give battle. They also voted I would succeed the Warlord, which was a cause of some concern to me, as I had no idea how one leads a tribe let alone a nation. The prospect that one day I would have the responsibilities my father and uncle had borne, terrified me. I knew nothing of politics. I had always been straight with others. Politics needs guile and for a guileless man the plots and machinations of leadership come hard.

I met Clotildis at the edge of the forest the following day. It was warm and dry and I could see her standing at the edge of the forest across the meadow. She wore a dark green gown and a black lace veil as if she thought it might make her unrecognisable to a casual observer. I waded knee-deep in yellow meadow flowers and cowslips or some such plant with my steps quickening in anticipation. We went into the forest and found a glade where we attempted to make love. The wound in my side made it impossible in any conventional way, but where there is a will there is a way and there

294

certainly was a will on my part.

Afterwards, we lay on our backs holding hands and looking up at the sky. A warm sun shone upon our naked bodies and made us sweat after the exertions of the torrid moment that passed. I turned my head and looked at her slim, beautiful body. Just one look aroused me again but she sat up inclining her head towards me.

'No more of that, until you become the Warlord. A man must have some ambition and so unless you do what is necessary you not will reap the rewards of your labours.'

'The Warlord still lives and as far as I can see the only way in which I can kill him would be to do something dishonourable. Nothing would persuade me to betray my conscience any further. I won't kill him unless it is in a fair fight.'

'That can be arranged.'

'I don't want any arrangements to be made; I have a war to fight and I will not be used. I will prosecute this war as best I can and to Hel with your meddling.'

I finally lost my temper and dressed.

'Galdir, my love, I did not mean…'

I left the glade and mounted Guntramm's horse, which I had commandeered since Valknir was not in a fit state for riding and Guntramm was in no fit state to ride.

Lazygis and Ayma met me in their wagon as I rode back into camp.

'Are you going somewhere?' I asked.

'Yes we must travel back to meet our army. We must tell them of the alliance. I also need to arrange for Ayma to get home to my country. Our women are strong but they are needed at home just like yours are.'

'You are coming back?'

'Yes, with the thousand heavy cavalry we promised your uncle.'

'We will meet again on the borders of Italia. The entire German army is moving south in two days and we have a small Roman army to fight on the way through Raetia. I don't think it will be a hard fought battle for we outnumber them three to one.'

'I hope we don't miss the fighting, it would be a shame to lead my men all this way just to watch the Marcomannii take all the plunder!'

'Don't worry I will save some Romans for you,' I said.

Two days later the camp began to empty. My uncle sent me with a squadron of cavalry to scout the approach to the north of Italy for his army. A group of scouts joined us from the other two main armies and we rode all day on the first scouting expedition. One of our healers had sewn up the spear wound in my side and it was just starting to be more comfortable when I set out. By the end of the first day, it had reopened slightly and was bleeding a little.

Duras studied the wound.

'It doesn't look too bad to me,' he said with a grin. 'It will, after all, teach you not to be so careless next time.'

'At least I haven't lost a bloody kingdom.' I said.

He looked at me with a frown and replied, 'No, but you have not gained one either and as long as your uncle lives you won't, will you?'

We looked at each other and the irritation passed, as it always did. We laughed and the mood was gone.

'If we locate the Romans then we have to get back fast enough to plan where to fight them,' I said.

'Yes, but they may not attack us. It is always easier to defend than to attack, especially with trained Roman legions standing firm when we assault them.'

'No matter, we outnumber them to such an extent it will be like killing sheep,' I said.

'Let us see what tomorrow brings. We have a saying in Dacia. No one knows what the dung smells like until the horse arrives.'

'Duras that is one of the most unsavoury sayings in your vast compendium of home-spun Dacian proverbs! We aren't talking about horse dung, we're talking about warfare!'

'It all comes down to horse dung in the end. The horses shit on the fields and grass grows because of it. We bury the corpses in the field and they all combine to make hay and fodder! A neat circle!'

'You're crazy,' I said and went to sleep wondering why I had taken up with a Dacian who drank too much beer.

The truth was I loved him as a brother.

*

On the second day, we found the Romans in the hilly country between our encampment and the northern borders of Italia. There were not many of them—only two legions, but I knew better than to expect them to fold easily. I sat astride Valknir in the drizzle and watched as they formed their lines. The ground was wet and slippery, and I could smell their body-smells in the wind as Duras and I watched. I wiped the moisture from my brow and flicked it away. There was a layer of mist in the vale below us and a crow cawed high above us as it circled, perhaps waiting for its inevitable feed.

'Compared to the size of our army they look like a tiny war band,' said Duras.

'All the same, if they aren't handled right they can kill a lot of men. Their discipline always impresses me. It's the way they fight in silence and they obey every command as if they

297

were doing a drill. If only our men were the same,' I said.

'Yes, if our men didn't just try to crowd and push they would be able to use their weapons. Maybe using our shorter swords will be more effective now.'

'My thoughts exactly. There can't be more than fifteen thousand of the proper Roman infantry. They've drawn up their forces sensibly though.'

'It'll be a steep climb for our lads.'

'They're fit enough.'

Duras said, 'With the numbers we've got it won't matter. Let's go and join the men.'

The two legions had a variety of auxiliaries with them who occupied the sides of the hill. They had Scythian horse archers, Balearic slingers, and a fair contingent of Gallic horse on either flank. They faced us in a line organised in a particular way the Romans often used. Their infantry were usually in a staggered pattern, the centre of the century behind covering the gap between the centuries in front. They had missile troops called velites who occupied the front ranks. These were tough, mobile and agile young men, who were trained to hit and run with the pilae the Romans used.

I should tell you about pilae, as Cornelius had described them to me. They were short javelins with a head of iron which, although the tip was hard as rock, the shaft of the head was of softer metal. When they hit their target, the head buckled and one could not throw it back or dislodge it with ease from either a shield or a hard part of a man's skeleton. The only way to defeat the velites was with cavalry or archers at a distance. We had plenty of javelin men and archers, so we saw no problem there.

We had drawn up in our vast numbers opposite the Romans, but I had ordered the cavalry, including the new

298

Sarmatians who had now joined us, so they could outflank the Romans on either side. The main body of cavalry rode around the hill and our infantry were to march forwards uphill but as fast as they could manage. Our men were fit strong warriors and with the shorter swords we now used, they were a true barb in the side of the Romans, even at close quarters. Our missile troops also had better bows and a greater range than at any other time in the past, thanks to the Sarmatians. I reflected we were, in a sense, becoming more like the Romans in our military style than any of us would care to admit.

It was a short battle. Our infantry hit the front ranks of the Romans hard. At the same time the cavalry, even charging uphill had a fearsome impact. With their armoured riders, they charged into the left flank. The Roman infantry collapsed and were routed almost immediately. The German cavalry rode up the hill at each side. They attacked the flanks and although there were losses, they hit the Roman troops hard there and they too were routed quickly.

I was on the right flank for the charge. With bloodied spear and later dripping sword, I felled man after man as they broke and ran. Oddly enough, it gave me little pleasure. They were frightened, fleeing men and I gain no pleasure from such slaughter. A hard fought battle with hand-to-hand fighting in which a soldier can distinguish himself and earn the titles he bears afterwards is always more satisfying. The honour men gain from a battle should be hard won, so it can be worn like a badge afterwards. This battle left me cold.

We captured a number of Roman officers and my uncle wanted to ransom them for gold. The Marcomannii, a cruel people, wanted only to torture then kill the prisoners and as was their religious need, hang the bodies on the trees afterwards. I must confess I thought this was typical of the barbarity they displayed.

Odomir bargained with them and the tribes shared out the prisoners according to the proportion of the army they contributed. We had charge of twelve such prisoners. We tied and gagged them and placed them outdoors in a horse pen. I accept this was not humane treatment even for a Roman, but at least they were alive – frightened, I admit, but alive.

After we had killed the Roman wounded on the battle-field and plundered the bodies I went back to the camp to try to rest. My previous wounds were bothering me and I gained little pleasure in the victory. I began to wonder what I was doing in this army. I had little enough control over the troops and I disapproved of the aims of the campaign in any case. I sat on a blanket on a grass tussock and waited for Duras to turn up. I knew he had enjoyed the fight for I had seen him chasing off the Romans and whooping with joy as he did so. He bore a great, long-handled battle-axe which he loved to wield. His whole appearance must have been daunt-ing to any enemy he threatened. He was huge and with a big brown beard and braids and the wild battle frenzy in his eyes it would take a very brave man to challenge him.

I started forward and rubbed my thigh, which was itch-ing. The wound was healing at last after being infected and oozing pus for a week. Duras suggested the arrowhead had taken cloth from my leggings into the wound but I thought it was unlikely since the arrow had gone right through. I began to think many different unrelated thoughts, for a battle does that to a man.

I thought of Livia and how she had encouraged me to go north to find my people and how Cornelius had taught me to fight. Then I came back to earth with the thought Clotildis was moving me in a direction I did not like. I knew I could kill my uncle in a fair fight but he was my blood kin whatever Guntramm had said before I defeated him. Odomir was misguided but he was still my uncle and I had no real thoughts of vengeance then.

Guntramm in fact, survived the horse injuries. His arm where the horse had kicked him remained useless to him. I think the injury did something to the ability to move the muscles but the arm hung limp and useless to him for the rest of his days. The injury to his face recovered partially but he had trouble eating and kept his face covered all the time. He rarely went out in public for his appearance had become terrible and children ran away in fear if they saw him. I confess that although I did not choose the fight nor did I inflict the wounds, I felt responsible, foolish though it might seem.

I was deep in thought when a voice interrupted me.

'You are Galdir?'

I looked up and the sight of a tall, once blonde man the size and age of my uncle greeted me. There were scars on his face and he wore a white bearskin, a rare and expensive adornment for any warrior. I had never seen its like even in Rome. He had a full, greying beard and as he approached, I noticed he limped. He shuffled up and sat with difficulty on the ground opposite me.

'Galdir. I owe you a debt, or perhaps one might say I never paid the debt I owed to your father. I am sure you do not remember me, do you?'

'No I have no idea who you might be. There are a lot of tall blonde men around here, in case you hadn't noticed.'

'This particular man is named Stator.' He said with a

grin, 'I was there the day your parents were killed and I swore to your father I would protect you as best I could even if it meant giving up my life. The Roman legionaries overpowered me and marched me to Rome bearing you upon my shoulders.'

'Yes, I think I remember a man like you but I was only five at the time and the memory is a fog in my mind. Why do you seek me out now? Maybe I should say to you "where were you all those years when I was a slave?" or perhaps you fared better than I did?'

'Lord, I have only ever been a warrior. I loved your father and although the Gods denied me the privilege of dying next to him, I confess I wept when I heard he was dead. He was a truly great leader and the most honourable man I ever met. We, his war band, loved him for he was kind when he needed to be and a fearsome fighter when war required it too. I have a debt to pay to his memory for I swore to look after you and I failed. They took me away to a gladiator school. I made a life for myself, which in the end resulted in freedom but I had no way to contact the son of my Warlord for I did not know where you were. All I was able to learn was you were in the household of the Piso family. Years later, I gained my freedom in the arena and made money in private life by trading. I confess I never found out what had happened to you.'

'Do you remember a gladiator called Cornelius Nepos?'

'Of course, he was the most famous of his generation. He defeated all the warriors pitted against him and the crowds demanded his release. He continued to fight until the Romans rewarded him richly. Rumour has it, he made so much money he retired with huge wealth and bought a farm in northern Italia.'

302

'Did you ever meet him?'

'Only once, but luckily it was when he was training others and I never had to fight him. I was lucky in that respect I suppose.'

'You were indeed lucky, for he is the man who taught me to fight, almost as if he took on the role my father tried to leave to you!'

'Lord, it has not been easy to find you. When I heard a tall blonde slave had killed the magistrate Piso, I wondered if it might be you. How many tall blonde slaves would such a family have? I was free at that time and working as a trader and it took another year before I earned enough wealth to come north. I travelled north in search of you. Against all expectations, I find now you are reaching for the position your father would have sought for you. It is an answer to my prayers and Wuotan has heard me. I am ashamed I have never been there to help but I will correct that now.'

The man raised himself and set his forehead on the ground in front of my feet. I was embarrassed, and bade him rise.

'I really don't know what to say to you. I have friends and they watch my back in battle, but I have no one near me who can tell me about my father and mother apart from Chlotsuintha and I suspect she is mad in any case.'

'Chlotsuintha? She lives? If she is indeed alive, then you have the most powerful witch in the land with you. Can I see her?'

'Only if your eyes and ears can stretch all the way home, Stator. She is not favoured by my uncle and she has been largely cast out by the council.'

'That is not good for our nation; we need the strong magic she alone can produce, to help with this war. Your father would never have started a war. He always said the Romans never accept defeat and if you once wage war upon them, they never forget. They come back time and again until they win.'

'Very true, but I am not the Warlord.'

'You should be and soon you will. I am here to do anything you ask of me. If you wish it, I will kill your uncle tonight. I owe him a death for what he did when he betrayed your father and allowed me to become enslaved. I am an old man now and limp from my wounds, but I remain an efficient killer of men, for the Romans trained me well.'

'Just wait a moment,' I held up my hand. 'I don't want you to kill my uncle or anyone else, thank you. I don't even want to do it myself. He is just about the only blood kin I have and to be honest, I don't think I have the skills to lead a nation. I don't really want to be Warlord.'

'You don't want…?'

Stator stared at me and he had a look of offended disappointment I will never forget.

'You young pup!' he said, 'Your father gave his life for his people. He did it with a smile on his face knowing he would go to Wuotan's Hall, leaving behind a strong son who would take his place. You do not have a choice. You are Galdar's son and you were born to lead our people. You owe it to your father, and if your mother's death means anything to you then you must do it for her memory too.'

'You are beginning to sound like a woman I know. As soon as I have arrived on the scene almost everyone I meet tells me to kill my uncle and become Warlord. None of you seems to realise I was a slave for fourteen years. Slaves don't think like that. Slaves are furniture and don't even have rational thoughts apart from obeying blindly. Where can my kingship come from? Thin air?'

'Galdir, it is inside you. You are your father's son and you must believe in yourself. Let me kill Odomir. He deserves it.'

'Stator, if you truly wish to serve me then please don't kill anyone at the moment. Let us await events and see what the fates will spin for us. Patience! If you wish to honour your oath to my father, then watch my back. Odomir has tried to kill me already but failed because a visiting Sarmatian helped me. It was only luck that spared me.'

'Whatever role your uncle has now, you are my Warlord. I will always obey you.'

'Then it is settled. Take no action. Await events and keep your eyes and ears open.'

A cloud obscured the sun for a moment and when it passed, the old warrior smiled. He grunted as he stood up and stared down at me for few moments.

'We need Chlotsuintha. We need her magic. Without it much ill can befall our people.'

He turned and limped away. I reflected there might be many who felt like he did. It made me shudder. I had no wish for power. Slavery does that to a man. It saps his will and his ambition and shaking off those feelings can be impossible unless circumstance thrusts it upon him. I sat long there, poking the fire and musing over the day's events. Flashes of memory interceded at times; the blood spurting from Guntramm's face; the cut on Valknir's back and the overwhelming cheering from the crowd, it all seemed so inappropriate. Was I not unworthy of such victory and such praise?

I knew I was not worthy to lead a nation.

It is not up to a man to decide such things, I know this now. The Gods move us around for their pleasure and nothing we do or say will change their minds. I might not have suffered so much in those days had I known this. Sometimes I think I have learned all my life-lessons too late.

CHAPTER VII

"When defeat is inevitable, it is wisest to yield."

— Quintilian

It took only two weeks to reach the Italian border country after defeating the small army in the Raetian hills. We raped the land on the way. Our army burned homes, killed, and overlooked no possible plunder. Our scouts had revealed there was an army waiting for us outside a Roman border town called Aquileia and it seemed to me that we hurried to reach our opponents.

Whether the haste was real or imagined I felt we should have taken our time for after Aquileia, no armies stood in our way. Some of the leaders had talked of sacking Rome as the Gauls had done many years before but there was little enthusiasm for this in the Frankish council and the wish to return home to families and farms was uppermost in many of the soldier's minds. Odomir would hear nothing of it however.

'We have come so far and defeated so many armies that to go home now would be a betrayal of all we have achieved. We must end this Roman domination of the world! We must stay intact. We must conquer!' he said in the council meeting.

The listening members of the council nodded agreement

until Eudes stood up. His wizened figure belied his voice as he spoke, 'Brothers, it is time for us to withdraw. We have homes and the men are restless. There is no long-term gain for us in this war. We can defeat the Romans, but to what purpose? We cannot rule their empire. We can see it wrecked but it would not help trade for our people in the north. We need peace so that prosperity will follow.'

'You speak like an old woman,' Odomir said. 'We have come this far and are on the verge of a great victory yet you want to go home. We must stay and fight. The Roman city of Aquileia stands before us and it is poorly defended. Its walls are falling down and they have not, in their arrogance, bothered to repair them. We can sack the city and then decide if we go on or not.'

The council appeared to like this and there was much discussion but as ever they did as Odomir wished.

On a warm summer's afternoon we saw them as we descended from the hills north of Aquileia. We spied an army. It was no ordinary army however. There were almost fifty thousand men and mainly infantry. A cloud crossed the warm sun as I sat on my horse looking out across the lush green valley.

'Quite a lot of them really,' Duras said, who rode next to me.

'Yes, they are almost half our number.'

'They have hardly any cavalry, which is unusual for a Roman army. If you look closely at the back of their ranks some of them aren't even properly armed,' he gestured with his hand at a long double line of the enemy. They were holding pitchforks and scythes and waving them in our direction.

'I don't think they are more than conscripts, old soldiers

308

and farmers. I don't understand why they are here. Surely, they know they can't hope to stop us. Ours is a huge army of warriors with heavy cavalry and trained infantry. Even the Chatti work like the Romans, fortify their camps, and carry entrenching tools and the like. How can these people fight against us?' I said.

'They are brave to try,' a voice behind us said. It was Horsa, one of the Marcomannii leaders.

'Are they brave or stupid?' I said. 'They will all die. Strikes me as stupid not brave.'

'A brave man,' Horsa said, 'does what is required whether he is afraid or not. Only a fool goes into battle with no fear. It is the fear that drives us on to do the things a warrior needs to do.'

'When do we attack?' I asked.

'My king is keen to do it now. He feels the very sight of us will rout the Romans and it will be such a short battle we will be into the town before nightfall.'

'Is the entire army drawn up behind? It would be a shame to find the first wave of troops is unsuccessful.'

'We don't need to outnumber them; we can take them even if they outnumber us!'

'At least persuade him to wait until the heavy cavalry turns up, that way the Romans will be broken up by the time our infantry contact them.' I said. For some reason I was being cautious, but it was obvious this peasant army facing us would never be able to stop us.

Horsa rode away and I could hear him shouting instructions to some of his men. In the event, we did not wait. We numbered approximately the same as the Romans but we had a contingent of German cavalry who we ordered to the rear. Their main goal was to come up behind and cause mayhem once the poor Romans had routed, as I was sure they would.

I had no taste for such a slaughter. I admired the spirit of the opposition. The Romans were fighting for their country and everything they valued in the world, but we wanted plunder and that too is a powerful incentive.

Duras and I stayed back at the top of the hill. This was not going to be a cavalry battle for there were no opposing horsemen. They organised our army so the centre consisted of Chatti infantry. These were fearsome, hardened fighters and had trained to become almost the equal of the Roman legionary. They carried smaller shields than the legionaries did but they had short swords and axes. I had seen them in action; they were terrifying. Our left flank consisted of only a few Franks, for most of our men were still arriving with my uncle. The right flank consisted mainly of Marcomannii tribesmen, wild unkempt and bloodthirsty, despite having been Roman clients for more than fifty years. Our army advanced at speed and the ground trembled beneath its feet. Each man screamed his war cry, waved his sword in the air, and sprinted towards the enemy. It was as if the hillside itself came alive, changing into some unbridled tempest, screaming and taunting, downhill at the quaking Romans.

German armies fight very differently from the Romans. Each man is a big fearsome fighter. We howl our war cries. We swing our weapons with the force of Donar's hammer. Against Romans however, this is not enough; our lack of discipline means each headstrong warrior tries to outdo his comrades in feats of arms. Our men are difficult to restrain once their blood is up. If you cannot control your infantry, they merely rush upon the enemy without following orders.

In contrast, the Roman professional soldiers had strict

310

discipline. They rarely broke or retreated unless it was in response to a charge of heavy cavalry such as the Sarmatians might mount. So far, in this campaign we had always vastly outnumbered every Roman force we had come across. We had walked bathed in Roman blood all over their corpses, using huge volumetric assaults.

As I watched, the Romans closed ranks. They stood shield to shield in the face of our approaching men. They looked staunch, undaunted; their helmets and shields in their ordered ranks were a firm unyielding barrier. They betrayed not a flinch as they faced the coming German storm. With a sudden concerted movement, the Roman front ranks let fly a hail of pilae arcing towards our men. It was as we had expected. The difference now was the spread of the missiles was minimal. It took me a few moments to realise. It occurred to me the Roman front ranks had heavier javelins than the two ranks behind. When they threw them together, the density of missiles stopped our men in their tracks. The front rank of our infantry was lying in the grass before the Romans, dying, screaming and bleeding, as if swept away by some mighty giant's scythe.

The second rank became disorganised. Some tripped over the dying and writhing men in front of them. Some had to clamber over bodies to get to the Romans. The ground was slick with blood. Our warriors waved their weapons. They screamed curses and war cries but they had lost their momentum.

They were closing on the Romans when the next volley hit them. This volley lacked none of the force and density of the first. More men fell. We expected the Romans had spent the two pilae each man usually carried. Not so. Another wave of javelins rose from the Roman ranks. It was like a dark storm-cloud, blotting out the sun over our warriors. Still further waves of wicked barbs descended upon our ranks. It had turned from an easy victory to a slaughter.

The Romans had not only changed the weight of their javelins to suit the occasion but they had changed the number. They were obviously carrying far more than two javelins. I thought that had to be the reason they had stood so long waiting for us. They were unable to advance with the number of missiles they were carrying.

The number of javelins slowly reduced but our army was now in disarray. It took precious moments for them to thread their way through the vast numbers of their dying and wounded comrades. Some tripped on the spent missiles projecting from the ground like a stockade. They tumbled headlong. They could not run.

Our men became angry. In a disordered mob and with audible fury they rushed the Romans. The suddenness of what happened next, made me twitch in my saddle. The ground before their feet seemed to open up. It was as if the new front rank simply disappeared from the battlefield tumbling to the underworld. The very earth in its anger at the futility of men's foolishness had swallowed them up.

We heard screams and cries. They were the sounds of men dying, men in the throes of agonising deaths. I saw it then. The Romans had dug a trench in front of their army. It was not a simple trench. It was a deep death-pit filled with spikes. They had covered it over with turf laid out on a wicker framework. It was so cleverly hidden it was invisible from a distance. The trench must have been huge and deep. The next few minutes became the most disturbing of all. I squirmed in discomfort in the saddle. I bit my lip. It was a disaster.

The huge press of men behind our second rank were unable to stop. They flew headlong into the vast trench, on top of the front ranks. It was of course, filled with what Julius Caesar had called "lilies". Spikes of wood sharpened and ready to impale the plummeting men in the bottom of the trench. Two whole ranks of our men fell that way. Those whom the lilies did not spike, were killed from above with more javelins or the weight of the men pitched on top of them crushing or suffocating them.

I could see it all from the hill. We could do nothing. Cavalry cannot charge across a trench. In our frustration, we watched the thousands die.

'They must withdraw,' Duras said.

'We can't withdraw, if we don't press forward across the trench the Romans will just stand there and laugh at us.'

'Better laughter than death. You Germans are the worst people I have ever seen for pride and stubbornness. They could even be defeated at this rate,'

'Maybe we could ride around the trench and attack their flanks.'

'I don't believe what I'm hearing. The trench stretches all the way around the Roman forces. If you lead a cavalry charge the entire squadron of horse will end up in a ditch and impaled,' Duras said.

He was right but I felt desperate to do something. There was of course nothing for cavalry to do. We had to rely on our troop's experience and hardiness.

Apart from a few Romans killed by our missiles, they had hardly lost a man. They stood ready, silent, and determined. I had never seen Romans fight in this way and I wondered who their commander was, for he had taken a rabble and with clever defences, turned them into a successful fighting force.

The trench filled up. Our men strode across the bodies of their comrades in their anger. They were determined to deal a deathblow to these arrogant Romans. The enemy had closed ranks apart from a few who were still hurling javelins from behind. They stood immobile. Our men had now lost their forward thrust. It was pitiful to see. They climbed to the Roman front ranks. The Roman short swords cut down many more as the Chatti came to their senses and formed a line.

The Romans now outnumbered us slightly. We had lost thousands of men to the javelins and the trench, but our superior quality of soldier began to tell. The front Roman rank began to buckle on our left flank and then it wavered and began to fold. Our men howled with this success. They started hacking, stabbing and killing. The middle of the Roman's right flank seemed without warning to open up. Our men began to pour in. They were ready to turn on the rear of the Roman infantry line. It was not so easy however.

While the infantry were fighting, the Roman peasants had gathered in huge numbers exactly at the point of the breach. They advanced. Although they were poorly armed, they were fresh. They had huge numbers. The peasants were now attacking our Franks in front and at the sides, where they had broken through. Hundreds died and the Roman shield wall closed again. The peasants did the same further towards their left flank. It was a neat manoeuvre. The Roman line appeared breached. It gave way. The peasants attacked and the line closed again.

Despite our losses, the quality of our men began to tell. We were pushing the Romans back and they began to give way in an ordered formation. It was not a rout but a retreat.

They fought like bastards all the way to their town walls. Close to the walls archers on the Roman defences began shooting. They fired over their men's heads. It bought enough time for the Romans to enter the town. They shut the gates in our faces and we pulled back. We had fought with fifty thousand. Almost nine thousand of them had died. The Roman casualties when we counted them, amounted to only one thousand. We had learned not to underestimate our enemy.

When the rest of the army had assembled there was a council of war. As night fell, leaders and kings sat in a circle several ranks thick around a fire and the flames rose in a ghostly flicker reflecting off the waiting faces of the lords of the German horde. There was a cool breeze fanning the flames and sending occasional sparks high above us. The sky was cloudless and as I my eyes followed the trail of a glowing spark upwards I could see Orion, my favourite constellation, bright and clear. He clutched his club; his belt shone clear and bright and I wondered if it was an omen. I thought it meant our people needed to leave.

The first thing the Marcomannii did was to decapitate the king who had ordered the attack, without ceremony, perhaps without rancour, in front of his own men. They did it in a matter-of-fact way and cleared away the body in silence. I cannot even recall his name, nor would I try for he was a fool. The entire German military operation so far had depended upon using the vast numbers of our amalgamated forces to crush any Roman army sent against us. We now had a siege to deal with and sadly, my people are not skilled at sieges.

We are a quarrelsome race. We have little patience for siege-craft and each individual warrior wants to fight hand-to-hand winning glory not sit around while the inhabitants of a town starve to death and hide their plunder. Maroboduus the Marcomannii king was determined to stay and besiege the town.

'The defences are poor and neglected. We can find a way in or we can starve them out. I would favour assaulting the walls for I think they will fall easily,' he said in council.

Maroboduus was an unremarkable man to look at. He oozed ordinariness. He was of medium height with mid-brown hair and a face neither kindly nor fierce. The thing making him exceptional was his brain. His dark eyes showed his intelligence as he looked at the other leaders. He could plan a war, read a map and he had a way of putting things to his people which made them back him without reservation. As his people's leader, he had organised his state and his army along lines he felt were a reasonable adaptation of Roman ways. This reorganisation held them together throughout the campaign. I was always suspicious of him for I knew with certainty from my own experience that beneath this veneer of civilisation his people were as barbarous as wolves and no less cruel.

'Brothers,' Odomir said. 'I for one, will support Maroboduus. We have come a long way and we have had more success than any other alliance in the history of our peoples. We cannot stop now. We must raise siege engines and ready ourselves for an assault.'

Hours of tedious debate followed with a number of disagreements and the council again decided to stay, but I knew the alliance would break up for that was as much part of our nature as battle. Despite this I was pleased we could stay in one place for longer. I had Clotildis on my mind. The old men talked and I thought of her body. Her breasts, her lips, her smell, all had me staring at the ground in a reverie. I reflected on the power she held over me and tried without success to understand its strength. The politics stopped suddenly and I was aware of silence around me.

'Galdir, pay attention!'

It was Odomir. I looked up and realised the assembled leaders had been waiting for me to reply to something. I stuttered in obvious confusion.

'Did they have cavalry?'

'Who?'

'The Romans, you idiot! You were there at the battle.'

'Er... No, they had very little cavalry we could see,' I said.

Odomir turned to the assembled kings and began to talk about his plans for an extended siege of Aquileia. Then I lapsed back into a comfortable vision of Clotildis, naked and beckoning; it was involuntary. I was a slave again. A slave to lust.

CHAPTER VIII

"Quick enough, if good enough."

— St Jerome

It was a dangerous business arranging trysts with a queen. Merely being seen alone in a private place more than once was indiscreet and we were both aware of the possible consequences. I rarely visited her now and we communicated by means of signals across the dining area or when walking together. I longed to spend a night with her but realised the risk would be too great. Although I blamed her in my mind the truth is, it was my own weakness depreciating my honour throughout my dealings with Clotildis.

My opportunity came sooner than I had anticipated. It transpired Odomir and his bodyguard were visiting the Marcomannii camp for another council. The boring nature of these council meetings meant I had no particular attraction to the political posturing of people for whom I had little respect. I hated the Marcomannii for what they had done in Lovosice. I often thought about Medana and prayed to Wuotan her death had been quick for the Marcomannii were cruel by nature. Although I had managed to keep the feelings hidden deep within me they threatened to surface when I heard the Marcomannii making decisions for my people, or at least for the future of my people.

I received a verbal message from Clotildis through a servant, very early in the morning on that day. It was to the effect that I should meet her by the stream, where the horses were watered and some of us bathed. My heart quickened in anticipation. I sometimes think half of the feelings that lust arouses in us base themselves upon anticipation for that expectation of pleasure heightens all sensations when they are finally gratified.

I walked through the camp with a feeling the entire world was fresh and new, hardly seeing the mud and the horse dung nor appreciating the smell of thousands of unwashed masculine bodies. I strolled in the damp grass reaching almost to my knees, hearing birdsong and seeing the birds soaring above me. My mind played the scene before my eyes: Clotildis partly clothed, my hands exploring her body, our lips wetly touching and her gentle moans as we made love. I hurried my pace. The little track I had joined turned a bend around a large rock and there she was. Fulfilment, anticipation, lust, all went through my head as if I was in a dream world.

The inanity of it all simply reflects how lust is capable of making foolish people do things that can only be the works of mischievous Gods like Loge, the God of fire. Chlotsuintha had told me the tale of how Loge had inflamed the heart of Wuotan with images of a giantess and how his lust made a fool of him before all the gods. Loge was certainly playing tricks upon me. All rational thought, I am ashamed to say, seemed driven from my head.

I rushed to her arms and we embraced. It was as if my expectations heightened the act of love itself and her frantic exploring hands and mouth were like fire on my body. The intensity of that act of illicit love rivals any such trysts I had with her, and it excites me still to recall it.

The second time we made love she sat astride me and looked into my eyes. There was a faint smile on her face and her hands rested lightly on my chest. With a speed that took me by surprise and in mid thrust, she stood and looked towards the path leading around a boulder by the stream. She said something in a low voice I did not catch and backed away with a look of horror on her face. Still recumbent, I turned my head and could see figures approaching but the length of the grass made it hard to see so I sat up and half turned despite my state of undress.

There were three men approaching rapidly with drawn swords. They were only twenty yards from me and I had little time to react. I jumped to my feet and pulled my tunic down over my rapidly fading erection. I had just enough time to pick up my sword and look at the faces of the approaching warriors. I realised then what trouble I had to face. It was not the fact of their presence, with their drawn swords and murder in their eyes, it was that two of them were my uncle's bodyguards and the third to my horror, was my uncle Odomir.

'How...?' I began to say.

The three men approached fast and I heard my uncle say, 'I want him alive! I'll geld him and blind him before he dies.'

I felt my heart beating in my chest, my lips were dry, and I noticed I was breathing hard. I cannot tell if the panic in my heart was due to guilt or that feeling before battle that winds us up and makes us perform.

I had to fight for Clotildis as well as for my life. Nothing drives a man harder than lust and danger and it was apparent in the way I now approached this fight. I knew I could not afford for them to take me alive for the outcome would be a slow and painful one. It made me less cautious than perhaps logic demanded but I came at the two guards with a fury beyond anything they expected.

Having surprised me in a state of relative undress they expected to have the better of me with ease. They approached side-by-side and Odomir stood behind. Out of the corner of my eye I saw Clotildis make her way around me to Odomir. As his guards struck the first blows I saw him open his arms and embrace her. The distraction did not last long for I had much to do.

The man on my left raised his sword. He hacked at my head as the second did the same from the opposite side. I crouched fast. I rolled backwards head over heels. I could not parry two blows at once. They knew it. As I regained my feet I sidestepped to my right and the man on my left came around his comrade to remain facing me. As he did so, I feinted at the right hand man. I followed through lunging at him on his right. Neither of my opponents had shields and this gave me some advantage. They were as vulnerable as I was. My blade connected with the man's waist. He yelped in pain. I withdrew my weapon. I sliced across the second man. His chain mail protected him from any serious injury.

They were both advancing again. I was retreating in the long yellow grass. It is hard to describe what goes through your head during a fight. I looked and listened as if my senses were more acute. My heart thumped, my mouth was dry. Anticipation is all in a sword fight. Maybe that helped me. A blur to my right as the assailant struck. A parry and curl of my blade bringing it up in a short circle to contact the man's face. Blood spilled; pain given. The other man striking. Sword flying and falling, parry, strike, parry, strike, and fall back. Assess the damage. Am I wounded? Attack, opponents weakened, limping, bleeding, a stab to the chest but parried, a slash at chest height, a return at leg level, a man down, attack again, swinging blade, forceful contact, second man down. Blood, moans, death. Another killing stroke.

I turned to Odomir. I stood, breathless and bloody with his two guards lying at my feet, the fight a blur in my mind. So fast; so clean, so exhilarating.

'Well?' I said. I was never one for long conversations when action beckoned.

'I'm going to kill you, you raping, cheating viper.'

'If you can you will. So stop talking and do it old man. I owe you a death for the death of my father and mother. My mother died screaming and bloodied; I will do that to you in her name.'

'Your mother was a whore. I took great pleasure in her death, for it was her whispering in Galdar's ear that took him away from me,' he drew his sword. 'He could have been a great man and led his people to glory and war. Instead he chose to negotiate with the Romans and he achieved nothing.' He circled slowly as he spoke. 'They killed him for the dog he had become and it left the road open for a greater Frankish state, one that will live forever. Not slaves of Rome, but side by side with the enemy, living in respect.'

'You're a fool. You are such a stupid damned Barbarian. The Romans will walk all over this country and its people. They can't be conquered by an uncivilised, uneducated rabble, like you and your men. You will never live to see Rome but if you did, you might understand. Rome and the Empire are vast. They have enough resources and armies to crush you like a fly and you stand before me arguing when all you should do is lead our people home. They need peace.'

'Liar!' he fumed, his face almost puce as he ran to me

with sword held high.

Odomir was a big man, not as big as Duras, but big enough to dwarf me and I am not small. He swung his sword in a downward stroke, which was forceful and fast. It was no trouble to side step and hold up my sword. I began to understand why Cornelius had described his Barbarian opponents as slow and clumsy with only brute force to help them fight. Odomir swore as he struck for he knew he had missed me. He had left himself vulnerable and exposed on his left side for a moment. I paused, for I had no real wish to kill him. He was my uncle and whatever he said, he was blood kin.

'Why don't we stop fighting you and I? You know I can kill you whenever I choose old man. You have become slow and it is no honour for me to kill a man in his dotage.'

I do not know why I spoke thus for I knew in my heart that after interrupting Clotildis and I as he had, there was no question of us both leaving the place alive.

'You dare, before all the gods to speak of honour? You try to rape a wife of the Royal House and you speak of honour? If Clotildis' maid had not told me of your evil intentions, I might have been at Aquileia with my men. I will have your head.'

For a moment, the thought that Clotildis had told him of our meeting made me hesitate. A myriad of thoughts flew through my head. She had engineered this; she had lied to us both. I was angry now, but not stupid.

'Since when does a woman get raped sitting astride a man?'

He paused for a moment as the truth began to dawn on him.

'You dare to besmirch my wife?'

His rage seemed to have taken away the little sense he had left and he swung his sword from right to left, then left to right and finally in a full circle, ending by bringing down the heavy blade aiming at my un-helmeted head. I merely stepped away feeling contempt and irritation.

His rage was getting the better of him and he kept swinging. He raised the sword high to strike at me again. As he did so, I stepped forward onto my left foot and turning, stabbed forward. My blade went right through him at the midriff. It happened very fast in a way I had once seen Cornelius do it. As I withdrew the blade, I stepped to my right, bringing up my elbow. The blade followed, striking my uncle's descending weapon. It flew from his grasp and he fell to his knees, staring at me in disbelief. I smiled coldly at the blue-grey eyes.

'My father and my mother are avenged; I will lead our people home and they will have peace, I swear it!'

My words were the last thing he ever heard and I always regretted not putting his sword in his hand before he went to the gods. He was brave but old and slow. We owe it to ourselves as we become older to remain strong and fast for one never knows exactly when we will need such skills even in old age.

I looked down at the body of my uncle with mixed feelings. I had become an adulterer and killed my own blood kin yet I felt elated. It is true I felt guilt but I was also convinced I had enacted a revenge the Gods planned for me long ago. Like Volsung; like Völund the Smith. Maturity has since taught me that to invoke the God's will every time something happens is a kind of dullness of thought. It is a mental mechanism to excuse to one's own unsavoury behaviour. I have learned since that it is better to assume responsibility for one's actions and face the consequences than to blame everything on fate.

I knew the truth might ostracise Clotildis and me completely if the circumstances were too closely scrutinised. If we were to survive then the events of that morning had to remain secret.

I now had to take my place as Warlord and I had a strong feeling it was not I but Clotildis who was the victor. I realised long before this that she was using me for her own purposes but had let her manipulate me simply for the pleasure of gratifying my lust. Infatuation, desire and jealousy all played a part. Oddly enough, I didn't hate her for it, nor did I wish her harm. I still think she had a haunting beauty of mind and body, which at the time could have made me forgive her anything. Despite her cold political soul she may have deserved better than the fate the Gods gave her in the end.

Had it not been for her entrapping me in her web I would never have evolved into the man I am now. Life is, after all, a form of evolution. We begin as very insignificant beings and emerge into our old age both as honourable and worthwhile, or not. Some would say it is only according to the apparent whim of Wuotan and the Gods, but I have my doubts; I think they do allow us choices.

It was time for action. Clotildis and I scattered my uncle's horses and we decided to leave the bodies as they were, for someone to find by accident. No one need know who had done the killing for the council had already chosen me as successor to Odomir. Clotildis appeared to have thought it all out long before.

We split up and went separately to the camp. As I reappeared, Duras looked up from his fire where he was cooking.

'What have you been up to? Another walk with Clo-tildis?' he smiled his knowing smile as we looked at each other.

'You're always making assumptions about things you don't understand,' I said with irritation creeping into my voice.

'Do you remember the time in my father's hall when I suggested you and Cornelius join me in finding a woman each? You said you were grieving for your dead Livius.'

'Livia, you fool. Livius is a man's name.'

'All right, Livia then. You seem to have lost sight of your grief and now seem to be seeking another. If you and Clo-tildis are so much as suspected, you will be grieving for each other.'

'There is nothing to fear in that respect. I can look after myself.'

'You think so?'

'You're mad,' I said.

'If I'm mad, why was one of the Warlord's body guards here only an hour ago asking where you had gone?'

'How would I know?'

'Galdir, you can't afford to be so complacent—it's your life you're gambling with.'

'I told you it is all taken care of, my friend.'

'I don't understand you at times. I'm going off to prac-tise, coming?'

We left the camp and engaged in sword practise. After an hour, we had news that some women taking their washing to the river had found Odomir's body. The rumour was it had been a Roman assassin. Who else would want to kill the Warlord after all?

CHAPTER IX

"Roman, remember that you shall rule the nations by your authority, for this is to be your skill, to make peace the custom, to spare the conquered, and to wage war until the haughty are brought low."

— Virgil

He was a clever man, Marcus Aurelius. He knew us better than we realised. Barbarians do not have the patience for siege craft and although Aquileia would have been a good base from which to invade Italia, the army began to lose interest. The Emperors did very little for a long time. I heard later they both came with their army; they moved north slowly. By the time they reached Aquileia, there were few Germans left. The Marcomannii stood alone then and had to retreat to their homelands with their tails between their legs.

There were no problems with my succession to my uncle's position as Warlord. The council named me as such, and there were no objections with both my uncle and my cousin removed from the scene. Clotildis took her time before she began visiting me regularly at night. We snatched moments at first but we were still cautious. If people had known we were lovers, there might have been some suspicions about my uncle's death.

The principal change with my accession was that I pushed the council to break the alliance with the Marcomannii and Chatti. We resolved to go home. Few of my people wished to stay and so we marched or rode from the army's presence like so many ants leaving a nest, our armour clinking softly as we departed.

We travelled north and west. For many it was a journey home to loved ones and family, for me it was a fresh start with Clotildis and a new role in life. A life I hardly understood. I could see the responsibilities but the mechanisms seemed to escape me and the only counsel I trusted were people like Duras and Stator, neither of whom I could rely upon if the politics became hard.

I was outwardly undergoing a transition, a metamorphosis. Before Odomir's passing, my people saw me as a young hanger-on. I had no particular influence with anyone, and anything I said at council meetings or even in conversations with the leaders of my people were ignored. Sometimes they even found my opinions risible.

Suddenly I was the Warlord. If I opened my mouth, people now took me seriously. If I asked for something, someone would provide it and if I wished to speak to someone, they came to me and not the reverse. I soon learned to keep my counsel and speak only when I had something to say. Although it is second nature to me now I had to learn that when you lead others you should think first then speak, for all too frequently in my past I had done the opposite.

With high rank comes not only great responsibility, but also privilege. I had the use of my uncle's huge tent, I was able to arrange for meals and entertainment, and we dined often. I was able to drink wine on the road north for I had only to ask and my people provided it. The biggest privilege was being able to spend time with Clotildis. She seemed so happy to be with me too.

Although the nights were wonderful, the days were frustrating in many ways. We travelled all day and in the evenings, there was the work of logistics and supply. Although I could delegate most of these matters others required me to participate. It was then I was glad to number Eudes in my group of advisors.

One morning, as I sat before the great tent, Eudes came to me. He knelt before me and I bade him rise.

'Lord Galdir, I served your father and knew him well. It will be my greatest pleasure to help his son. In the weeks to come I can tell you a little about him if you wish for he was a great man with high ideals and great honour.'

'Friend Eudes, you honour me with your offer of help. I am very new to all this and any help offered will not be scorned.'

'I am glad you have Stator by your side, for he too served your father and served him well until the end.'

'Stator has some strange ideas, but I am assured of his loyalty. I know that during my uncle's time as Warlord when he was directing the Nation's politics, Stator held true to the principles my father held. Like you, I want peace and I want the best for our people. It seems to me we must move them to the west of the Rhenus where the climate and land are better. That is my main wish at the moment.'

'It is something we cannot achieve with ease, Lord. The Rhenus is wide and we would need boats. Do you realise how long it would take to make boats for all our people? We would have to employ Gauls and Frisians to make boats and it would take years.'

'I think we could do it quicker than that. The problem is keeping all the tribes supplied while we move them. I need someone with knowledge of logistics and supplies. If we encamp the whole nation with the army for a time we can move them all in sections. Half the army can go first and then the people. The second half of the army can follow. I am sure the present occupants of that land will not welcome us and it may require fighting to establish ourselves in that part of Gaul. The Romans are too busy fighting the Marcomannii to mount serious opposition. This makes it an ideal time if we hurry.'

'It will be done, Lord,' Eudes said.

When the old man had left, Duras came to me. He had a serious look on his face and I viewed it with foreboding.

'The time has come to part I fear, my dear friend, Sextus.'

'My name is Galdir now, my time as a slave is past. Do you really mean you will leave me with this pack of wolves? I had hoped you would return with me and help me relocate my people on the west bank of the Rhenus. I need your advice and maybe your strong right arm when the Romans come, for of their coming I have no illusions.'

'No, my friend, I cannot,' Duras said solemnly. 'I swore an oath to regain my kingdom and that is my destiny. I have helped fulfil part of yours. Now it is my turn. I think you will manage quite well without your drunken Dacian, unless of course you want to lend me your army. I can then re-enter Lovosice with ease.'

Duras smiled knowing I had no power to provide what he needed especially now the Romans were on the march. I leaned over and whispered into a servant's ear. He went to do my bidding.

'Duras, we have fought together over the years and you are my blood-oath brother. Throughout you have never asked me for anything but friendship. One day I will visit you in your kingly hall, but there is little now I can do to aid you. I can give you gold with which to raise your army and that I do willingly. I also have a gift for you. It was a gift freely presented to my uncle and he insulted its bearer. I give it now to you to be the first truly regal possession of your house and beg you to keep it safe.'

I took the sword from the servant and held it out with both hands to Duras. There was a tightening in my throat as I did so. I know not why. We looked each other in the eye and he took the gift from me. I could see a tear appearing in the corner of his eye too and I looked away. It was the end, or at least a pause, in a deep friendship. Duras drew the blade and it had lost none of the lustre it expressed when Lazygis gave it to Odomir. It was a kingly gift and well deserved, I felt.

'Where will you go and when?'

'In the morning, I shall depart to the forests around Lovosice. The Marcomannii will not have many men there and if I raise an army of Dacian warriors I should be able to storm the town without difficulty. It is the Romans I worry about for I don't know whether they would regard me as friend or foe.'

'I think if you defeat the Marcomannii at Lovosice then the Romans will offer you peace. It is well worth considering, for in the south I think they will defeat the German tribes. I hope they won't come north because they will overrun us without much difficulty. We are a small nation.'

'You know, I don't think it is just the size of the army but how they fight that counts. Your men are brave warriors and there is always a chance you can win.'

'I must lead my people across the Rhenus first. Let us feast tonight before you depart and then bid each other farewell in the morning. To-night we will remember old times and departed friends.'

We did feast that night until almost dawn. Duras took his leave of me and I, drunk as I was, felt tears run down my cheeks. I remember that. I, a tall, fair, strong warrior— weeping. It must have been the beer or perhaps the wine but I was a more emotional man in those days. Maybe the trials ahead hardened me, but I do not shed tears anymore for who can cry when they have lost so much in life?

My friend set off in the morning and he took a spare horse. I provided him with a purse of gold coins, not enough to finance an army but enough to see him through to the end of his journey home and contribute to his efforts. Seeing him depart brought home to me how singular and alone I was. Whom could I trust?

I loved Clotildis even more then and clung to her as we stood side by side for I was grateful for her presence. We waved as Duras departed although I knew she did not care for him since he had always told me not to trust her and she knew it. I was no fool however and I realised her main reason for wanting me had been to remove my uncle. In this of course she had been successful and my lust for her showed no signs of diminishing.

Organising the gathering of a whole tribe was more than my poor intellect was equipped to carry forward and my reliance upon others became as normal as any other habit in my life.

Maharbal, Hannibal's cavalry commander once said of him that the great General knew how to gain a victory but did not know what to do with it afterwards. So it was with me. I often think how the realisation of power is not the same as wielding it, for without people around who you can trust it is all a form of play-acting. In my pretence of king-ship, the royal pantomime became part of my life.

I was then no more a king than Duras, who dispossessed, was perhaps more royal than I have ever been. For who was I really? Perhaps just an escaped slave with an inheritance he was barely capable of taking in his trembling hands.

It was during this time of uncertainty that Ranulf ap-peared. Clotildis had told me often how she had no surviv-ing family and I was surprised when she introduced me to him.

'Galdir, this is my cousin Ranulf. You know I have few blood kin. Well, I asked him to come for my comfort. A woman should have her kinsmen around her and he is one of the few people who shares my blood. He is my mother's nephew.'

'Of course he is welcome here,' I said. 'Any member of your family has a place at our fires.'

'I knew you wouldn't mind! Galdir, I am so pleased he can stay with us. Perhaps he can help you with the planning of the emigration of our people.'

'I don't need any help, but thank you all the same. Where is he?'

My guards showed Ranulf into the tent. He was a tall blonde man with no beard and a look in his eyes I found hard to trust. I never liked him, but some of that may have been jealousy.

He bowed before me and smiled a disingenuous smile. I frowned, but put up with his presence for Clotildis' sake. It was a stupid name anyway for Ran is the goddess of the sea,

Ulf means wolf and there are only human wolves at sea not four-legged ones.

When I say I never liked him, I should have said I detested him. He always smirked in a disrespectful way in my presence. I tolerated him because Clotildis said she loved him as blood-kin. Since she and I were to be married it was customary that her relatives had always to be welcomed into my home whether I liked them or not.

Ranulf always seemed to express a silent disapproval of anything I said or decided. An example would be when I suggested he ride to a nearby town. I asked him to take my instructions for the gathering and find out how many people there were. He simply refused. He said he had no time to do that and perhaps it was better suited to Stator or one of the servants. His refusal did not offend me; it was the expression on his face. He showed no respect; he treated me as if I was some fool.

Stator asked for an audience. Yes, even my most trusted people had to arrange to see me for Clotildis had instructed the guards they could admit no one to my presence without a prior announcement. She assured me this was a simple matter of security, since any ill doer could smuggle a knife or other weapon into my presence. When he came, he stood in front of me shuffling from one foot to the other as if I might send him away if he said the wrong thing.

Pattering rain on the tent canopy above competed with his voice as he said, 'The boats are nearing completion and now it seems to be time for the collection of our resources and an assembly of the people. Eudes has gathered all the information and needs to discuss the mechanism of the crossing with you; he asked me to tell you he has had difficulty in getting an audience.'

'Difficulty? What do you mean?'

'He has been turned away by your bodyguard twice in the last week and knows of no reason why that should be so.'

'I don't understand. Send for him now then.'

'It will be done Lord.'

Stator turned to a guard at the entrance to the tent and whispered in his ear. The guard left.

'And stop calling me Lord. If there are two people in this nation who are entitled to call me by name, it is you and Eudes.'

'Yes Lord, I mean Galdir,' Stator smirked.

'Oh and Stator?'

'Yes Galdir?'

'Send the captain of the guard to me.'

'Of course.'

Stator turned and strode out of the tent into the sloping rain. He left me pondering. I made up my mind to speak to Clotildis again. I felt I could not have my closest advisors barred from my presence. I realised it was only out of her concern for my safety, but it was not good enough. I supposed it was all part of my adjusting to a partnership with my beautiful consort. If you love someone enough to live with them and then marry them I supposed you have to take heed of their thoughts and wishes. I had a warm moment inside as I pictured her naked and enticing.

CHAPTER X

"It is not because things are difficult that we do not dare, it is because we do not dare that things are difficult."

— Senecca

'But my love, I think only of your security. If anyone were to impersonate one of your advisors he could attack you. The guards are so sloppy in their attitude to searching visitors.'

'That isn't the point. And you know it,' I said.

Clotildis reclined on the couch, bedecked with furs, as if she were already queen and I her consort. She irritated me then. We were not even married and she was already ordering my life and determining whom I should see and whom I should not.

'Clotildis, I am the Warlord. Have you forgotten?'

'No, I forget nothing. If it wasn't for me, you would still be bowing to Odomir and Guntramm would be his successor.'

'Yes, but it might have been much easier for me. Had you thought of that in your schemes?'

'Let us not quarrel. It is so vulgar. We are the nobility in this tribe and we need to be seen to be above petty squabbles.'

'You are right of course. I still insist though, that you stay out of my affairs. We will emigrate and I need to have the

336

counsel of my ministers.'

She reached for me then and soothed my brow with her hand. Surprising as it might seem it reduced me to soft clay in her hands. I became pliable and moulded by her fancy. We made love. It was tender I thought, but truncated by a noise outside as of men scuffling.

I made to rise but she held me to her. My lust delayed me then. It is hard after all, to break off at certain points in the act of love and I was a weak man. When we had finished, I dressed and lifted the leather door flap, but she spoke to me again.

'Galdir, when shall we be married?'

'Soon my sweet,' I said.

'How soon?'

'I don't know. Is there any hurry?'

'Yes, I want it to be before we leave to cross the Rhenus. It would be fitting after all for us to start a new life as husband and wife in the fertile plains of Gaul would it not?'

'I will make some arrangements and we will talk about it tomorrow.'

She smiled that wistful smile and as ever I was charmed by it.

When I left, I saw the two guards posted outside Clotildis' tent dragging away a body. There was blood oozing from it and a pool of it lay congealing outside the entrance.

'Hey! Wait a minute!' I called.

The two men looked round; they were startled to see me and they dropped their burden. The bloodied body lay in a crumpled heap between us. They knelt before their Warlord.

'Who is this man?' I enquired.

'We don't recognise him Lord,' one of the bodyguards said.

'What happened?'

'We searched him as instructed and found a hidden knife. He tried to attack me and Peppin here killed him. It was over in a second, sire.'

'And you don't recognise him at all?'

'He is dressed like a Frank but his hair is black and his skin unlike ours.'

'Have you searched him?'

The guards looked at each other anxiously.

'You can keep it,' I said, 'I only want to know who he was.'

'He had gold coins on him, can we really keep them?'

'Of course, you did a good job.'

They dragged the body away, leaving me wondering who would want me dead, now that my uncle and Guntramm were both out of the running.

*

The wedding took place four weeks later. People came from all over the Frankish lands. There were representatives of local tribes from our borders and we spent the whole of the day before the nuptials, greeting guests. The only member of Clotildis' family was Ranulf and he seemed to make himself scarce, but the reasons were obscure to me.

On the day of the wedding, we had a hailstorm. I remember looking out of the wooden doorway of my hall and seeing the dancing, bouncing lumps of frozen rain as they landed on the steps. The ice-balls were large and took time to melt. Soon, a white carpet of ice covered the ground. I wondered then if we should postpone the wedding. The ceremony itself, if I can call it that, was supposed to take place out of doors but the weather was hardly conducive. We congregated in my uncle's huge tent instead. I had them erect it in front of the Great Hall in which Clotildis and I now lived.

I looked at the assembled guests. They were dressed in their finest clothes. We Germans wear no fine silks but we like bright colours. Our guests wore tunics and gowns of red and green wool and their silver belts and cloak-pins, fine torques and arm rings flashed in the torchlight of the draughty tent. Servants lit braziers all around or it would have been miserably cold. Someone knocked one of them over onto the wooden boards we had laid down, and there was a commotion as servants rushed about with pans of water to extinguish the escalating blaze. Without the wooden boards, the floor would have been a mire of mud and slush. The ground sloped slightly and it was with annoyance I had to get servants to scoop away pools of water from one end as the hailstones melted outside.

A priest to Wuotan said some prayers to the Allfather and he sacrificed a pig in a muddy ceremonial pit in front of the assembled congregation, outside the tent. The pig squealed and defecated in the mud. It struggled and ran in circles and knocked the priest to his knees in the muck. Many shook their heads as if this were a bad omen but the priest quickly recovered his dignity and cornered the poor beast at the far end of the pit and slit its throat. They buried the pig, for we do not eat sacrifices.

I think this is equally true of even the Marcomannii but previous experience with them had shown that they sometimes even performed human sacrifice.

Effigies of the newlyweds were then pinned with mistletoe stakes to a tree at the edge of the forest to encourage the favour of the forest spirits and the celebration began.

Clotildis looked every inch a queen. She had a beautiful

crown of dried flowers and her dress was dark blue, tied with a belt of gold. Around her neck, she wore a golden torque made especially for the occasion. It was light in weight, but elaborate and set with coloured gemstones as befitted a queen of our tribe. The entertainment varied between singers, dancers, and swordfights. At weddings, mortal combat is forbidden for fear of invoking ill-luck, so no one died.

The feast was the usual drunken brawl into which German weddings always convulse. We over-ate and drank huge quantities of wine and beer for two days and nights and at the end Clotildis and I went to bed as husband and wife.

Although a few fights broke out in the wedding party afterwards, it was mostly a convivial time. We retired to the comfort of our wedding-bed drunk, sated and I thought, happy. As we undressed, Clotildis fell onto the bed giggling. She lay there motionless on the furs for a time and I looked at her face. It was radiant and her beauty made me, in my drunken state, close to tears as I lay beside her whispering in her ear.

'At last we can be together for all time.'

'As long as we both shall live,' she said.

'And beyond,' I said.

'Yes my love. We have at last achieved all the goals set by our destiny. You are the Warlord and I am your Queen. Soon we will rule over a green and prosperous land and no one can take it from us as long as we have the army.'

'The army, yes,' I mumbled.

'When we go, we have to burn all our towns and villages to make certain the people are committed and cannot return.'

'Yes, yes. It is all taken care of.'

'Will you make sure they know that if anything happens

to you, I will rule in your place?'

'Yes, rule in my place.'

'It's just that you have been so very tired lately and I dread to think what would happen to our people if they were left leaderless. I will rule if anything happens to you. I would be the first queen of the Franks. I pray every day for your safety; I love you so.'

We were both too tired to make love that night, but enjoyed being able to spend a whole night together. She was such a beautiful woman and only the third woman I had slept with in my life. The night held a deep meaning for me and I felt Clotildis had special feelings for that night too. I clung to her as we fell asleep in each other's arms after a long drunken conversation about the members of the ruling council. I remembered little of it myself but Clotildis, even when drunk, never forgot what she heard.

She was not there when I awoke and I recall shouting for her but my head was so painful I desisted at once. I slept again and then awoke in the late afternoon but I was still alone.

Five days after the wedding, I fell ill. It was a strange illness and manifested itself with stomach cramps, headache of a severity I had never experienced before, and a strange blotchy rash. I could barely raise my head from the straw bed on which I lay and I shivered continually. I had dreams of battles and demons pursuing me. I could keep no food or water down for days and Clotildis who sat with me kept trying to feed me and give me drinks. It seemed odd to me I had such an illness without fever for until then, my stomach had been as reliable as if it was made of cast iron.

Despite starvation and dehydration I recovered and began to show interest in the work of collecting all my people together for the exodus across the Rhenus.

The Frisian shipwrights had finished their work and we mustered the army. The outlying towns and villages had begun to assemble at the points of muster that Eudes and I had chosen. They were well supplied with food but I knew we had to move them soon lest disease and starvation set in.

Throughout the preparations in the subsequent weeks my illness persisted in some form. The stomach cramps returned from time to time and the rash waxed and waned. I began to wonder if fate had cursed me with a lifelong illness now, for it had been with me for weeks. Gradually the pain and sickness began to fade. I ate only sparingly and drank milk direct from a cow's udder. My physician had recommended no human hand should touch anything crossing my lips for otherwise, the Gods might curse it. I thought this was rubbish but when I followed the advice I seemed to improve, but milk alone is no diet for a man and I had to have meat.

I called a farewell feast. A farewell, on the eve of our departure, to the sticky mud-mire we had called home for over a hundred years.

Bright torches lit the hall and a huge fire burned in the central hearth. I was feeling good for the first time since the wedding feast a few weeks before.

Everyone of any importance attended. Stator sat on a low stool at my feet and eyed everyone as if they might be potential assassins. Clotildis, my wonderful, beautiful queen sat with me as the feast began. I drank ale for the first time for weeks because we had depleted the wine stores some weeks before. It did not matter for optimism seemed to fill me and I thought that in our new home we would prosper, if the Gods willed it. I remembered the prophecy Chlotsuintha had whispered to me with such reverence. The Franks would become the rulers of the whole of Gaul but first we had to suffer defeat by the Romans. I now hated the Romans with a fervour akin to religious belief. I saw them as the evil men who had enslaved me; the rulers of the known world.

That night was a better feast than my wedding. There were no ill omens and everyone there had the same positive outlook that I had. Perhaps my enthusiasm was infectious but I stood to give a speech at the end of the meal and my people greeted my words with reverend silence as I rose to my feet.

'My people,' I said in a deep and grave voice, 'My people! My father bade us go, and go we shall. We go to a better place but may have to fight to keep it and even fight to take it when we arrive. It does not matter. It is our destiny. The ancient prophecies cry out for us to fulfil them. I know some of you see my accession to power as a bad thing, but I promise you all: I am your servant. I am here to rule and help you all. There is not one among you who I would not die for; you are my people and I will lead you to a better place and we will prosper!'

I sat down to tumultuous applause and cries of 'Galdir! Galdir!' but the truth is that I meant every inebriate word. I felt I was following the path my father had shown me through all that had happened since that day in Rome when I had clubbed the judge Piso to death.

I am sure it was my finest moment as Warlord because the events that followed were not what I would have predicted nor did they follow the prophecy in the way I had understood it.

My heart leapt as I sat down from my speech. My people cheered me not because of what I had said in my ham-fisted way but because they had a leader whom they realised, cared for them. I really meant every word of what I had said but talk is cheap and wine costs money as I recall the barman of an inn in Rome used to say.

I looked at my beautiful queen. She smiled at me, but her smile differed from the one she usually gave me. It was powerful, piercing too, in its way. I looked into her eyes at that moment and I swear there was a coldness there, stabbing me, striking me and making me shudder. I cannot describe that look. It was a kind of hardness. I always knew she seldom betrayed the workings of her mind, yet what had I to fear? I knew she loved me as I loved her. We had been through so much to be together.

That night, as I slept in Clotildis' arms Livia came to me. It was a strange dream. We were in a field and she had her bow. She smiled her radiant smile transforming her face in to an almost beatific countenance in the bright sunshine. All was bright around her and I had to shade my eyes from the radiance.

My heart leapt as I looked at her and I asked her how she was. She did not speak but beckoned me by gesture to follow her. I could not catch up and I kept calling her name. She only glanced at me in silence for a moment over her shoulder smiling as she walked further and further away. I followed her into an olive grove. It could not have been in Germania but had to be in Italia, I remember thinking, as I followed her. The grove became darker and darker and the grass instead of being green became black and slimy. I stumbled over gloomy, gnarled tree roots. It became dark; there were flashes of lightening. Thunder deafened me as I struggled to plod on through the dark slime engulfing my feet. She glanced over her shoulder at me again, still smiling. The black grass stuck to my feet and I had trouble following. I felt distressed.

The black mud and grass continued to ensnare me until I could trudge no further. I could not move. Livia turned then and nocked an arrow to her bow. Her face changed and I saw her features turn into those of Clotildis. She pointed the arrow at my stomach. In the dream Clotildis fired the arrow straight at my gut and as it struck me, I heard her laugh and turn to someone in the background. A man came; I could not see his face in the gloom. Pain from the arrow in my guts consumed me then but I knew he was there. I awoke.

The pain in my stomach was real enough. I was sweating. I groaned, doubled up with pain, and rolled over falling from our bed. Clotildis seemed distressed and called for help. The pain was a searing, burning agony and as I looked at my arms I realised the rash had returned.

I prayed to Wuotan. I cursed. I groaned rolling about the bed, but the pain was unrelenting. I remained in that condition for three days. Pain, vomiting, prostration. My physician came. He gave the same instructions as before. He forbade me to eat meat. Only milk from the cow's udder, direct into my mouth. The milk seemed soothing and I did not object. It all puzzled me. I had been a strong, fit warrior. My muscles seemed to waste away and it was a struggle every day even to raise myself from the bed. One might greet the idea of having to lie under a cow for sustenance as ridiculous, but I can remember it as the one thing helping me.

Clotildis seemed beside herself with worry. She stroked my forehead with her gentle hands when the spasms came and kissed my forehead so gently.

I recovered again but had to be careful what I ate. The pain returned intermittently if I ate anything solid at all and all I could keep down was milk. To this day, I hate milk. I think I drank a lifetime's worth of milk in that period. Eudes took charge of the exodus. I was barely able to stand most of the time as we ferried our people across the river. The timing became a blur to me. Illness does that to a man but I do recall I was among the last to make the trip. Half the army went with me and I could see in their faces how they had already written me off. They looked at me and when I looked back they shifted their gaze and muttered. I seldom saw anyone smile.

On the west side of the river we had to travel many miles to a place where we felt we could start the process of building our homes. The place we chose was close to a river. It ran into the Rhenus miles from where we made our settlement.

The local people were the Eburones. Since the Romans defeated them a hundred years or so before, they had never recovered sufficiently for them to mount any serious opposition to our encroachment. They were not up to fighting anyone, let alone a heavily armed force of hefty German warriors. They did not exactly welcome us but they were content to negotiate the distribution of their land, which was under-populated in any case.

Clotildis insisted we build a grand palace for the reigning Warlord. I had my mind set on a more modest building than she did, but love wins through every time and I acquiesced.

It took many months to build the great palace. It was not like any construction in Rome of course. We did not have the skills or resources to build with stone unless they were rough buildings, which often collapsed. Instead, we built a huge Great Hall in the true German fashion but larger than any seen before. A living oak tree supported one end and beneath it was a dais where I, the Warlord, would sit to preside over banquets and give judgements.

The hall itself was massive. The hearth in the centre of the Great Hall was square and each side was the length of a fully-grown man. The smoke from the hearth rose upwards to a wooden funnel taking it out of the roof, a thing I had seen in Dacia years before. I remembered Moscon and the gaiety of the feasts in his hall and how well Cornelius and I were entertained by Duras' father. I was particularly proud of my roof. It was made of wooden tiles slotted together in a cunning fashion and pegged to cross-timbers holding the roof up. The individual bedrooms opened off the main hall and at the back was a walled compound large enough to ride and train horses. I loved it but my physical state made it impossible for me to ride for I had become ill again.

It was spring by the time we had the hall built; my people had distributed themselves across the land and built their new homes too. They had begun raising herds and planting crops. The soil here was different to the soil of the land we had left. It was darker and richer and the place was not subject to the flooding we were used to in the east.

I was only sorry my health did not allow me to visit the outlying countryside for I was desperate to see how my people were faring. I began to see things others did not. I had shivers and found my eyes were unfocussed and blurred. I stuck to my milk and allowed only my doctors and Clotildis to feed me. I was in despair.

CHAPTER XI

"A man whose life has been dishonourable is not entitled to escape disgrace in death."

— Lucius Accius Telphus

I was in the bedchamber of the new palace, if a wooden hall can have such a title. It was morning and I recall there were birds singing in the world outside. As I awoke, I remember wishing I could be outside riding Valknir and breathing the cool spring morning air.

I recall seeing and hearing it all but being unable to move. What happened next came as no surprise to others but it came as a complete revelation to me. I am astounded sometimes by how blinkered I had become. I make excuses to myself by thinking about how ill I felt but I am sometimes honest with myself and admit I denied the truth all along, because of my infatuation. I was guilty of a long self-deception and denial.

Fool! Stupid fool!

They had propped me up in my bed. Both my arms were lying on the blanket in front of me, but I could not move more than to twitch my fingers. Clotildis stood before me. She was with Ranulf and I saw them laugh together. My mind was a little confused at first and I wondered at first whether I was dreaming. His presence puzzled me.

'I'll do it now my love,' Ranulf said.

348

'He's awake,' Clotildis said, her voice echoing in my mind.

'So? He can't move and I doubt if he can even whisper. What did you put in that milk?'

'A mixture this time. He seems to have become resistant to the Belladonna. I used a mushroom as well. The one with the red cap and the white stalk.'

Ranulf's face presented itself to me smiling inches away from my eyes. If I could have spat, I would have. My anger and frustration made my head swim. The realisation of the depth of the betrayal and my naivety hit me as hard as any poison.

'For a stupid man he seems to be very strong. It's taken such a long time to do this. I can now force the council to make me queen. There is no-one else, now that Odomir and Guntramm are out of the way.'

I tried to protest but no sound came from my lips. I was as passive as it is possible to be, limp. I felt almost as if I was outside my own body watching and listening. I wondered then whether I had already died and was looking at the two of them through the eyes of my spirit.

'Unintelligent people are often strong,' he said. 'I can smother him now if you like.'

'Kiss me first. I doubt if he can see us but if he can, I would like him to know what a fool he is. To think I would want a man like him when I have you!'

She reached forward and her arms encircled Ranulf's neck. They kissed slowly, passionately. They were in no hurry. I looked on with horror and my eyes moistened. I wondered how long they had been lovers but realised it must have been long before I even met her. My arrival on the scene must have been an opportune moment for them. I had become the instrument they could use to remove both my cousin and my uncle and it all seemed to happen at the right time for them too. I cursed inwardly, for no sound came from my throat. I felt as stupid as they had made me out to be.

I heard her muttering endearments. The words stung my mind like a curse. She said all those things she used to say to me but I knew now she meant them for him. The clarity that comes with revelation is cruel and cold and I knew I had not long to live. I had no chance to fight, you see. The anger in me was violent but there was nothing I could do to move even a twitching finger. She turned to me then and laughed.

Ranulf said, 'Don't worry fool.' He smiled as he approached, 'It won't hurt, suffocation isn't the same as slitting your throat which is what I would have enjoyed doing to you even more.'

He held a bolster against my face and as the light disappeared the last thing I saw was her hand on his shoulder. That hand rested there with a gentle grip perhaps with love, as she watched him suffocate the life from my weakened body.

The blackness lasted only a second or two. The bolster fell away. I could see Ranulf's face. It was gripped in a strange contortion. My first thought was they were playing with me and they were going to frighten me first but I realised as he turned away it was a grimace of pain. He slipped down out of my view. I saw Stator. He raised his fist. He struck Clotildis in the face. I remember seeing her crumple to the floor and Stator looked at me and spoke to another in the room.

'Is he dead? He doesn't move.'

'No, not dead but the poison has made him still. We must work quickly. Bring the potion we prepared last night girl,' a voice said.

I knew then it was Chlotsuintha. I even knew to whom she spoke, for the small girl Frija was always her helper when I had first met her seven years before, in that hut in the Frankish town, so long ago, on my return from Rome.

Everything faded then, as if the Gods had shown me all they wished me to see for no better reason than to teach me a lesson, and now they needed me to see no more. If that is so it shows their wisdom for it was a lesson well learned, at least for a time.

It was the closest I was to come to death for a long time but not the last.

I awoke to an odd feeling. Women were manhandling me. Not that it could be interpreted as an unpleasant sensation, but it would have been different if I had possessed any control over my body. The slightest movement in any muscle caused an exquisite pain and made me desist immediately.

'That's it! Knead those muscles. The fungus causes damage to them and we must restore the circulation Frija. Harder!'

Chlotsuintha's voice was welcome and familiar to me. I opened my eyes and saw a glimpse of her wrinkled face. It looked older and more wrinkled than ever I had remembered it. Her skin was like the brown bark of an ancient tree and her mouth drooped at the corners making her face seem stern and proud. When she spoke, it was as if most of her face moved up and down at once for all her facial skin sagged like a bag. Her voice was cracked and high pitched but I knew she was honest and had only good intentions serving as a kind of mouthpiece for the Gods as she would say. She had rolled up her sleeves revealing wrinkled, sagging, tattooed skin and I could smell her where I lay. She was small, standing with an angled back no higher than my waist, but her mind was clear as spring rainwater.

Chlotsuintha had reached an age where no one knew her ancestry and no one had lived as long as she had in the entire Frankish nation. She weaved her spells, cast her rune-stones, and muttered of her visions of the future only to a few. The older men revered her because believing in her power was a part of their childhood upbringing. She was old enough to be a tradition among the Franks.

'What happened?' I asked in a voice which seemed to have surprising strength considering the state of the rest of my bony frame.

'You have been exceedingly stupid, Galdir.'

They rolled me onto my side and Chlotsuintha slapped my bare buttocks with her hand, none too gently either.

'I think I know that now.'

'You should have understood what was happening long ago. Blinded by the weakness of your flesh, you were. You should learn from this, a long-lived man thinks with his brain and not the part of his body adorning his nether regions.'

She cackled then as only an old woman could: at her joke and at my expense, but I did not begrudge her that humour for I had learned she was right.

'Frija, rub the potion into the muscles a little harder, dear. He can't bite you, you know.'

Rolled again onto my back, I looked at Frija. She was a small slim girl, her raven hair hung loose in straggled locks about her shoulders. She was no beauty; in fact, her features were quite unremarkable except for one thing: her eyes. They

352

were the bluest eyes I have ever seen even to this day and Chlotsuintha told me they were a window to Asgaard, the home of the Gods through which all were invited to look, but few could truly see. When Frija looked me in the eye, I understood she was no ordinary girl. I realised then the power she possessed for her eyes were not cold like ordinary blue eyes. They seemed to burn with an iridescent blue fire penetrating to the back of my skull and maybe beyond.

Frija smiled then and I was embarrassed. I had the uncomfortable feeling she knew all about me, my innermost thoughts; yet she smiled. There was no contempt in her smile—it was pure girlish humour and I knew she directed it at me without her saying a single word. Some people are like that. They can tell you more with a look than others can tell you in a speech.

They massaged and pummelled my aching limbs until I thought the pain would never go but I soon found I could move them a little.

'You owe your life to Stator,' Chlotsuintha said quietly.

'Stator?' I said puzzled, and then I remembered the tall man who had been in the background after the attempted smothering.

'Yes, it was he who sought me out, he was desperate. It was he who waited behind the door until he knew the truth and it was he too who killed Ranulf. That is of little import, for he owed you that for your father. He never did anything for you when you were a slave in Rome and now he feels he has earned his keep! What he did for you that was important, was that he roused me from the slumber that has kept me from being your witch. I will not abandon you again my boy.'

'Faithful Stator. I owe him much then.'

'Perhaps.'

'Will I live?' I said.

'Live? You have the constitution of a horse, of course you will live, you idiot!'

'And Clotildis?'

'Never mind her. I can think of a few things to do to her I won't bother to frighten you with,' the old witch said. Frija looked away.

'No. I will decide what will become of her. I don't want her hurt!'

'Has the poison reached your brain, boy? She must die and painfully, for she is evil and does not deserve to live.'

'No! I am the Warlord. Your Warlord! You will obey me in this. She is to be held prisoner until I have my strength back and I will pass judgement on her. I loved her you know, Chlotsuintha. Maybe you don't understand.'

'Look at me Galdir. I am so old that worldly pleasures have no meaning anymore. It is only the will of the Gods driving me on to live, as they express their will to me, and force it upon me. It does not mean I have never loved or cannot understand. There was a man once,' her eyes stared into the distance, across my naked body but in the same moment, she seemed irritated by her thoughts for she raised her voice, eyes wide. 'But that is none of your business! I will ensure your men carry out your wishes but I think you are foolish. If only you could know what I know, or see with my eyes, you would not spare her a second thought.'

I spent three weeks lying down most of the time. The first week I could not stand and by three weeks, I could stand and walk with assistance. Chlotsuintha spent most days with me supervising my physical treatment and giving what she called spiritual guidance.

354

I was still in some pain for the immobility had created a sore on my left buttock and urine and excrement had infected it. It healed eventually but it was a long time before I could sit in the saddle comfortably. Oddly, the pain made me curse Clotildis every time I sat upon Valknir to which the poor horse if he could speak, would probably not have objected.

'Wuotan is angry with you,' Chlotsuintha told me.

'What?' I looked at her with surprise. Her wizened face and dwarfed stature seemed to move slowly but achieve much. Her eyes were sunken deep in the excessive wrinkled skin of her face and they seemed tiny, but saw everything.

'I cast the blood runes last night, for the first time for some years. I use them seldom.'

'Yes?'

'Yes. They spoke to me.'

'Yes?' I said louder, feeling impatient. It was like squeezing water from a stone. Witches are like that, they do not function in the same time scale as normal people.

'The stones have been created many years before I was born. They were wetted with the menstrual blood of each of seven generations of witches, and seven is a sacred number.'

'You've told me before Chlotsuintha,' I said feeling more impatient still.

'When I go to Hel, the half monster and half human, Frija will take the stones and anoint them with her menstrual flow and become part of us. There will be eight witches moving the stones for Wuotan then and the power of her runes will wax.'

'Frija? She will be your successor? I suppose you want me to marry her. Well I desire no women now, I can tell you. I loved...'

'You are not listening. You hear but don't listen Galdir!' she seemed annoyed.

It is unwise to anger a witch, so I shut up.

'Frija has learned from me for ten years. She was just a child when she came to me. At first when her mother and father gave her to me she was sad but I treated her as my own daughter and she has learned all I can teach her. She will be more powerful than I have been and will serve you well if you listen to her rune magic.'

'Chlotsuintha, I do not entirely believe in any magic, I believe in the Gods but not much more. I don't want to marry again and frankly although Frija is an attractive girl, I have a burning grief inside me. Please don't ask this of me!'

I owed Chlotsuintha my life, but my irritation was clear from the tone of my voice. I was tiring then for I could only have short conversations without going to sleep at that time.

'Impatient is what you are! It is because you are young. I will tell you plainly now for you don't listen. Frija is only of value as long as she remains untouched. Her powers will wane if she is tempted by man's flesh. It has always been this way amongst us witches. Keep her safe when I have gone and she will serve you well.'

'I thought you said there was a man in your past.'

'There was a man, whom I could have given all of it up for, but I chose this path instead.'

'Who was it?'

'Your grandfather, he was like you. Impatient and strong and sometimes stupid!'

'Why is Wuotan angry?'

'You have dishonoured yourself with that woman! You took another man's wife, you killed her husband, and worst of all you abandoned the Gods.'

'I realise all this, but I felt powerless. I loved Clotildis. Maybe she cast a spell on me?'

'The only spell she cast on you was arousing the contents of your underwear. You must learn from this. Control your lust, listen to your advisors, and above all keep your honour close. It is what you owe your bloodline.'

I was silent after that. I had not really needed a witch to tell me what a mess I had made of my honour. Unfortunately, I was a man who learned little from his past and my life has been a cycle of the same mistakes; their lessons soon forgotten each time. Had I known it, such dishonourable behaviour was to become the pattern of my life again. Chlotsuintha knew I was weak, and maybe her foreknowledge was what made her talk to me in this way.

I slept. I had dreams of my mother. I am sure it was of no importance then, but she smiled at me and caressed me as if I took refuge in her face and touch. I was so young when the Romans killed her and I am uncertain whether my recollection of her face was accurate, but it was a kind face and I remember her gentle caress with vivid accuracy.

CHAPTER XII

"Time is flying, never to return"

— Virgil

Witches are strange people; ephemeral in a way, if you know what I mean. When you expect to see them, they are not there and the converse is equally true. The day I gave judgement upon Clotildis, Chlotsuintha was absent. I think she was so disgusted with me for keeping my wife alive she could not face me that day. I knew exactly what the right punishment would be. I had known it all along.

A combination of the central fire and many bright torches flaming in their holders all along the walls illuminated the hall. There was a faint smell of stale beer and vomit emanating from the straw covering the floor. I thought vaguely as I waited that it needed changing. Stator sat on a stool at my feet. He had never left me on my own since the poisoning. When he was not physically in my room, he was outside and slept across the doorway.

She had her hands tied in front of her and two guards walked with her, one on either side. I noticed despite her unkempt and unwashed appearance, she walked straight and tall. She was a proud woman and it showed in how she held herself even in those circumstances. I remember also thinking she had courage for she showed no signs of weeping or fear.

Clotildis stood in front of me and looked into my eyes. There was the same hardness I had seen before but had always ignored it before. This time, that solidity in her convinced me I was doing the right thing.

'I hope they have not treated you badly,' I began. My heart still ached for her.

She continued to look at me and smiled a wan smile.

'No, not badly,' she said looking down at the soiled straw beneath her feet.

'Clotildis, after all we went through, why did you do it?'

'You don't understand. Ranulf and I were lovers before ever I had the chance of marrying Odomir. Ranulf was my one real love. He was a man. He was clever, witty and strong. He was so far above you and any member of your family, you will never understand.'

'So when did you decide to kill me?'

'We always planned to kill you. From the moment you walked into your uncle's hall that first day with Duras. You were the perfect fool to use.'

'I loved you, you know.'

'Then you are a bigger fool than ever I took you for. I never loved you; I wish Ranulf and I had succeeded. I am almost relieved to die now for he has gone before and waits for me. I meet death gladly for I will be with him again in the afterlife, forever. You wouldn't understand. You don't know what real love is.'

She was quite wrong, I thought, but I did not correct her.

'The guards killed a man who tried to get in with a knife a few days before the marriage. Was it you who arranged it?'

'No, it was Ranulf. He was getting impatient. I told him he had to wait until I was queen before killing you. We almost quarrelled over it for it could have ruined the whole plan. I wish now he had done it. I would not be here in this position if he had.'

'Have you no remorse?' I said.

'None. I regret only my failure.'

I still had feelings for her. I almost attempted reconciliation because I wanted her love more than I wanted revenge. I missed having her in my arms at night and I missed her humour. I longed to hear her voice whispering to me as I had become accustomed to in our talks late at night as we lay in each other's embrace. If she had given some indication of regret or even the feeling she had some kind of regard for me it might have turned out otherwise for us both. Her attitude of hardness and scorn and her admission she had planned my death all along made me come to my senses. Perhaps Chlotsuintha was right and she should have died in pain, but I could not bring myself to give such an order.

'I am not going to kill you Clotildis.'

She looked up at me then uncertain for the first time since she walked in. I returned the look for I knew what to do.

'When I was dying in front of you and Ranulf was going to smother me, you called me a slave. I have been a slave for a large part of my life and so it does not offend me. I am the Warlord of a great nation now and I do not need to have you put to death. I have arranged for you to go far from here. You will have no chance to destroy anyone as you tried to destroy me. Maroboduus has agreed to take you into his hall as a slave. There, you will serve others and never experience the luxury for which you thirsted. The Marcomannii do not treat slaves well I fear but such is the fate you have earned.'

Her face changed then. It cracked into a puckered grimace and she began to wail, leaning forward, her face thrust out at me.

'No! No! Kill me, please Galdir kill me.' She screamed it repeatedly and the noise became frightful. Stator stood then and slapped her in the face. The hysterics ceased. She simply looked down at the ground and sobbed still begging me to kill her.

It might seem vindictive but I felt she would suffer more if she was alive and feeling her failure daily. I did not want her blood on my conscience in any case and slavery was, after all, tolerable. Had I not lived through it myself? She would have to become part of the furniture like any slave and maybe she would learn a bit of humility at last, I thought.

As they dragged her from the hall, she was still begging me to kill her. I can almost hear her voice now, an echo from the past. She had broken my heart that one, but something hard had repaired it. Hard as revenge; for I knew I could never have her affection.

It was the end of a chapter in her life and mine but strangely enough, it was not the end.

I heard many years later she was an efficient slave and well liked among the Marcomannii. One of their noblemen took a fancy to her in the end and freed her. I heard he married her, but soon regretted it for she became a shrew. He had no rest unless he obeyed her demands in every way. I remember smiling when I heard the tale.

CHAPTER XIII

"Happy is he who dares courageously to defend what he loves"

– Ovid

On the day after Clotildis departed for the land of the Marcomannii, a flock of starlings flew twice over the palace. The flock was in the shape of an eagle with outspread wings. I knew then a storm was brewing. I knew also that the storm was Rome. We had news that Marcus Aurelius and his brother Verus had gathered a huge army and they were marching north to Carnuntum, a large town in Noricum. It was rumoured the Chatti and Marcomannii had allied again to defend their land but I knew it was futile. Rome cannot be defeated. If the Romans fight a war and lose they simply gather more armies and return in greater strength until they win. They never accept defeat and their empire continues to spread as a result.

We Germans also suffered from a peculiarly stupid cultural disadvantage. We formed alliances but retained our dislike of one another. It meant such allegiances were short lasting and quarrelling always terminated our campaigns. The Romans in Gaul fought each tribe in turn after their tribes quarrelled and this made their conquest gradual, but complete. The Germans were in no way different to the Gauls in that respect. I had premonitions of the same thing

362

happening to us.

I sacrificed a white ewe to Wuotan in the night, in a deep pit. I recall the sticky warmth of the creature's blood as it flowed onto my hands and how its heat brought neither solace nor reassurance. As I nailed it to an oak tree, I hoped he would bring us peace. I called Chlotsuintha to me.

She was all doom and gloom about the future but told me any details of what she feared.

'I need to know when they will come. Can you tell me or not?'

'Galdir, you have to be patient. My gift does not work in a way that allows me to tell you the exact timing only a general picture for it is formed from visions and portents and runes. The Gods may not wish you to know. It might alter their plan if you change course.'

'Not much use to me then is it? The Romans are marching to Noricum to fight the other German armies and all I can find out is it will happen. I would guess the alliance will fall, but how long it will take and how long before the Romans march north is only guesswork. We need to prepare in any case I suppose.'

'These are not things for a witch to comment upon. You must ask your councillors and spies.'

Frija helped her from the hall for she could only just walk. Her frail and bent frame belied her sharp mind however and I wondered why she was so uncooperative. Perhaps she was testing me. She may have wanted me to face the Romans myself and win or lose as the Gods willed it, or it might have been a blind acceptance of the future she had seen in her dreams.

I arranged a council meeting in which we planned how to defend our new land. It would not be easy. We had spread far and wide since the exodus.

We decided every man who could bear arms would be responsible for his own attendance and those who were too young now but would within a year or two, be able to bear arms had to be trained in their use. We were to become a nation of warriors. Such training was beyond me. I was good at hand-to-hand fighting, but I had based my military knowledge on a few battles with the German alliance and was not up to the task.

Eudes knew how to rally our men and arranged muster points for warriors from all the villages. We passed information by word of mouth for we had no writing, as the Romans had. It made information a little unreliable but we could get messages out with relative speed and we estimated we could rouse our troops quickly by using a series of beacons to alert the villages and order the troops to muster.

We had fortified the settlement in which we built the palace, but only with a high and strong wooden wall. I had them dig a trench outside it, deep and wide enough to make ladders difficult to use. We placed stakes of sharpened wood in them to prevent a full frontal assault and we dug many potholes to trip unwary cavalry in the fields around the town.

I look back on our defences and knowing what a Roman army can do, I despair of my people. Our defences were puerile compared to the engineering skill of even the average legionary. We had no ballistae. We had no onagers. All we really hoped to challenge the Romans with was our men. They were strong. They were valiant and brave, but valour is not enough, not these days.

There is a certain moral value in discipline which I admit, sadly, is lacking in us Barbarians. We have warriors who want to prove themselves before Wuotan and they die gladly for that reason. They think a glorious death is the only thing required of a man. I have doubts about that now, although at the time, I was just one of these Barbarians who hoped to die valiantly with a sword in my hand. Valhalla was where we all hoped to end our lives. Feasting and fighting would allow us pleasure and laughter for the rest of time or so we thought.

I still think this is a better philosophy than that of the dreary White Christ who has come and insinuated his doctrine of peace into our every council and meeting. An after-life in which there is no struggle or pride would be tedious to me. Better the old Gods, the real ones who have personality and anger, jealousy and love.

It was a long summer. One in which we reaped wonderful harvests and the cattle grew strong and fat. My people prospered. I was able to tour the outlying towns and farms and everywhere I went my people greeted me with respect and hospitality.

It was in the autumn he came.

The farmers had gathered the harvest and it was a time for celebration. I was sitting in the Great Hall eating with a number of my best warriors. Big men, strong positive attitude and a good sense of humour.

We drank wine and laughed. I heard the doors at the far end of the hall bang open and a chill wind seemed to come from nowhere. I looked along the torch-lit room and could see a man, cloaked and hooded, striding towards us.

'Where is Galdir?' he sounded impatient and disrespectful. He was not addressing me in the manner he should, whoever he was.

I stood. I raised myself to my full height. I put my hand on my sword and glared.

'I am the Warlord. This is my hearth and you would do well to use a more polite tone. We do not treat strangers badly for we believe in hospitality, but if it is abused we punish quickly.'

There was silence as the man approached. He threw his hood back and stared straight at me.

'Lazygis?' I said.

'Galdir, my friend,' the Sarmatian said.

He stumbled then and nearly fell.

'Lazygis.' I said again, 'help him, he is a friend.'

One of my men got up and helped the Sarmatian to a seat. I got up and sat beside him on the bench,

'Lazygis, what has happened? Are you wounded?'

'Just in the arm.'

His face was drawn and pale. He leaned on the table in front of him with his left arm. He looked thinner than when we had last parted company and I could see his supporting arm shook with the strain. I had always seen him as a strong man and I could guess what had happened.

'They have slaughtered everyone.'

'Who did?' I said, but in my heart I knew the answer.

'Aurelius and his army.'

He spoke almost in sobs. I gave him wine. He gulped it as if it was a source of reclamation.

'The Romans came in the night and their army took us by total surprise. The whole army and families were annihilated. Dead.'

'Ayma and Panogaris?'

'All dead,' he said and stared straight ahead. I waited.

There was not much to say then. I understood what he felt. I had lost too and there were no words to help at a time like that. I put a hand on his shoulder and looked in his eyes. They revealed the depths of despair. We sat silent for a moment but I had to know.

'What happened?'

'I can't talk about it now. They came and killed us all. I have only eight hundred men left. We came here to see if you will help us. There is no place left to go.'

'What about the German alliance?'

'They quarrelled like dogs in a pit. If they organised themselves properly they could defeat the Romans, but all they do is fight each other. Maroboduus is dead. He was the only one who could hold them together. They are now just a fragmented bunch of tribes who don't work together.'

'Maroboduus dead? That is bad news. How did it happen?'

'No one is sure. They found his body outside the camp one morning. Whether it was the Romans sending an assassin or one of his own chiefs in a power struggle isn't known.'

'Perhaps we were right to leave when we did,' I said.

'They are not happy with you Franks. They say you ran away from them in Aquileia and you are hiding here because you are afraid.'

'And what do you say, Lazygis?'

'I say you are wise. You will never defeat the Romans. They will sweep across all this land and kill everyone. They spared no one.'

'Where are the rest of your men?'

'They're coming behind. Maybe two days away. We split up and arranged to meet here.'

Lazygis broke down. I placed a hand on his shoulder again and poured more wine. I had them summon Frija and she tended his wound. It was a deep sword cut at the top of his shoulder. We gave him a room but he refused and went

out to sleep near his horse for Sarmatians do not like sleeping in buildings.

I pondered the news until late. I could only hope it
would take time for Marcus Aurelius and his brother to
defeat the other German tribes and we would have enough
time to create adequate defences.

I began to realise I was behaving no better than the other
Germans. I had refused to fight alongside them and they
held it against me. German against German as usual. Perhaps
it was our nature and even I, brought up in Rome, could not
change that.

There was little point in pursuing a peace settlement with
the Romans. They would hardly go to the trouble of fighting
us for years and then give up when they had the upper hand.
I did not want to become a slave of theirs either. I bade
farewell to that with the death of Piso. Like my warriors, I
would rather die fighting.

I wondered how Duras had fared, for I had heard no
news of him since he left. The Romans would have taken
Lovosice by now, since they had gathered their armies at
Carnuntum to the south east of our country.

Perhaps he was now a Roman puppet King, but at least
he would be a King. Better a puppet than a vagabond with
an inheritance. No. I could not surrender. I would not sue
for peace. If I made it hard enough for the Romans to take
our new land, they might eventually leave us in peace. It had
happened before.

I now had eight hundred Sarmatians on my side, but
they required food and fodder. I decided to split them up
and house them in groups of fifty in the various settlements
in the new Frankia.

It was a question of waiting now. Waiting to see how the

Marcomannii and the Chatti fared in their struggle. It seemed unlikely to me they would be successful and the Romans would come. But when?

CHAPTER XIV

"To refrain from imitation is the best revenge."

– Marcus Aurelius

It was a gentle winter. Snow came only a few times and the westerly winds did not bring the ice and snow its cousin the east wind usually carried. It was still a time of general tension. The whole nation knew the Romans would come one day. Like children, they carried on with their daily lives and their childish optimism carried them through.

My heart was heavy. Lazygis told me at length about the fall of the Sarmatians. The Romans had all but wiped them out. Those who had lived escaped north to their own lands but that was only a tithe of the original migration. The remainder of their army was now with us. It made little difference to our preparations, which had stalled over the winter. The one area where we had to adjust our plans was to fill in the horse-traps we had dug before our town. We now had enough heavy cavalry to attack any besieging force and we could not risk injury to our own horses.

With the arrival of spring came news from the Marcomannii. They had fought a massive and decisive battle at Carnuntum. It happened as soon as the winter snows were over. Marcus Aurelius' army crushed them like a miller crushes corn and the German armies scattered like the chaff. They tried to sue for peace but the Emperor refused to hear them and demanded complete capitulation. The Romans enslaved many of the tribes in their entirety and some they put to the sword. We heard also the joint Emperor Verus had died and Aurelius was now sole Emperor. It worried me. His reputation showed he was a cruel man, or else he was a man who made no compromise with his enemies. He knew Rome would win and he annihilated any opposition in the same way opposing forces would have exacted revenge upon him and his people. He may have been an educated man, but I thought him an educated killer like all the high-ranking Romans.

We realised the peace and tranquillity we once enjoyed were about to come apart at the seams and we posted small groups of lookouts on the approaching roads far beyond the borders of our own country. We needed the intelligence early, to gather our forces. We stored up great quantities of grain and salted meat in the town and we did our best to renew the defences.

'You should send an emissary,' Chlotsuintha said one day.

We sat in the Great Hall. The oak tree I had incorporated in one end of it had grown a little and the roof was now under threat. So much for the skills of Germanic engineering. I listened to the drip of rainwater as it trickled along the oak and dropped to the dais beneath. It irritated me.

'I don't think the Romans will listen to any words I might send,' I said.

'Galdir, it is usual to send emissaries before great battles. It has always been so.'

'What for?'

'You may learn about your enemy. Your father would have sent one.'

'And who,' I said, 'should I send? I need all the kings.

Anyway, there are few enough men in my court I can trust. Since that business with Clotildis I have become cautious.'

'Send Stator. He is old, he is not threatening to them, and he speaks good Latin. Besides he used to trade with the Romans and he knows their ways.'

'And just what is he supposed to say to them? Please don't attack us? It's laughable.'

'He could say something like that, but I would think that if he is accompanied by Frija, she will be able to learn more in one day than a thousand Stators. She sees everything.'

'Maybe I should just send a spy. Someone who can gain access and find out what they intend to do.'

'No, Galdir, listen to me. Talk first. There is always some chance of peace but at least we can find out what they intend.'

'I will consider your suggestion.'

I should have known she would have her way in the end. Chlotsuintha always did.

I did send Stator and Frija with a guard of ten of my household troops. I also sent a present to the Roman general out of politeness. It was a brooch, cunningly made, which flipped open and could be used to contain a lock of hair or something of that nature. It had never been used, for we Germans are superstitious about such things and fear our hair could be used to weave magic spells around us. It was not what a German would ever have given to another German as a gift. That would have been like sending poison. I felt it was a good gift to a Roman.

As spring moved on to summer I heard about the Roman army long before Stator returned. An outlying watcher came back from one of our south-easterly lookout posts. He came to me as soon as he arrived.

'Well, Fredgund, what news have you for me?' I asked.

'There is a great Roman army coming this way Lord.'

Fredgund was not as his name of peace-spear might have suggested him to be. There was nothing peaceful about him at all. He was a big man and had a scarred, serious face and a temper known among us all to be best placated.

'How great is this army?'

'I cannot count them for they are too many. They are as many as the ears of corn in a field, and they come with great engines of war on wagons.'

'Fredgund, how many wagons did you count?'

I knew each legion would have about twenty wagons for their tents and corn and a few more for the ballistae and onagers, maybe forty wagons per legion. I did not expect Fredgund to be able to count thousands, for we Germans, would be stretching our mathematical ability too far.

He held up both hands.

'This number twenty times, Lord'

I presumed this would indicate about four legions with auxiliary cavalry.

'Where did you see them?'

'I have taken five days to ride here. At the pace which they travel, it would take them ten or more days to come within sight.'

'Well done Fredgund. You may go and get some food now.'

Fredgund made his way to the kitchens. I arranged for a meeting of the council. I had to send for Eudes, since he lived in another newly built town, a day's ride from where my hall was. When he arrived the next morning, I felt we needed to lay our plans in more detail. We had lost a day.

'No news from Stator?' Eudes said.

'No, not yet. It's very odd. He should have returned long ago. I can only assume he is held prisoner or dead.'

'A pity. How many men have they?'

'Maybe four legions. That means they have at least forty thousand, if you count their cavalry and auxiliaries.'

'We can muster maybe that many, but it will include boys and some women. Did you know many of the women claim the right to fight if there is a battle?'

'Yes, I heard. They intend to stand behind their men and chant and throw axes. I can't see the Romans running away from women's tongues, can you?'

'Have you met my wife?'

'No, Eudes.'

'If you had,' he smiled, 'then you would not question what they can do with their tongues.'

We both laughed at that and then went about the business of checking to be certain all our messages had been sent to outlying towns and villages. It was my intention to muster all my army in and behind the town, where I had built fortifications. In the bend of the river, there was a huge unassailable area. The river bordered three sides of it, and the fourth was the wall at the back of the town. We could put the army there in tents and I knew I could defend the place for a long time. We had prepared well.

'Eudes, I plan to go out to meet these Romans. If I talk to them, I can discover what they want. Maybe there is a peaceful way to deal with them without giving up our freedom.'

'Galdir, you sound like your father. He tried to reason with those wolves. He was destroyed.'

'Perhaps so. I intend only to talk with a soft and reasonable voice but carry a firebrand in my hand.'

'I do not trust them. They have played us false so many times in our history. You make peace with one army and another takes its place a few years later and wages war if they think they can gain profit. We should fight.'

'We will without doubt fight the Romans, but I need to see their army close up first. It is wise to know one's opposition; they may have weaknesses we are unaware of.'

'With Stator gone, who will you take with you?'

'I will take Lazygis, and half the Sarmatian cavalry. We should also take about five hundred of our mounted men. If it comes to a fight, I intend to hit hard and get away quickly. They have only light cavalry. They are no match for us on horseback.'

'I thought you were going to talk, not fight.'

'It depends upon many things. The simplest way to see it is that if they continue into our lands and want a fight, then we give them one. If they refuse to go, then I will use the men I take now to wreck their supply lines. They are a long way from home this far north and a big army like theirs is a hungry beast. If we hit their supplies, we can delay them. Any delay will suit our side.'

'I don't think they will be so stupid as to leave their supplies unguarded.'

'What do you think I want so many men with me for? To parley? Have our people destroyed all the crops and grain between us and the Romans?'

'Yes, and they have taken with them what supplies they can, leaving nothing behind.'

'Exactly. The Romans will depend on the supplies they bring with them and a supply line stretching south. If we hit that, they may not be able to last out a long siege.'

'Galdir, it is a good plan, but it does not need a Warlord

to carry it out. You are needed here.'

'Don't question me. If I stay here, I will go mad. I need to be out and I haven't had a fight for two years. Do you know what it does to a man?'

'Do you think I am a stranger to that? I have fought more battles and skirmishes than you have had women!'

'Rather more I am afraid,' I said in truth. 'No more arguments! I will leave in the morning as soon as Lazygis arrives.'

*

On the second day after I received the news of the approaching army, I set off from Sicambra for so I had named the capital of my realm. It was a name derived from Sicambri. The Sicambri were the tribe originally forming the basis of the Franks and it was in their honour I named our main town. I can hardly call it a capital.

There were almost a thousand warriors. They were all mounted and all armed to the teeth. The Sarmatian heavy cavalry rode at the front, flanked by our riders. I loved them. They were strong men, with a positive attitude, and all of them battle-hardened veterans of the wars we once fought beside the Marcomannii and their alliance. It seemed to me now to have been an age ago. Lazygis and I rode side-by-side at the head of our war band.

It took four days of riding before we saw the first of the Romans. They were a group of light cavalry. No doubt they were a piquet sent out ahead to spot any enemies. As soon as they saw us, they turned and galloped away. My men jeered and called them many names until I told them to be quiet. I had to explain we were there to talk and not to fight in the first instance. I doubt if they understood however and the Sarmatians were sullen and quiet at the news.

'Why are your men so reserved, Lazygis?' I asked as we rode along.

'It is because they have blood scores to settle with the Romans and they want to fight and die. Many have lost as I have, and they pray every day to Ma for vengeance. It is the way of my people to never forget a wrong.'

'You can reassure them they will kill Romans in plenty once the real battle starts. For now, we talk. Then we ride south.'

We camped on a small plain flanked by woods with a shallow stream trickling across it. The stream was useless as a barrier since even a child could wade through it, but it was a source of water and made a natural barrier of sorts if the Romans attacked.

I had difficulty sleeping. It was not the discomfort of sleeping on the ground, but bad dreams pursuing me. I had the one where Livia turned into Clotildis but there was no stomach pain. Maybe it was my mind trying to warn me. I had another dream of a woman in a Roman gown, with beautiful green eyes and rounded hips. I awoke during the night and could not get to sleep again.

I sat and looked at the sky. It was high summer and the stars shone clear and bright above me. The moon was a gay smiling crescent above and its light made the trickling water seem silvery. Above the moon was a star. It shone, bright and clear and I realised I had never seen this combination of star and moon. I took it as an omen. To me it meant we would win through.

Lazygis snored in his sleep nearby and I realised how hard a man he was. With all he had been through he managed to keep a semblance of that old pride for which I had always remembered him. He did not intend to give in until he had avenged himself upon the Romans. I shared his feelings. The slavery I endured during my early life had been enough to teach me to hate the Romans and if I could have, I would have killed them all to a man and not parleyed a single word. That I wanted to talk to them at all seemed strange. It must have been some sort of mantle of responsibility I had acquired now that I was a leader instead of a follower.

I watched the dawn as it shed its light across the little plain. The grass threw long shadows as the sun began to peep, pink and mauve, upon the horizon. I heard the birds then. They seemed almost to surround us as they trilled their melodies to herald the new day. It was a new day to them which they did not measure by death and battle. For them it was just another day. The dew made the ground-spiders webs shine like silver plates all around us and as the men began to stir I wondered what the day would bring.

We ate and were packing up our belongings when one of the Sarmatians pointed to a small group of riders approaching across the grassland.

Lazygis and I stood and watched as their shapes became clearer and I recognised Stator. There was no difficulty identifying him for he dwarfed the horse he straddled, his feet almost touching the ground. There were three riders with him. I could not see Frija and wondered what was going on.

They dismounted on the far side of the stream and I noticed Stator had manacles on his wrists and one of his captors held a knife at his throat. I felt rage rising within me but for once I managed to put it away. One of the Romans approached.

'Who can I deal with in this shit-faced rabble?' he said.

I recognised him for an officer; he had a tall horsehair

plume and he carried no shield. His red cloak flowed behind him as he walked through the stream; its hem was dark, wetted by the icy cold water. He frowned.

'I am Galdir,' I said, 'I am leader of the Franks. I wish to talk with your commander.'

'You would do well to use a more humble tone, Barbarian. We come with four legions and we will fight for this land. We know you harbour Sarmatian rebels and if you do not give them up we will attack you.'

'Is this how the great Romans address their enemies? Do you have no wish for peace?'

I said this with a very clear and polite accent. It seemed to dawn on the officer that my Latin was good.

'Does everyone here speak such tolerable Latin? Have you all been traders with us?'

'No. Only Stator and I speak Latin here. I see you have made him prisoner. Is this how you treat emissaries? He came in peace and you have betrayed that time-honoured law.'

'Don't talk to me about laws. You rebels have no laws.'

'All the same I want my man back. He came to you in peace and you have chained him like a common criminal.'

'He's worth nothing to us. You can have him back for all I care.'

He turned and indicated they should release Stator. They pushed him, still in his manacles, and he stumbled into the stream, where he fell. Two of my soldiers ran forward and picked him up and he shook them off violently. He was not a man who accepted help readily.

'Who is your commander?' I said.

The Roman looked me in the eye and said, 'The Legate Marcus Licinius Piso, and he won't want to speak with you.

He has been sent by the Emperor himself to subdue this land and that is what he will do.'

'Perhaps you should return and ask him if he would like peace. I also want the girl who came with my emissary. She is close kin and I would not like any harm to come to her. Clearly I cannot trust in the honour of you Romans.'

'You talk of honour. You Germans have no honour. We have fought you already and you are nothing in our eyes but Barbarian scum. We will crush you. As for the girl, I'll see what the General says.'

'I will wait here with my men for two hours but after that I will seek recompense in blood. Do not trifle with me.'

He looked over his shoulder at me as he walked to his horse and I realised he was grinning. It may have been his scorn making me do it.

I shouted after him, 'If you don't give me back my cousin I will take some of your women hostage in return.'

It was a weak and silly thing to say. I regretted it as soon as I said it, for he knew as well as I did it was an empty threat. There were no women around for me to take prisoner. The Romans seemed to be holding all the dice. If we sat and waited, they could ignore us. They could even kill or rape Frija. There was no time to waste but it seemed I could do nothing to the Roman legions as they approached our capital.

I decided our original plan to harry their supply lines would be a way to demonstrate to them we were not toothless. I needed to get Frija back, but had no lever to spring on the Romans, political or military. I mulled it over in my head as we waited. I was determined to make them regret their dishonourable behaviour and I knew we could do it, but at what cost I could not tell.

We waited for what we thought was about two hours and the Romans ignored us. I learned from Stator that the general in charge of the army was Licinius Piso. I wondered if he was the same Licinius Piso whose father I had killed when I was a slave, but it seemed unlikely. Why would such a rich man become a soldier?

If it was the Piso I knew would he know who I was? It had to be impossible. I could imagine he would hate Germans, but all Germans? It seemed unlikely.

They say you should know your enemy and Chlotsuintha had insisted I would learn more of them by trying to parley. The name of the commander seemed to pose more questions than answers to me. His family had not enslaved me; they had bought me after the event. If it had not been a Piso, it would have been someone else. They did not treat me any worse than any other slave in their household. Beatings and whipping were the norm after all, and in retrospect, I wondered if my killing the Praetor had perhaps been an excessive response to my situation. I recalled the little girl's screams however, and my uncertainty disappeared. I knew I had been right even if I had done it in a temper.

At least I had Stator back. I could not understand why they had held Frija. It made no sense. She would only seem like an ordinary girl to them. I hoped they did not abuse her. I was content to wait and see. Vengeance would be mine if they had hurt her. I would do anything to get even if they had.

CHAPTER XV

*"Since love grows within you, so beauty grows.
For love is the beauty of the soul."*

— St. Augustine

They had not tortured Stator, merely held him prisoner to stop him from going ahead and warning us of the approaching army. Frija had disappeared as soon as they entered the Roman camp and Stator had no knowledge of her whereabouts at all. He had not seen her since.

My guess at their numbers seemed to be correct for Stator had counted four eagles. At least we had confirmed their numbers, but achieved little else. I explained my plan to Stator.

'If we head south and attack their supply routes there is no guarantee we will ever be able to get back into Sicambra. They may cut us off,' Stator said.

'There is always that risk but we need to disable them somehow. It won't be possible to attack an army of forty thousand men with only one thousand mounted soldiers.'

'True, but maybe we should return home and wait.'

'Stator, I'm sorry. That has already been decided. You will return home. I need someone who can organise the defences. Eudes is a strong man but he is old and I need you to go.'

'I was left behind by your father to guard you all those years ago. That oath is still upon my shoulders. Do not send me away.'

I looked at Stator. He was serious and there was little else I could say to him to persuade him. He stayed with us and in the end, I did not regret it.

We mounted up and rode south. The land sloped upwards and we came upon forested slopes hiding us from the Roman army. Our aim was to skirt them and come up from the south to harass their baggage train.

We had ridden most of the day and it was late afternoon, when we saw their vanguard. I was surprised the Romans in their arrogance had not sent mounted auxiliaries to follow us. We were a small band, but we were the cream of our warriors. There was not a man there who had not fought the Romans before and many had been victorious before and after Aquileia.

We sat on our mounts at the edge of a wood looking down at a broken gulley, transected by a shallow stream. The Roman wagons were moving slowly in the stream bed in the absence of any road or track. Several hundred cavalry flanked them and there were at least five hundred infantry with them, half of them auxiliaries.

The auxiliaries were not important; they were light infantry and their morale would not be good. The Romans would have imported them from other parts of the empire and they were only fighting for Rome because their own lands had been conquered.

The three centuries of Infantry were the ones that mattered. There was one in front, one behind and one split in two, marching either side of the supplies.

We attacked with terrible speed. Unfortunately, one cannot stop Barbarians from doing just that. The Sarmatian cavalry went in first. They charged directly at the century in front of the wagons. We had four hundred cavalry and they had only eighty men at the front. By the time the rear and flanking infantry could respond, it had become a slaughter. I saw Lazygis let fly an arrow that penetrated a legionary's chest. He hacked with his sword. Another man fell. A man raised his shield and the Sarmatian pulled his reins taught. The horse responded. He had trained his mount for this. Its hooves came down with such force they crushed the soldier beneath his shield and the beast trampled upon him as a man might crush an insect with his heel. Blood oozed onto the ground from beneath the futile wooden protection, so useless to its owner. The Roman cavalry were riding towards the fight and we hit them then riding fast from the forest. Lazygis fared well while we destroyed the Roman cavalry.

He withdrew his men and loosed a volley of arrows. It depleted the Roman ranks and their auxiliaries were routed, seeking protection from the woods either side. The Sarmatians followed up by killing the fleeing auxiliaries to a man. Their swords flashed bright in the setting sun's rays and blood dripped and spattered as only it can in battle. My heart leapt, for it was a beautiful sight such as only a warrior could appreciate.

When a soldier runs, his back is exposed and he cannot use his weapons. Mounted cavalry can thus ride among them and commit slaughter; like a dog in a rabbit warren. We were left facing only about fifty men who surrounded one of the high sided and covered wagons.

Our approach was slow and we formed a line. The Sarmatians drew up on the other side. They charged and the Roman circle broke. We killed every one without remorse. We offered no quarter. Lazygis would not have allowed us to take prisoners unless they were for torture and I would not allow this. It is not in my nature. I am no Marcomanni and although I hated the Romans, I could never emulate my crueller cousins in other tribes.

I rode down to the wagons where my men were beginning to burn the Roman supplies. I heard a scream. It was a woman's voice and it seemed out of place. It came from behind a wagon. Two of my men had hold of a woman. As I watched, they had dragged her down onto the ground and one lay across her as the other began to lower himself onto her with his tunic lifted. The white of his bare buttocks was a ridiculous sight in the wreckage of the Roman convoy. It brought to mind a scene from my past. It was as if I could see and hear my Livia in that moment. I saw her struggling beneath the brigands and it kindled anger and disgust.

The woman struggled and screamed. Surprised, I noticed a knife flash in her hand. The man laid on top of her clutched his arm and rolled away and the would-be rapist paused as the woman held the knife at his throat.

As I approached, the knife flashed again and my man grabbed the hand wielding it. The woman's left, clenched fist struck him on the temple and he rolled over to his left, still holding the woman's wrist.

I dismounted and took the knife from the woman. I kicked my warrior away.

'No rape. I don't mind what you do to the soldiers, but leave any woman you find alone! Hear me?'

Both my men stared at me with a look of complete incomprehension at first, but it was soon replaced with clear and mounting anger. They must have thought I was mad.

'Warlord. You cannot by any right, stop us from taking her. We claim this right by law. You know this.'

'Yes Fredsein,' I said.' But I can kill you if you do not

obey me. Do you doubt that I will?'

'Warlord, we will not obey, we cannot. You are too soft to lead men such as us.'

I drew my sword. They had their weapons in their hands too and both approached me. The wounded man had blood running down his left arm, but he held his sword steady in his right.

I had not expected to be fighting my own men but sadly it is common for German warriors to fight over the spoils of war. They approached slowly. All around, I could hear the sounds of men dying, as my men finished off the wounded Romans. There were also the sounds of them ransacking wagons and horses whinnying. I realised the woman was crawling away under the wagon. I thought she would be safe there. There was a smell of burning, rank in my nostrils.

I attacked. Fredsein was a tall man. The look on his scarred face seemed to express more confidence than I expected. He ran straight at me. He raised his sword above his head. He brought it down with a hard vertical stroke. I parried. I stepped back. I felt reluctant to kill him but had little choice.

He kept swinging his blade. He turned full circle. His blade flew out at my neck. I ducked. I stepped forward onto my left foot. I twisted as my blade shot forward and up, accurate and straight. He seemed surprised when my blade entered his throat. The tip of my sword went through and through. It projected for a moment by inches through the back of his neck. Fredsein's sword fell from nerveless fingers for he died in an instant. It was not even a quick move and certainly not one to celebrate. I had to tug the blade hard as I pulled it from his spine, but it did not stick.

The second man, whose name I did not know was more

cautious. He seemed to have a look of doubt on his face.

'Do you really want to die here and now? For a Roman woman who would not have given more than very temporary pleasure? Leave it alone and I will let you live!'

The blade in his hand faltered and he replaced it at his belt. He knelt.

'I apologise, Warlord. It was all in the heat of the moment. A lust was upon me. I am your loyal soldier.'

He turned and walked away looking for other spoils. I looked down at Fredein's body. It was a meaningless way to die, killed at the hands of his own leader for disobeying an order. I had lost a good man and it irritated me. Why had he not backed off? Had I not given him enough time? He had attacked me after all. Perhaps he had translated his sexual excitement into blood lust. I could not tell. It left me wondering, as I wiped the blood from my sword on his cloak, what I had risked my life to save. I had no doubt it was some plump Roman matron, for I had not seen her with clarity.

I looked under the wagon. She looked back at me with steel in her eyes. She did not attempt to crawl out, so I just stood and looked at her for a moment or two. There was nothing plump or matronly about her.

'If you stay under the wagon my men will burn it and you will roast. Not a very good end for a Roman woman, is it?' I said in Latin.

'You speak Latin?'

'Well are you coming out or roasting?' I said smiling.

She emerged from her protection and stood facing me. She was my age and betrayed startling good looks, despite being somewhat bedraggled. She had striking green eyes, cold as winter, but she did not seem humourless for the little horizontal creases at the sides of her eyes showed she laughed frequently. Her black hair was loose around her shoulders and her body a matter of conjecture, for she had loose-fitting clothes suitable for travelling. I recognised those eyes. I had seen them in a dream.

'I am Galdir. I am the Warlord of the Franks.'

I bowed pleasantly.

She looked at me as if I was a worm. There was no hint of fear or concern in her expression.

'If indeed you treat women prisoners properly as you say you do, then you will let me go,' was all she said. I noticed she was looking at the ground.

'This is yours,' I said proffering her knife, which I still held in my left hand.

'Thank you,' she said, secreting the little blade in her gown, I know not where.

'We will release you when we have reached a safe distance from your army.'

I noticed she was wearing a necklet. On closer inspection, it seemed to be the same one I had sent as a gift to the Roman commander.

'Where did you get that?' I said pointing to her chest.

'It was a gift from my husband. I believe it is of German workmanship.'

'It is certainly not of German origin. I sent it as a gift to the commander of the Roman army, but why I should have bothered escapes me, for he held my emissary prisoner and still detains a woman, a cousin of mine,' I said frowning.

'I'm sorry I did not know. Do you want it back?'

'Of course not. Besides, we Germans do not wear such things. What is the name of your husband?'

'Marcus Licinius Piso. He is legate of the Second Legion and has been sent by Marcus Aurelius, to subdue the German uprising in this part of Gaul.'

'I wasn't aware there was an uprising. We are only defending our homes.'

'This land belongs to Rome; we conquered it a hundred years ago.'

'True, but that was a hundred years ago. Rome has shown no interest in it since and we have moved because we needed better land for farming. We are peaceful and don't want to fight your husband's army.'

She smiled then. 'I do not think attacking our wagons is a particularly peaceful act. Do you?'

'It was solely in response to your husband's refusal to talk and his holding my cousin hostage. It is not honourable to take emissaries hostage, even in Rome this is so.'

'You seem to know a lot about Rome.'

'Yes, I grew up there. My name is Galdir and the Roman name they gave me is but a bad memory.'

'What did they call you?'

'I was Cornelius to the Romans. My father was a trader,' the lie tripped from my tongue as easily as riding a horse.

'What will you do with me? Can you not let me go?'

'I'm sorry but you will have to ride with us until we are well clear of the Roman army. I will see to it you are as comfortable as we can make you under the circumstances. If you give me your word not to escape I will not tie you up.'

'I will give you my word, as long as I am not threatened in any way. Can I trust you to protect me from your men?'

'I killed a man to protect you, is that not enough?'

I frowned as I spoke and she said, 'Yes, I'm sorry, I did not mean to offend.'

We left the smouldering wagons after making sure the Romans could not use or salvage any of the supplies, and rode east. My intention was to turn north again if there was no pursuit. I puzzled over what to do with the woman. She told me her name was Lucia Claudia Piso. I thought she seemed haughty and arrogant. That I had to return her to her husband was never in doubt but I did not intend to do it soon. I was having too much fun making him sweat over her absence.

We captured a survivor of our attack on the baggage train so I sent him with a written message to Piso indicating that if he let Frija go I would consider releasing his wife. If he refused, I would release her one piece at a time. Of course, there was no danger of that but Piso could hardly count on it.

We rode until dusk and then made camp on a flat-topped hill where we could see any approaching troops. Although our campfires were visible from below, our view of the surrounding valleys and forests was such that we could escape fast if anyone launched an attack.

I sat by the fire with Lucia beside me. We had rigged a makeshift shelter out of wood and loose branches. My men had complained endlessly at having to drag the materials up to the hilltop. It had been put together with the epitome of German engineering skill by which I mean it fell down if there was a gust of wind and had to be resurrected between some tall rocks. Happily, the night was still enough for it to remain upright.

Lucia and I talked of Rome. I told her I disliked the place and why. She seemed surprised.

'But Rome is a wonderful place. It is full of life,' she said.

'So is an anthill, but that doesn't mean you have to live in one.'

'You really dislike Rome then?'

'I do not have pleasant memories of my time there. I spent most of my time in the Subura and there is nothing there but overcrowding, poverty, and nasty smells.'

'But Rome is so much more than just the Subura. The Forum Romanum for example. It's a hive of activity and socialising. Even if you don't like that, for a young man there is the Campus Martius where the troops train and races and sport are practised.'

'I was never allowed to do those things.'

'Rome is also the religious and intellectual capital of the known world.'

'You have the wrong gods for me to worship there!'

'What did you do in Rome?'

'Not much.'

I felt it was silly to tell her I had been a slave there since she might make the connection with the death of her father-in-law.

'My father was a trader and so I saw little of Rome apart from the Subura.'

'But you speak very good quality Latin for a German trader's son who grew up in the worst part of the city,' she said and her green eyes searched mine.

'My father was fanatical about spoken languages and even now I have managed to keep his hobby alive, though he is long dead,' I lied.

'Did you never go to the chariot races or the arena when you were there?'

'Yes a few times. I had to go with my mast... I mean my father. The races were good but I always thought it was a cruel way to treat such beautiful horses. Many of them broke legs and some were badly hurt just for the pleasure of the crowd.'

'You're a strange man for a Barbarian. You speak good quality Latin and you feel sorry for animals. Do you feel equally sorry for people then?'

She was mocking me and I knew it.

'Only when they can't fight back. I believe a man has a duty to defend the weak. Your people killed my mother when I was a child and I have never forgotten it. Your soldiers did that. It is why I would never allow a woman to be harmed if it is within my power to prevent it.'

'You should not look down on women like that. I don't need your protection. What makes you think we women are so weak and powerless? Some of us are stronger than men. Maybe not here.' She pointed to my upper arm, 'but here,' she said pointing to her forehead. Her eyes flashed and I thought she looked like a cat, for there was something feral in the depths of them. Perhaps not a cat, but some feline creature all the same.

We talked more until it became late and I discovered she was fun. She made me laugh. I had not had so much simple fun talking to anyone, since those early days with Clotildis.

'It is late and we have an early start in the morning,' I said. 'I will walk you to your bower.'

We stood and then I walked with her, still talking, the few yards away from the embers of the fire. It was not cold but she shivered. I involuntarily put an arm around her shoulder. She did not reject it and I wondered what was happening to me. I was the Warlord. I was her husband's enemy. The fact there was an attraction between us confused me. It was hard to shake off.

At the shelter, she turned and stood close. She looked up at my face, lips parted, head tilted slightly back. It was an invitation I was powerless to refuse. I reached down and took her in my arms. Our lips met. I had not kissed anyone since Clotildis and the feeling was like touching the Gods. My heart beat faster. I looked at her. We caressed each other and I saw she was smiling. I still do not know if it was a smile of mischief or of pleasure.

We made love; she was passionate, forceful, and almost aggressive. She seemed hungry for it as if she was taking, absorbing from me, and loving it. I remember her nails scraping my back as I thrust into her. Her gentle murmurs as we made love, her teeth biting on my shoulder, all drove me to heights of pleasure I had never imagined possible. She was no weak or dainty girl; this was a woman who knew her mind. I think she enslaved me. I began to wonder who was the prisoner now, who the slave?

Chlotsuintha's warnings reverberated in my mind. I knew what she would say, but I ignored her voice in my head. I owed no debt of honour to the Roman Legate and my attraction for this woman fostered no guilt in me. There could be no serious consequences of this sally into romance and Gods know, I needed it. Clotildis had hurt me deeply and I had lost Livia and Medana so now I sought to assuage my torn and ravaged heart with this Lucia. I have always deceived myself over such encounters but it was always an enjoyable weakness. Perhaps all weakness is such.

Afterwards we lay breathless next to each other in the warm night air, with the silent sleepers all around. It was as if we had taken something illicit or forbidden and it seemed to excite us both. I wanted her again but she pushed me away. It was as if my being in control of her destiny gave her the right to choose mine. I could not persuade her and I realised I was happy to obey.

'How long before you must take me back?' she whispered, her hand toying with the hairs on my chest.

I looked at her. There was humour in her eyes as she spoke. There was no sign of fear or concern. I smiled too and spoke softly.

'I suppose there is no great hurry. Your husband is bound to start his war soon, but until then I can spend some time harassing his troops with my men and there would be no need to return you to him. Besides, you are my hostage.'

'I am in your power. Am I a lover now or a hostage?'

'I want him to return the girl who came with my emissary. She is important.'

'Is she your lover?'

'No, nothing like that. She has an important destiny in our tribe and cannot be replaced.'

'Do you have a woman?'

'No. Only you!' I smiled again and kissed her. This time she allowed my advances and we made love once more. We held each other after that until dawn, when I returned to my blanket by the dead fire. I did not want my men to know what had happened.

Stator sat up and smiled in the dawn light.

'My lips are sealed,' he said raising one finger to his lips still smiling. He lay down and turned over.

So much for secrets.

CHAPTER XVI

"What makes men indifferent to their wives is that they can see them when they please."

— Ovid

Lucia! I speak her name and it stirs me like no other. I will never meet another like her. In the days following the burning of the wagons, it was as if she had become one of us. She rode next to me and I soon discovered she was an accomplished rider. She stayed watching the skirmishes from a distance as we harassed the Romans and killed their cavalry and auxiliaries. We were never foolish enough to attack any large bodies of infantry since they were the real core of the Roman forces.

We followed their army and attacked whenever any of them fell behind or were left to attract us. The heavy Sarmatian cavalry were a boon. They could attack infantry or cavalry. They could harass light troops with their arrows and break an infantry line with the ease a scythe cutting corn. I started riding with them on the attacks. My skill as a horseback archer was developing well too, according to Lazygis. He was always at my side in the battles and I took comfort from that. Stator, despite his age, kept up with the Sarmatians but there was little he could do apart from watch my back, for his horse was not armoured like that of the northerners.

We were camped on a hill when the messenger came. It was a Numidian rider. The Romans had a small group of Numidian horse-mounted javelin men with them but they were lightly armoured and could do nothing against our heavy cavalry.

The rider dismounted fifty paces from our camp and stood still waiting for a response. Lazygis and I approached with the proud demeanour I had learned from my German people.

'Who are you?' I said in Latin.

The rider looked at me. I had seen many such men in Rome but Lazygis stared at him in wonder. He had never seen a black-skinned man and he frowned as he looked at the messenger.

'Lord, I am Arcas. I am from a far off land and I ride with the army of Rome.'

'Well?'

'I have a message from Marcus Licinius Piso, illustrious leader of the forces of the Emperor Marcus Aurelius. The message is to one Galdir, the leader of the Germanic forces.'

'I am he,' I said.

'The message is this: "In exchange for my wife I offer the Germanic woman Frija. If my wife has been harmed, the woman will be crucified before the walls of your nameless town."'

'Tell Marcus Licinius Piso I have heard his demands and need time to consider. I will agree to the cessation of hostilities for one week and will then give my answer. I would ask you to return then to this place with the hostage Frija and the exchange can take place providing the General comes unaccompanied and I meet him with my hostage, unaccompanied also.'

396

'I will take this message,' the Numidian said.

'When he comes, tell him to go to that hill,' I pointed to a small hillock on the far side of the river in the vale below, 'and I will come to him with his wife.'

As the messenger rode away, I felt a strange regret. It would be the end of my relationship with Lucia. In such a short time, I had become more attached than I would have cared to admit.

We were sleeping together every night and my men knew it. I suspect they joked about it behind my back. They regarded it as a natural consequence of capturing such a woman. I was the Warlord after all and could do as I pleased. There was no one who could gainsay me. What they did not realise was that she was willing and it was I who felt the emotional pangs not she.

I knew she liked me. I had no illusions she was in love. It was not her nature to love in that way. I was perhaps a diversion. A physical distraction from the clear and present dangers of her predicament. Perhaps I felt love for her because of the recent loss of Clotildis and I was transferring my emotion. How this sat with my detestation of Rome was an enigma to me. I hated the Romans for what they had done to my family and me, yet Lucia was irresistible.

Chlotsuintha would have explained it by invoking my weakness and my lust but there was more to it than that. I found Lucia's company truly amusing. We talked and laughed and it took away the emotional pain I always carried deep within me. We were lovers and friends.

For her part, she seemed resigned for our situation to change and for her to return to her husband. We talked little about him but she did tell me there had never been much between them. His main interest was his political aspiration and hers was simply to enjoy the life her Gods had given her. I think I was only a rough amusement and a temporary distraction. That it kept her safe in a dangerous predicament had not escaped me either but I wanted her to feel secure. I would never have tolerated anyone abusing her even if we were not lovers.

We remained camped in that place. The hill looked down upon a valley cut by a river, with a hill opposite whose grassy slopes had dense bushes either side. There was a ford between the two hills but it was narrow, which was why I picked the spot. If the Romans came in force, the river would delay them and we could easily escape, since we all had mounts.

I spent the days of that week enjoying Lucia's company and at night, I enjoyed her body. Making love to her was unlike lovemaking with anyone previously in my life. She was forceful and demanding, but I loved that in her. It was almost as if I had a need for her to lead me. I think such a woman would be hard to live with for a Barbarian like me. She could have made me do anything with her force of opinion and strength of personality.

By the end of that week I wished anything would happen to delay the exchange. The thought of losing Lucia when I had only known her for such a short time ate away at me. I was tempted to simply abandon Frija and take Lucia with me to Sicambra but I knew it would never work. She was not a woman whom anyone could persuade to anything she did not want and besides there was a Roman army to face too. My people needed me and I could not desert them for a sexual fantasy.

My responsibility to my people won through in the end and I became resigned to losing this wonderful woman for the sake of my people. Losing is perhaps the wrong description for I think I never truly had her. It was she who possessed me.

The night before the exchange, we made love all night and neither of us slept. By morning, I was in a quiet and unhappy mood. We dressed in silence for there was little to say. Our little romance had ended and I was as powerless to change these events as I had been in their nascence or their evolution.

Piso did indeed come alone. He rode a beautiful white stallion and led Frija, bound, on foot behind him. When I was sure there were no troops with him I was tempted to capture him and take Frija back, but the obvious dishonour of such actions prevented me. I was tempted all the same.

Lucia and I rode down to the river and forded the cold grey waters. We climbed the slopes of the far hill but I had a feeling this would not be the last time I would see her.

As we climbed the hill, she turned and smiled. She simply mouthed, 'thank you', and rode on. When I arrived at the summit I saw she had dismounted and was in his arms. I felt like killing him but knew it was only a fleeting anger.

'You the leader of these brigands?' Piso said, looking scornfully at me.

'I am Galdir, Warlord of the Franks. There is no need to insult me. We have treated your wife well and you will notice she was not dragged here bound. She was allowed to ride, in contrast to my cousin here.'

Frija appeared unconcerned. She did not look as if she had been mistreated. She smiled when our eyes met and I wondered what she guessed.

'Yes, quite,' the Roman said. 'I am Marcus Licinius Piso. Marcus Aurelius our noble Emperor had charged me with pacifying this part of Gaul.'

He looked at me with a firm expression on his face. He was of a similar age to me and dressed in the armour of a general. He had a handsome face with dark eyes staring into mine in an aggressive way I disliked. He seemed arrogant and churlish.

I dismounted. 'We are here to exchange prisoners, that is all,' I said.

Lucia looked away at the hill where my men were camped. I read nothing in her expression unless it was boredom.

'If you have mistreated my wife…'

'You can see that has not happened. We may be Barbarians but we do not mistreat women prisoners, despite anything you may have heard.'

'Your Latin is good. Where did you learn it?'

'I was in Rome for a while.'

'Then you will know we do not tolerate armed insurgency. The Emperor has instructed me to annex the entire area and send all of you back where you came from. If you refuse you will be defeated and killed.'

'You take much for granted. You do not have enough men to make victory certain. You have no heavy cavalry. My men have fought you before right up to Aquileia. We are not afraid of you.'

'If you prove strong, which I doubt, we have another army from which I can get re-enforcements. You will never defeat the might of Rome.'

'Perhaps we should have peace and then no one will die?'

'Peace! You talk of peace, when you have attacked us continuously for weeks?'

'If I brought a large army into Italia and refused to speak

to you after taking your emissaries hostage, what would the Senate do? Invite us for a dinner party?'

He looked at me and I could see he was trying to control his rage.

'General,' I said, 'we have no wish to fight your army. Leave us alone and all this unpleasantness can be avoided. We have done you no harm as far as I can judge.'

'No harm! No harm! You filthy Barbarian. You Germans have played us false for years and attacked us many times. A Barbarian like you killed my father. Do you really think I will let any of you live? When we sack your towns, we will burn and kill everyone in our path. The strength of Roman justice is formidable.'

I said, 'Roman justice does not exist. There are only narrow-minded imperialist policies aimed at subduing everything that is different and making it Roman. You plunder our lands and think you can rule us with steel. You can't. We have pride in our culture. Germans will gladly die for it as our fathers did before us, because we will never submit to the Roman yoke. We will fight you then, but beware: I am no toothless old dog. Many will die. Do not say I did not give you the opportunity.'

Beyond the Roman on the far slope of the hill, a movement caught my attention. It was treachery. There were at least four squadrons of light cavalry riding as fast as they could up the slope towards us.

I mumbled an oath at Piso and mounted Valknir. Frija mounted behind me, holding onto my waist. He stood smiling at me, holding Lucia behind him with one hand, and the other on his sword. We rode fast as Wuotan's shield-maidens down the slope towards the river. We penetrated the cold, brown, muddy water with a splash and Valknir made short shrift of it. The nearest of the pursuing cavalry was ten yards behind when I turned.

The Sarmatian archers I had hidden in the bushes by the stream launched their first arrows. Those composite bows could fire an arrow so fast it sometimes penetrated armour. The pursuing equites drew up suddenly and several of them fell from their horses, stuck with arrows. The power of those arrows threw them from their dying steeds. They pitched, horse and rider alike, into the river. It became a mass of spraying, whinnying, bleeding mounts and the following horsemen struggled to halt their steeds. It was bloody, splashing chaos.

They reformed on the far side, about four hundred of them. With faces distorted by rage, they renewed their charge. The remaining three hundred Sarmatians flew down the hill. It was a full charge. They looked as formidable as they sounded. The drumming of their hooves was like thunder on that hard ground. I could feel it beneath my feet. I could hear their war shouts. A huge mass of bright steel, black chain mail and brown war-horses.

I left Frija on the horse and she walked it calmly up the hill. She had nerves of steel. I joined the standing Sarmatians who had formed up in a rough square. Some fired bows, others fought on foot with spears. It took only moments for most of the Roman cavalry to cross the river. It was long enough for the Sarmatians to break on them. They drove a wedge into their formation. They cut right through the Romans, up to the river. Then they turned, fighting all the time with spear and sword and blocking the Roman retreat.

We had routed the Romans. They were unfortunate for they could not re-cross the river except at the ford. It was blocked by their dead in any case. They headed to their left, to skirt the hill. Arrows flew and many of them fell, black Sarmatian shafts of death projecting from their backs.

Then half of my remaining men, mounted Franks, met them. I had hidden them in two groups at the far side of the hill. They were ready for just such a Roman betrayal. It was a slaughter.

Trapped between two hundred heavily armoured Franks and the equally heavy Sarmatian cavalry they tried to reform. They achieved some semblance of order but they had no chance. They were between a hammer and an anvil. Barely a handful escaped up the hill. The remainder were dead or dying, squirming in blood and mud by that river with their horses scattered.

Lucia and her husband could see it all. I was glad to show them both we were not amateurs in this business of slaughter and blood. I raised a mocking hand in farewell.

I had to argue with Lazygis to limit the number of heads the Sarmatians took for I did not want to spend too much time there. They made do with a trophy each and they hung the heads from their saddles. Sarmatians take the heads of their slain and make cups of them. I have seen many such cups but never drunk from one. It has never been a habit of the Franks to mutilate their enemies' bodies for we do not like handling the dead. This is the only custom we ever had in common with our Roman enemies.

They had gone when I looked up at the hill. I wondered where Lucia was going and whether she would remain with her husband for the rest of the campaign.

There was much truth in what Piso had said. Defeating one Roman army was nothing; they always came back with more men and fought until they were victorious. There seemed no way out for us. Negotiation was clearly not likely to work and in truth, neither side trusted the other enough now to repeat a parley. My feelings alternated between elation and sadness. I was elated to have won a victory against the Romans, but bitter in the knowledge I had handed back my lover to her husband. I missed her company at my side and I knew I would miss her lovemaking at night.

We decided to ride home to Sicambra. We had now spent three weeks harassing the Romans and there was not much more we could do. We had lost fifty men, half of them Sarmatians. Lazygis however was undaunted by this.

'They have gone to Ma and Pan. They fought well with honour and they died gladly. For many it was simply a matter of joining their ancestors and loved ones.'

'I hope my men too will be with the Gods. We believe when you die with a sword in your hand you go to the halls of the Allfather and there feast with him and fight until the end of the world.'

'It is typical of you Germans to you want to spend all your time fighting each other even after you are dead! I always knew you were mad.'

'It is a pleasant madness all the same, because like you, we never fear falling in battle.'

As we rode on in silence, I thought again of Lucia. A deep regret filled my mind. I had fallen for another married woman and I knew inside me it was not honourable. The difference was, this time, although she was willing I had no illusions she felt anything for me. I guessed that to her I was just a pleasant diversion at a time of discomfort and fear. I missed her already and fool that I am, I thought of her all the way back to Sicambra.

CHAPTER XVII

"Do not yield to misfortunes, but advance more boldly to meet them, as your fortune permits you."

— Virgil

The Romans had made a fortified camp a little more than a mile from our walls. They had not made any attacks and we did not guess their intentions. They were clearly not in any hurry. Time was on their side as long as their supplies were intact. We had destroyed most of the food sources ahead of them as they marched, but they must have had reserves and could easily have sent for more. I sent out groups of riders to disrupt the supply lines but with only limited success.

Much discussion took place but like true Germans, my people were impatient.

'Stator, if we go out and attack their camp we will be destroyed. They have deep trenches around the camp and they are lined up in such a way the path between is staggered. A frontal assault is not possible without great losses we cannot afford,' I said as we sat in the Great Hall. It was a cold and windy evening. The roof was leaking again and what felt like a gale blew around the fire drawing us like moths to the centre of the hall.

'Then how do we get rid of them?' Stator said.

'We have to assemble the army and mount a challenge,'

Eudes said.

'It would look stupid if we stand there and they don't come out and fight,' I said.

'How about setting fire to their fortifications?' Stator said, who clearly knew little of warfare, despite being a formidable fighter.

'No we can't get that close, besides we have too little oil or pitch to burn their stockade with.'

'Then what do we do?' Eudes said.

'Our best way forward is to isolate them. We put forces all around them and whenever they venture out, we attack. A siege of a siege. They will have to come out and attack in the end or run short of supplies.'

'But Galdir, we have been harassing their supply lines for weeks now and they still just sit there waiting for us to attack. I am not sure how long I can restrain my men,' Eudes said.

I stood up and looked down on my friends and advisors. It was aggravating me as much as it irritated them.

'Look, I am the Warlord here or have you forgotten? I know these Romans. They think we are childish and impatient. They only wait for us to attack them in their fortified camp. We will adhere to my plan and if they come out, as they have to in the end, we can fight. Until then we lay siege to them. We need to have sufficient forces in the field surrounding them to give battle to any sizeable force leaving their camp.'

Even Chilperic agreed to the plan and the following day we marched almost half the army and cavalry out of the town to surround the Roman camp.

After two days, the Romans began to form up in their camp and three thousand infantry marched out to give battle. They deployed themselves in front of their fort and their cavalry occupied the flanks but they only used about two hundred on either side. They marched forward towards the town.

The half of my infantry, who were ready, formed up between the Romans and the walls of Sicambra.

The Romans had ballistae and onagers, which slowed their progress and they began firing as soon as we approached. Each bolt from the ballistae skewered all in their path and we began to take casualties. It was terrible to see. The long iron bolts cut swathes through the ranks and we had to order the men to spread out to minimise casualties.

My soldiers were in disarray because they had practised forming up in set patterns and the effect of changing their formations caused a good deal of confusion. My Frankish army split into four. One group at either flank, one in front and the forces that were already deployed either side of the Roman fortifications.

The Sarmatians and other cavalry were on each flank and waited to take out the Roman equites. As the two flanking groups closed on the Romans, who were only a quarter of the total Roman force, our men began shouting their war cries and an occasional individual would run forward sword in hand at their shield wall. These men were undisciplined and died like heroic fools against an unbroken bank of shields and gladii. That it was a meaningless way to die did not matter to them. They went to Wuotan and we hailed them as heroes.

The Roman centuries at the back had turned, so in effect, they formed a square, with artillery in the centre and a solid wall of legionary scuta, their big shields, all around.

I felt nervous about attacking; particularly with three

quarters of the Roman forces still inside the Roman's camp since I thought they could emerge on our rear if I used the surrounding forces to attack the smaller group from the rear.

I had never before commanded large forces like this and found it more difficult to do in practise than in theory.

Our troops took the matter out of my hands. They were so eager and restless they attacked anyway without waiting for the horns to sound which had been our signal to advance. I was furious, since a full scale frontal and flank attack all in one go, might well crush the three thousand Romans, but would leave our men exposed to the troops still in the Roman camp.

At least the cavalry obeyed me. I advanced them on the flanks almost level with the Roman fortifications. Our infantry fared well at first for they outnumbered the Roman legion almost five to one. The lines of legionaries began to buckle under the pressure of our numbers. It was then that disaster almost struck. Predictably, the remaining Romans emerged. Their gates were wide enough to allow whole centuries to emerge at once. They dropped bridgeboards across their trenches and crossed in straight lines. They fell upon our men.

The Franks caught between the first Romans and the newly emerged forces, were now beset on two sides and this went badly for them. Some turned, some did not, but the Roman lines gradually came together and the men between were slaughtered.

There are many frustrations in life but for me, there is none as bad as a plan going wrong on the battlefield. I was unable to communicate with the infantry and they did not withdraw and form up.

I cantered to the right flank and joined Lazygis and his

men. We rode hard and formed up on the flank of the fresh Romans. The other Sarmatians and our Frankish cavalry did the same on the left. As our infantry's numbers began to dwindle we charged both Roman flanks simultaneously.

We rode knee-to-knee with spears ahead straight into the Roman forces, which although they outnumbered us, were facing the Franks in front of them. We hit them hard. My spear became stuck in a Roman shield and I left it. I drew my sword and wielded it to left and right, felling men with each stroke. There was a tumult of shouting, ringing steel and horses whinnying. It was deafening.

Our heavy cavalry broke into the enemy. They could not stand. My men in the centre recovered enough to mount a weak attack to the Romans who had come behind them but it was enough. The Romans furthest forward who had first engaged, had been so reduced in numbers they posed little opposition. We withdrew our cavalry in order to rest the horses for they were blown. The Roman line began to move imperceptibly backwards. They remained in their formations and our men were attacking still, albeit in a disorderly way.

We sounded the horn blasts for withdrawal. The Romans outnumbered our men now as more and more of them poured out of the camp. We made one further cavalry charge but they were ready for us this time and we had much less impact.

We withdrew. It was not a rout. Our cavalry followed at the flanks. When the Romans saw us retreating they surged forward to reap the rewards of their fighting skills. We charged them at the flanks again and this time they slowed down and reformed, having learned some respect for the Sarmatians.

We continued in this way until we reached the gates of

Sicambra and then entered. It reminded me of the Roman retreat at Aquileia, but that time it was the German forces trying to get in and not the Romans.

We now had to endure the expected siege. We took many casualties that day and no doubt the Romans would have greeted the day's events as a victory.

I say it grudgingly but I suppose they won the day. We had not slaughtered them as I had hoped although it seemed likely they now had a little more respect and had discovered we were not the Barbarian hordes they were anticipating.

When night fell they bombarded us with onagers and many houses caught fire. We had prepared for this and we had a system of buckets and ladders ready. We could draw water from the river behind us. In this way, we were able to limit the damage.

A siege is a terrible thing especially for us Germans. We become restless as the monotony of it wears on. We had food and we had water, but we could not leave the town. My men were so under-employed they asked constantly for permission to raid the Roman camp that stood so close to our walls. The Romans could not storm our walls with any ease, because of the ditches but they must have known the only way the town would fall, would be if they assaulted. Their forward camp was much less well protected and as such, vulnerable to night raids with infantry or cavalry.

We still had men outside the town harrying the Roman supply lines and this seemed to be effective for we were better provisioned than the enemy was.

We could see the Romans from the walls. Some of their tactics consisted of trying to wear down our morale. At one point, they used onagers to bombard us with the heads of our dead. It was an ignorant mistake however; although we abhor handling the dead, our priests were glad of the bombardment. It meant they could burn the heads. Since the original owners had died with their swords in their hands, they had gone to Valhalla anyway. Burning the heads was symbolic, releasing their souls on the journey and was in fact the best thing our enemies could have done for us. Instead of expressing dismay, my people greeted the flying heads with cheers to the undoubted consternation of our foes.

Most nights they fired burning missiles, containing pitch or oil in earthenware pots. Occasionally these burst overhead on the Romans and jeers and laughter from our watching guards always accompanied the mishaps. We soaked our thatch every night and as summer wore on towards autumn, it began to rain often, preventing the spread of fire. Our priests said this was because Wuotan was on our side but I suspect it was luck and nothing more.

We knew we could get through the hardships, but the monotony had the greatest effect. I held sword-fighting contests, dancing contests and some of the bards held a rather poorly attended exhibition of spoken storytelling. I did not have juggling. Juggling reminded me of my uncle Odomir so I took it off the menu.

For my part, I whiled away the time thinking of Lucia. I imagined what it would be like to have her by my side. I thought about how it would be to have her in my bed and I dreamed of her at night. For a man of my age, I was thinking like an adolescent.

I think the Romans must have been as bored by the whole business as we were. They launched punitive attacks from time to time. On one occasion, they approached from the river in boats. They did not see the thick, angled, wooden pilings we had placed just beneath the waterline in the summer. The river was fuller now with the autumn rain and the rows of wooden stakes with their fire-hardened tips were a good defence. They lost boats and men and our soldiers had great pleasure in firing arrows at the escaping attackers.

Perhaps it was not the tedium by itself but the restriction of movement. There was a lack of privacy for most. There was nowhere to walk where there was any solitude. The restrictions of space and overcrowding caused fights and dissent. My people were used to their freedom so they reacted poorly being cooped up like this. Germans make poor slaves and worse prisoners for the simple reason they are in tune with nature and relish a ride in the open air, a walk on a mountain or the feeling of the fresh wind in their faces and hair. Without that in their lives, the feeling of confinement is sheer torture for them.

Germanic people do not have the patience besieging others either. Even if the fates had reversed our roles and my people besieged the Romans, it would not have lasted long. Impatience and a dislike of rigidly imposed restrictions of movement always take their toll and I have never known Germans keep up such lack of activity for long.

In the end, none of us could stand the boredom any longer. It happened on a cold morning, in which the sun tried to shine its cold and gloomy rays into the far end of the Great Hall. The branches of my oak tree groaned in the wind and I sat cup in hand on my carved wooden throne. My trusted kings and commanders assembled as had become our habit now, and we gathered, talking and planning. Apart from talking, we ate bread with weevils. Those insects seemed to invade my town with greater eagerness than the Romans at our gates and it was no good being squeamish about eating them.

412

Eudes was the first to speak. He stood up, wiping his mouth with the back of his hand and he looked around the assembled leaders.

'Galdir, we must take the fight to the enemy,' he said. 'We sit here skulking behind our walls like women. No one can come to our aid and I think we should fight them while we have the strength.'

'Eudes, that is exactly what they want,' I said. 'They out-number us after that terrible battle at the beginning of the siege and our men don't have the discipline needed to defeat the enemy in a direct confrontation.'

'We must do something.'

'We can continue with the night raids. This time we will make a big one. We can take all our cavalry. The horses need the exercise. If we do it right, we may even kill enough of the Romans to make an over-all difference to the siege.'

'But you can't mount a cavalry charge in the dark!' Lazygis said.

'Why not?'

'Horses don't like to run fast when they can't see ahead of them. They just won't do it!'

'We don't have to charge until the infantry have set alight to the tents. Then there will be light enough for the horses.'

'You seem to have all the answers tonight,' Chilperic said. 'I would hardly have recognised you as the same man who led us in defeat on the first attack.'

'Chilperic, are you questioning me? Do you wish to fight?'

Chilperic scowled at that for he knew I would kill him. He had always supported Odomir in council and now he was being obstructive. I began to distrust him for he seemed to argue against everything I suggested.

413

In the end, we all agreed we should mount a night raid of sufficient size that all would feel we had accomplished something worthwhile. Morale is, after all, everything in a siege. We laid careful plans and when the meeting broke up we all knew our roles in the forthcoming raid.

We gathered our troops in silence behind our side gates that night. It was about four hours before dawn and a time when soldiers are tired of their sentry duties and most people slept their deepest.

Lazygis had charge of the cavalry and he took them out of the side gates slowly and as noiselessly as possible for the raid had to surprise the Romans who should have been watching those side gates, but no alarm was raised.

We sent a thousand infantry in light armour. They blackened their faces with mud to hide the pallor of their skin. Their job was to fire the Roman tents and cause panic and confusion. If all went according to plan, we would wipe out most of the Roman besiegers who made up almost half of their forces. They had their reserves of troops in the encampment but not close enough to call up reinforcements in time.

I needed a success that night. The previous defeat had not improved my hold over the army and a Warlord needs his men to feel successful or he risks them replacing him. There were many who complained about the entire strategy of resisting the siege and wanted a full-scale attack for good or ill. They felt it was dishonourable to hide behind our walls despite my pointing out it reflected only prudence.

The night was dark and cloudy but no rain fell. Clouds obscured the moon most of the time and I felt optimistic our men could fire the besiegers' camp. I rode with the German cavalry on the left flank and Lazygis with the Sarmatians were on the right. One in ten of the infantry carried earthenware pots with hot coals, which could be used to fire torches when the time came.

Our people are suited to this type of fighting. It did not involve disciplined formations or obedience to complicated manoeuvres just bravery and staunch warrior skills. They emerged from the front gate quickly. In the dark, it would have been difficult for the Roman lookouts to see the gate open the tiny amount necessary to allow our men to spill out silently into our trenches. The wooden spikes were all directed forward but it still required time for the men to negotiate them and the cavalry waited with impatience for the first signs of the fighting.

In the dark, spread out as they were, my foot soldiers must have surprised the unsuspecting Romans. It is unlikely their sentries were sleeping since punishment for that was flogging or death but the darkness enveloped us like a thick cloak spread by the Gods over all our activity. There was a light mist which also proved beneficial. The tension in the cavalrymen spread to the horses; they became restless. I sat on Valknir and calmed him by gently stroking his mane and talking to him in soft tones. He relaxed with no difficulty, but the surrounding horses were more of a problem. I realised we had to attack soon or the noise would carry. We walked our mounts along the Roman's right flank hoping they would not see us in the dark with the trees behind us to break up our silhouettes. If the horses were tense so were the men. I could feel a dryness of my mouth, a quickening of my pulse and my breathing was fast and shallow. I looked at my nearest companions and realised they felt much as I did for even in the dark surrounding us I could feel the tension. I pictured in my mind the white knuckles gripping bridles and the jaws clenched in grim anticipation.

The action started fast. Things often transpire that way in battle. I always have a feeling that no mental preparation is adequate for such action. There was a sudden noise of men shouting to our right. We saw flames in several places. We heard men fighting. There were metallic sounds as swords rang and human sounds too as men screamed. We rode.

We took our horses towards the fires at walking pace. We gradually picked up momentum as the pace increased. My men had thrown down the palisade in places. We were able to enter the camp at speed. What we saw reassured me. The Romans were emerging from their tents. A yellow glow illuminated them for some of the tents were on fire. There were a few of our foot soldiers in small groups fighting with the disorganised Romans in the smoke. Our foes could not form up into their centuries because of the swiftness with which we were attacking. We rode through the camp, killing all who stood before us. We meted out death upon our hated enemies with bloodied swords and spears. Even with success in one's grasp there is no room for complacency in battle. One should never underestimate one's foe. We knew the Romans would re-form and we had anticipated that.

CHAPTER XVIII

"And once sent out, a word takes wing beyond recall."

— Horace

In the centre of the huge camp lay a wide muster field. That was where the Romans drew up in their disciplined ranks, those who still lived that is. They were in difficulties because our men harassed them all the time. Arrows flew from our ranks and the Romans threw their javelins in reply.

Our raiders formed up in front of the growing Roman cohorts. We attacked them at the flanks with cavalry. Lazygis followed suit. In the dark, the Sarmatians must have seemed terrifying to the half-awake Romans. Their dark horses and black clothing made them seem demonic in the light of the burning tents. Men screamed as they died. The smoke wafted odours of burning goods and bodies amid the debris of the broken camp.

There were too few of us to cause a real rout and we had to withdraw. Valknir's hooves made soft splashing sounds as I rode him back towards the walls and I smiled to myself. The after-glow of success seemed to carry us along. It was a delight to have had the better of the enemy in the brief fight. The confusion of the darkness and the suddenness of our attack had been the main reasons for our success. Each horseman picked up a foot soldier and we rode out of the

417

Roman camp with whoops and catcalls. The Romans did not follow: they were too busy putting out our fires.

We re-entered our town through the side gates. We were laughing and feeling happier than for a long time. Our people lined the narrow streets. As we entered, they cheered and shouted. Torches lit our path to the Great Hall and a huge crowd gathered to cheer us in. It had been a fine raid and it warmed all our hearts after the long boredom we had suffered.

We only lost a handful of men that night and they were mostly among the foot soldiers. Their leader was a man called Stigulf. I had chosen him because he possessed more discipline than most of my leaders and I could rely on him to obey my orders. In the event, he followed the plan to the letter and so I rewarded him with gold.

He told me they had no problems killing the Roman guards and pickets in silence. After they gained entrance to the fortifications, they split into four groups, two to tear down the palisade and two to start fires. The groups met up and started killing the emerging soldiers. It sounded as if it had been easy but I was sure it had not been. I assumed the long siege had blunted the normally sharp discipline of the besiegers but they would now be twice as alert and further attacks would have to wait for months.

It only took the Romans a day to repair the damage to the palisade and to renew their onager's attacks at night, but we celebrated the victory for weeks after. We felt we had dented their pride and their morale. The bards made up songs of our heroism and they told stories of the night attack until even I felt tired of the whole business.

Barbaric people are like that. They only need an occasional success and they inflate it out of all proportion.

The siege had continued for three months when they attacked in earnest. I stood on the walls and watched them. They began with a redoubled missile assault, but we were used to that now and my people regularly dampened down all the houses. The bombardment had demolished the houses nearest to wall long before.

The Romans constructed long ramps of timber and used these to cross our trenches and pits. They brought ladders. There were thousands and they came to take the town once and for all. It must have rankled that we had stood against them for so long and the night attack had been fodder to their bitterness. We knew they were here to kill us all and we were defending our homes and families. Perhaps this was why we fought as we did. No one shied away and even our women lined the walls and cast missiles at the attacking Romans.

There was an initial cloud of arrows but we took few casualties from it, since we had high walls behind which to hide. As soon as the hail of arrows ceased, our men knew the Romans were placing ladders. There was a strange silence then. A calm before the tempest. A Cornicen, as the Romans call their signalling trumpeters, broke the silence. I was on the wall over the gate and as I looked out, I could see rank after rank of helmeted soldiers waiting to climb to their death or glory.

As soon as the first Roman mounted the ramparts, we stood ready to defend ourselves. We started by using what pitch and oil we had, in earthenware jars. When the clay pots had broken and smeared the enemy and their ladders, we threw down torches, lit from braziers placed at intervals along the wall. The effect was terrible to see. Burning men fell back among their comrades. They too became smeared. They caught fire. Our men howled with satisfaction as the Romans burned.

A few of the enemy got up onto the wall, but we cut them down with swords and spears. We had some javelins and we hurled these all along the wall into the massed ranks below. There were many Romans but our men lined the wall densely. We fought them off as they tried to climb up.

We did not attempt to push down the ladders although we had long poles with which to do so. We had enough men to prevent the Romans getting up in any sizeable numbers. We wanted to kill as many of them as we could. We needed to deplete their ranks. We wanted them to pay—and pay they did.

They had a battering ram, but it broke through their boards and stuck there, it became unusable.

We fired arrows into their midst. It did not achieve very much for their shields protected them well. It did serve to slow them down and make them cautious. The attack continued for hours. Neither side gained any advantage but the Romans still persisted. Many of them died. At one point they managed to get twenty or so legionaries over the wall and they were fighting fiercely, back to back, keeping our men at bay. When I joined the fight, I think my presence alone was enough to encourage my troops.

The leader of the Romans was a big brute of a man: all muscle and snarls. I pushed my way through my men and stabbed at him. There was not much room to swing a sword, but I had a shorter blade in my left hand. He pushed with his shield. I stepped back. He pushed forward stabbing with his gladius. I had the range, but he was a big man. He stabbed to his right as he raised his shield. This time he cut

420

down a man on my left. I brought my long sword down on the rim of his shield. It was a mighty blow. It dented the shield and it lowered for a short moment. I stabbed with my left hand at the exposed eyes.

He ducked and I struck again. It was not such a heavy blow. His shield arm must have been tiring for it lowered again. He stabbed at my groin with his sword. I turned. His outstretched arm tempted me. I struck it sideways with my long sword. I hit my mark but the shield struck me and I fell. In a crush of men, sitting on the wooden wall-walk, it is all but impossible to regain your feet.

I still held my blades. I was able to stab at my enemy's legs with both. He tried to bring down the edge of his shield on my neck.

I rolled aside. I scuttered on all fours through the blood and mud, back towards my own men. I regained my feet. The big Roman was on his knees. I realised I had all but severed his hand above the wrist. It was why there had been no deathblow as I had fallen. One of my men finished him off easily enough. We attacked again and those Romans we failed to kill hand to hand, we pushed over the edge of the wall-walk to be despatched by the women below who waited for this to happen.

Frija was among them. I looked down and could see her looking up at me, those knowing blue eyes looking through me. She smiled a secret smile as she brought down an axe on the head of a crawling Roman at her feet. I knew she was not normal, she seemed to be part of the earth and stone. Hard and strong, yet beautiful in her own way.

The fighting raged all along the wall for several hours. I had to replace the men on the wall-walk in the end. It is a tiring business fighting in armour and chain mail. The fresh troops made a difference. They joined the fight happy to be allowed into the fray. They whooped and made war shouts as each Roman came up. The enemy did not tire and perhaps they too had refreshed their assault troops but it was to no avail. The fact the ground was muddy and it had begun to rain again disadvantaged them. They slipped on the ladders and many had a hard time maintaining an upright position once they had gained the wall. The mud so caked their steel-studded sandals they slipped and slid on the rough wooden planks.

The rain became steadily heavier and eventually the Romans withdrew under cover of their archers. We did not waste time or effort in throwing our precious javelins, but appreciated the fleeing Romans with the usual abuse my men were used to offering them. One man was unwise enough to bare his buttocks over the wall at the withdrawing enemy. He regretted it however because a Roman archer made it his business to use the exposed rear end for target practise. The arrow produced only a flesh wound, but it was perhaps a lesson well learned and the man gained little sympathy for his discomfiture.

It was a long night. It was cold and the first frost had begun to stretch its frigid fingers across the landscape. We knew the Romans would want to terminate the siege before winter set in because in Frankia the winter is bitter, hard and cold. We had no doubt at all they would return the next morning.

When we weighed up our losses, we found to our delight that we had only lost about fifty men. Most of the bodies on and beneath the wall-walk were Roman. We threw them over the wall and left them there. Disease from dead bodies was unlikely in the cold weather and they were well away from our people in the ditch around the wall. It gave us some satisfaction that the attacking troops would have to fight across the rotting bodies of their comrades.

We met and discussed the day's events while eating a frugal meal in the Great Hall.

'Galdir,' Eudes said, 'our men stood firm today and I am sure we can hold them again tomorrow.'

'I am sure too. They are the ones who suffer from the cold and wet not us. How many times they will attack of course before they obtain reinforcements I do not know.'

I cut a piece of salted pork from the slab in front of me and then broke off a piece of bread. It was hard and crumbly and fragmented as I ate it. The long table hosted two rows of elders and kings. It was one of those nights in which however much we fed the fire, it seemed inadequate. It was still raining outside and I could hear that irritating drip from the roof near the oak tree. It rankled.

'I think they will have difficulties if we can hold their attacks even for a few days. With winter approaching and our bands of horsemen harrying their supply trains they will, as you say, suffer,' Chilperic said.

'I don't think they will send for reinforcements. I think the Roman General is arrogant and wants this victory for his political status. If he calls for help his reputation will suffer,' I said.

'What, even more than it has already? His wife was captured, he had his camp raided and he failed to storm the city successfully. Not a very good record is it?' Chilperic said. He was always upbeat when talking about war. I think he was an ideal soldier, even if he and I never saw eye to eye.

'Maybe if we hold out long enough they will sue for peace?' I said.

They all looked at me in surprise.

'Never,' Eudes said.

'Peace with these dogs is unthinkable,' Lazygis said. 'Better to die than share a world with these men.'

'We have to consider the women and children. If we lose here, there is not a man, woman or child who will survive. Do we accept it will be the end of the Franks?'

There was silence then. I broke it myself.

'The whole point of this armed resistance is to force the Romans into a position where they will agree to let us live in peace. I will achieve that if I can.'

'You talk of peace? We should attack them and finish them off,' Chilperic said.

'It's impossible. Our troops aren't disciplined enough to take on the Roman infantry and we don't have enough cavalry to crush them. Let us hold the city and hope they capitulate. I have spoken.'

The meeting broke up. Lazygis and I remained, eating and talking.

'We both have reason to hate the Romans but we need peace with them to protect my people. I know you have vengeance in your heart. I remember your wife, Ayma and your little boy, Panogaris well, but I cannot drag the Franks into ruin for that reason.'

'I understand that. When we first met, you were just a rough soldier in your uncle's army. You make decisions now like a real leader. Your father would be proud of you I think.'

'We should rest tonight. There will be fighting tomorrow.'

'I hope so. I want to take many more Romans with me before I go to Pan.'

I slept well that night and dreamt of Livia. She smiled at

me and I realised I had not dreamt of her for a long time. I needed awakening in the morning which was unlike me. The servant who brought me a cup of watered honey said the Romans were drawing up in front of the gates and they needed me.

CHAPTER XIX

"So many men, so many opinions"

— Terentius

The morning brought the same events as the previous day. The sun shone faintly between grey clouds and although there was no rain the mud in front of our gates again hampered the attacking Romans.

This time they had another battering ram and they made sure it would reach the gates. We had prepared for them this time. They tried to keep our heads down with archers but we had made up arrow-breaks, wicker shields we used to protect the defenders as they leaned out and dropped torches and pots of pitch and oil. The shield over the ram burned and they had to abandon it.

The Romans continued to lose men. They climbed the wall and we killed them as they came up. They came in greater numbers but we had no difficulty killing them too as they ascended. It is very hard to fight at the same time as you hold onto a ladder especially when the defenders drop rocks and your comrades' bodies down upon you.

They tried to fire the wall. They ran forward one at a time to lay dry wood and pitch against the wall in one place. We poured water onto the wood and it failed to ignite. We cheered when they died trying to light their fire and we laughed at them. The taunts and jeers must have been infuriating for them but still they came on.

We were running out of arrows and javelins and were restricted mostly to hand-to-hand fighting. I directed this from ground level. Shouting up to the wall-walk encouraging my men and sending up fresh swordsmen where needed.

I replaced the wall defenders by midday. I saw Stator climbing down a ladder. He looked happy and tired.

'It seems to be going well,' I said.

'Yes. I think it is impossible to attack a wall like this if you don't outnumber the defenders.'

'I think you're right. They're dying in their hundreds. I don't think they can breach the wall and climbing up ladders is useless to them.'

'It's a shame they don't learn that they can't win.'

I said, 'Is it?'

'Maybe you're right. The more of them that die the better,' Stator said.

'They have kept coming all day now. They must be more tired than we are,' I said.

'Then they will die quicker. We can hold them Galdir. I know it.'

'If we reduce their number enough we may be able to come out and destroy them, but I want to wait until our victory is certain. I don't want them to beat us back. We will never launch a second counter-attack. Too many of our men have died already.'

Lazygis interrupted us.

'Galdir, I think you should see this,' he said.

'What?'

'I don't know what they are doing. Come up and see.'

We walked to the wall and both climbed to the boards of the wall-walk.

I looked out then, to see the Romans had withdrawn to a safe distance, but they had not retreated to their camp. There was some activity in their rear and I could see them erecting a wooden wall some ten feet high and several layers of stakes thick.

'What are they doing?' Lazygis said.

'I don't know. Maybe they are bringing their artillery closer and hope to protect it with that wooden wall.'

'It makes no sense. Ballistae would not even dent the wall. It must be some other weapon we do not know about.'

'Yes, but what?'

'We will find out in due course. Meanwhile we wait and rest.'

We climbed down and made our way to the Great Hall. A servant came to me then as we were about to sit and eat.

'Lord, Chlotsuintha is dying. She sent me to get you.'

'Dying? Is she ill?'

'No, Lord, but she said to tell you she was dying and would you come.'

'I will be there presently; go to her,' I said.

I made my excuses to the gathering leaders and made my way across the courtyard with a feeling of dread. Chlotsuintha had been my strongest support, not in military matters, but in almost everything else. To lose her now would be a sore blow to my morale. I needed her advice and never more than now, with the Romans closing in like a pack of wolves around a campfire. It began to rain again and I thought how it was to our benefit in defending the wall.

Chlotsuintha lived in a small hut inside the central compound close to the Great Hall. I raised the leather flap covering the entrance. My eyes adjusted slowly to the gloom and I heard her before I saw her. She coughed a small dry cough and I identified her little wizened body sitting on the edge of a small cot. Standing beside her was Frija. My feet crunched on something unpleasant as I entered, but I could not see what it was. It is best not to examine the floor of a witch's hut too closely.

'Have you no light in this place?' I said.

'Hush now, Galdir,' her voice was thin, cracked, and old. I had never heard her sound so ancient. It stopped me in my tracks.

'Chlotsuintha, what is happening? I was summoned,' I said. 'I came because I was told you were dying, yet I find you very much alive and sitting on the edge of your bed. I am too busy with the Romans to spend time in idle chatter.'

'Galdir, Galdir, when will you learn? All is not what it seems. My dear boy, so weak, yet so strong. Come, sit here for a last time and hear my words. Frija, fetch a stool.'

She always talked to me that way when she had something serious to impart and I sat down in silence for I had learned it was useless to challenge anything she said. I owed her my life, after all. I could make out her furrowed features in the half-light. The wrinkles seemed smoothed in the dimness.

'I am going now to join my six sisters who went before,' she said.

'You look all right to me,' I said.

'Galdir, I am tired. I am too tired to continue. The All-father has spared me until this time, but he has heard my prayers. He has spared me the defeat of my people. He beckons and I wish to go. I am so weary of it all. Everyone I ever knew has died long before and I am the only one left. There are young ones now who move their limbs fast and who can do what I can do.'

She looked up at Frija and I could just make out a smile on the old witch's face. She said, 'My dear sweet child, you know what to do when I have gone. I have taught you well, but there was much you knew already. You will be stronger and more powerful than I ever was if you choose to be. If you weaken as I almost did once, you will lose your power. You must swear loyalty to Galdir, for he alone can lead our people through the defeat that comes.'

'Defeat!' I interjected.

Chlotsuintha held up a hand and said, 'Silence! You do not understand. Through this defeat we will become victorious. You will not see how for many years, but it will happen. You must travel far but do not trust the woman with the green eyes. Listen to her words carefully and you will understand. She seeks only to entrap and enslave you. For once, life would be so simple and easy for you if you forget that part of you residing between your legs.' She cackled faintly then, but began coughing.

Once she had settled, I said, 'Chlotsuintha, we will defeat the Romans. It is going well.'

'Marcus Aurelius is not one to be defeated by a rabble of Germans! You cannot win this battle. You may win the war in the end but you must make sure that if you lose a battle you do so to the advantage of your people and it may then set the scene for winning the war. Aurelius knows this; he has done it all his life.'

'How do you know anything about the Roman Emperor?'

'I can feel him in the spirit world and I know him well, my boy.'

It seemed obvious to me she had gone mad. I thought she was rambling. I loved this old witch. She had become part of my world and she was part of the fabric of our history. I thought she might die soon but I was unprepared for what happened next.

'Galdir, take my hand,' she said. I did as she bade me and she lay on the cot propped up on a bolster. She took Frija's hand in her other and she said, 'Wuotan! Take my spirit. I have served you well, and I know you respect that. These two people with me are my greatest treasures. Welcome them when it is their time, the warrior king and his witch and bless them as you have blessed me.'

She closed her eyes and I assumed she was sleeping. Her hand became limp in mine and I realised she had gone. I saw Frija weep then. Tears and bitter sobs. She had lost someone who had cared for her and taught her from the age of ten and I understood her loss. How Chlotsuintha predicted her end with such accuracy remains a mystery to me but it was so; I swear it.

I took Frija in my arms, next to the body of my old witch. I stroked her hair as she cried and I could feel her breath on my shoulder and the firmness of her breasts as she pressed against me. I gained comfort from the contact and I think she did too but she pushed me away.

'Galdir, go and fight your stupid war. This is no place for you. I have funeral rites to perform and no man may enter here. I will serve you now when you need to see what the Gods want you to see. I will always serve you and my people. There will be no others in my life; by Chlotsuintha's life-fire and spirit I swear.'

She pushed me out of the hut. As I walked back to the Great Hall I began to grieve again. So many deaths and each time I lost someone I had to grieve for them all. I thought of Livia. I pictured her wonderful smile and realised how much

I missed her. I thought of Cornelius and I thought of Medana. All gone. And now, Chlotsuintha. Frija gave me no comfort for I hardly thought she had enough experience of life to advise me. But there was something she did have; some power, some skill perhaps. I had always known how special she was but only ever half-believed it.

I had no time to feel sorry for myself. I had a war to fight and I would not allow the old witch to be proven right. I would fight. I believed in myself. I believed in my people. I believed we could win and fight off these Romans. All I needed was patience. I had that and I had a strong right arm and good comrades. I looked across the table at Lazygis and I was sure we would win. I was as certain of that as I was that sunshine comes after rain or that the dead never return.

The Romans did not renew their attack. The rest of the day was quiet and the silence was almost worse than the attacks. We wondered what the night would bring. As I stood on the wall-walk and looked out at the battlefield, I wondered what our enemies were doing. I mused on how they might feel in the cold and icy night. Did they feel as we did? Were they resting? Were they concocting some other means of destroying us? Perhaps they had a secret weapon. I had heard of Greek weapons making loud noise and spreading flames over all in their path but I had never thought the Romans had such things.

I sent for Frija. She came to me. Her eyes were tear-stained and sad. I knew what she was feeling for I shared the loss. It was only that I had other matters to deal with and one does not show the weakness of grief to one's soldiers.

'What are the Romans doing?' I asked.

'I don't know. I'm not a Roman,' she said. She was clearly becoming more and more like Chlotsuintha. Difficult.

'I thought you could read the future?'

'That is not how it works. I have dreams and they sometimes tell the truth.'

'Have you dreamed recently?'

'Yes.'

'Well?'

She smiled and said, 'I dreamed last night of rabbits.'

'Frija, are you mocking your Warlord?'

'No, I dreamed I wandered in a mist. A rabbit looked at me. It was standing on its hind legs and it looked at me then ran away. I had a feeling of curiosity and I followed. There was a queue of rabbits waiting to dig. They were digging to get under a farmer's fence. The farmer stood on the opposite side and smiled. He had a wide-brimmed hat and only one eye. I thought he looked like the Allfather. He poured water into the tunnel and all the rabbits drowned. That was all I dreamt. Can I go now?'

'Rabbits?'

'Yes.'

'Go then. Tell me if you have any other dreams. Perhaps we can entertain the children with them while their families are being slaughtered by Romans.'

The hint of bitterness in my voice betrayed my disappointment. If I was expecting some clarity greater than Chlotsuintha's cryptic magic, it was clear I was going to be disappointed. I stood looking out at the Romans lined up in their centuries and the wooden walls they had erected. There were three of them at equal intervals along the trenches.

My mind was mulling over what Frija had said and a sudden realisation came to me. I had become stupid. They were digging like rabbits!

They were making tunnels.

CHAPTER XX

"True nobility is exempt from fear."

— Marcus Tullius Cicero

'Tunnels?' Lazygis said.

'Yes, the wooden screens are to prevent us from seeing what they are doing,' I said.

Night was falling as we stood in the Great Hall, Lazygis, Eudes, Chilperic and I. It was warm by the fire on the broad hearth and I could smell the remains of our roast lamb as it languished only partly eaten on the wooden plates. Rainwater dripped from the roof and as I looked at it I could have sworn that damned oak tree grew an inch as I watched.

'They can't dig that deep. Our trenches are ten feet deep and the pilings for the wall go even deeper,' Chilperic said.

'I know all that, but they are engineers such you have never seen the like. They can do it,' I said.

'Then what do we do? We can estimate where they will come out and we can wait for them. They will lose a lot more men than we will.'

'They may attack the wall at the same time to distract us,' I said. 'We would have our hands full.'

'What then?' Lazygis said.

'We will dig a ditch.'

'A ditch?' Eudes said.

'Yes even our people can do that. It will transect the line

the Romans take and we will direct the river water into it. It will need to be deep. The Romans will dig deep beneath our walls, but must then come closer to the surface because of the rock. If we dig at least a ten foot trench, filled with water, either it will seep into their tunnels or they will dig into it.'

'Have we time?'

'Of course. They can't use all their men for digging and we can. A tunnel requires only a few men digging at a time. A trench can be dug by hundreds at once.'

'My men won't dig. They are warriors not slaves,' Chilperic said.

'They will do what the Warlord says.' I looked at him with eyes of steel and I meant it.

He backed down and did not speak again. Eudes took charge of the trench digging. He was wise and after discussing it with some of our technically minded builders, could estimate where to dig.

The work proceeded. It took only one night to dig a trench at least fifteen feet deep and flood it with water from the river. Every able-bodied person in our town helped in some way. Women and children carried the rubble away through the mud and the warriors set to, with shovels, axes, buckets and any implement available, some using bare hands. Thousands of people, with only one aim in mind: to dig.

They finished the trench before dawn and when it was completed, we sang and prayed to Wuotan. He had after all guided Frija in her dreams and she in turn had told me in her half-hinting way.

A pale sun rose above us as we waited. We had men on the wall and men standing on the town side of our deep,

435

water-filled ditch. It was a waiting game now. Both sides waited for the Romans to finish their tunnels.

I stood and watched from the gates of my Great Hall. I knew we could do this. Any Romans who succeeded in emerging from their water-filled tunnels would die as they climbed the slopes of the ditch. I praised the Allfather under my breath. Through Frija he had given me a plan and was helping me execute it.

It was midday before we realised what was happening. The water level in the ditch remained the same for it filled directly from the river. We understood what had occurred because a stream of wet and clearly unhappy Romans emerged from behind the wooden walls they had constructed. We never found out how many had drowned in the tunnels, but it must have been a terrible experience for them. I pictured them standing in a queue underground, waiting to emerge. Then a torrent of water, drowning out all light and air. I did not envy them.

The Romans were in disarray. There must have been cohorts of them underground and it was then the rest of my plan unfolded, for we counter-attacked.

The Sarmatian cavalry came out of the left gate. My German horsemen emerged from the right. We opened the front gates. While the enemy was disorganised and wet, we attacked with our infantry. The Frankish infantry had learned their lesson. They obeyed their orders to a man this time. They kept tight formations against the spread out Romans who tried desperately to form up. It was impossible, of course.

Our men advanced, making use of the Roman wooden ramps. They threw our short javelins and the cavalry attacked each flank. The right Roman flank collapsed first. I could see Lazygis from the wall. He rode among the enemy, sword in hand, stabbing slicing. I saw a man raise a spear towards him as he approached. I had a sudden fear and my heart beat fast. The spear broke on the horse's chain-mail kirtle and the horse struck the man a cruel blow with its front hooves. I heard my friend whoop with joy as he rode into a group of Romans. There must have been ten of the enemy, but he rode on anyway. I was sure it would be his end. He rode through them and three of the Romans lay dead or dying. Lazygis turned and did the same again until they were all dead. I knew he had a death wish, but it was not his destined time. The same happened all over the battlefield. Sarmatians and Franks alike were dealing out death to the Romans.

Lazygis' cavalry turned then on the Roman rear. They loosed a volley of cruel barbs from their vicious composite bows. They charged then and drove a wedge into the disorganised foe. It was a slaughter. Not that the Romans ran, they tried to form small groups and fight their way out. It was of little use. Our men stabbed and sliced them whether they were facing towards us or turning to fight the cavalry.

It took only an hour before it was clear few Romans had survived. We formed up again in front of the town for we knew we had only destroyed half of the besieging army. The remainder of the Romans emerged from their fort and were ready to give battle. I could feel my heart beating fast and my mouth was arid. I could hardly believe victory was so close and I had planned it all. Chlotsuintha was wrong after all. I could sense victory, almost taste it in my kiln-dry mouth.

We now outnumbered them and it was a different fight from the disastrous battle we fought months before. I had arranged my infantry as if they were the horns of a bull. The centre of them was further back than the flanks in an effort to surround my enemies. I had learned this from Roman history, foolishly taught me by the slaves of the commanding legate's father. The irony did not escape me. Hannibal had used inferior numbers to do the same as I planned to do. A weak centre and a strong flank. When the centre gave way, as it must, the flanks close and the cavalry attack front and rear. It was just such a battle.

My flanking infantry were the fiercest fighters and they had spread so wide they occupied the slopes of the hills on either side. When they attacked, they did so downhill with all the momentum running down the slopes would give them.

Meanwhile, my cavalry reorganised into two groups. The Sarmatians at the rear were ready to charge any Romans who fought their way through, and the Frankish cavalry flanking on our right were ready to hit the rear of the Roman forces.

It was a wondrous thing to see. As the Warlord, I was not allowed to stand among the fighting soldiers. I bit my lip with frustration. I sat on Valknir and looked down upon the fight. I feasted my eyes upon it. It made my heart fly, for my plan had come straight from the Roman texts, and it unfolded in a classical manner. Few of my people fell. I was proud of them and more elated than I had ever been in my life as I saw the Romans try to flee. They ran through the ranks of my cavalry to escape the death my men meted out. There was blood and there were screams. I have heard it said somewhere that there are three good things in life. To crush your enemies, to see them flee before your army and to hear the wailing of their women. The Romans had no women but otherwise our victory was complete.

We followed them. They ran, and my men now broke formation and ran after them. It surprised me how few of them we caught, encumbered as they were with their armour and weapons, but I should have realised there was something not quite right about the scene.

A fleeing man drops his weapons to run faster. It is the only thing giving him an edge, that, and relinquishing his breastplate. These Romans ran as if they were ready to turn and fight again, which seemed ridiculous to me. The cavalry formed up behind my spread-out infantry, preparing to take over the killing when the foot soldiers ran out of energy. I smiled as I watched. We had won.

The far end of the valley turned a corner and was still overlooked by tall grass-covered hills with pine forests half way up the slopes on either side. We lost sight of our fleeing enemies for a moment as we reached the far end of our vale. My men followed. They knew the Romans were beaten, but they wanted to make sure they would never return.

There was something bothering me still. I was exalted at the victory, but something seemed to be wrong. I could not place it. Perhaps it was Chlotsuintha's final words or perhaps it was instinctual. I reined in my horse on the right hand hill. Lazygis joined me.

'There is something wrong,' I said.

'Wrong? We have a victory! The Romans are utterly defeated and we have a chance now to annihilate them completely.'

'Lazygis, none of them have disarmed as they fled. Have you ever seen a routed man hold onto his shield, armour and weapons? Call your men back.'

'You are foolish Galdir. Let them enjoy taking the heads of these Roman pigs.'

I looked at him. My expression must have been enough for he signalled to his horn-blower and summoned his men. They drew back immediately for their discipline was staunch. They began to ascend towards us when I realised my mistake.

I was walking Valknir along the slope and could see more and more of the valley below. I saw my men running back. It was now their turn to flee. To my undying horror I saw why they fled.

It was a vast Roman army.

There must have been four or five legions with thousands of auxiliaries and there were flanks of cavalry riding the slopes either side. There must have been fifty thousand Romans, fresh and ready, marching in quick order along the valley floor. The fleeing Romans formed up in front of them and turned towards my men. We must have had twenty thousand infantry to their vastly superior numbers. We had to flee. I signalled to retreat.

My foolish people disobeyed me then and it was our undoing. Perhaps they felt they could not face another siege or perhaps they wanted to die fighting and go to the Allfather's side forever. I cannot understand it now. I saw Chilperic rallying the infantry. I saw Stator walking through the ranks shouting orders or encouragement, I could not hear. I had to do something, but knew there was nothing I could do. I had only seven hundred Sarmatians at my back and no other troops. We waited. The Roman forces dwarfed our troops. They were closing in on our dispersed men and it was over almost before any counter attack could begin.

'Lazygis, you came to die fighting the Romans and now my friend, on this day, we will both go to our respective ends. Your wish it seems will be answered.'

'Yes, Galdir it is a good day for it. It has been a red day and a hard day, but it is one the Romans will not easily forget and we must take many of them with us before the end.'

'Shall we begin, Brother?' I said.

'Why not? Brothers in blood, brothers in death! Ayma! Panogaris! I will see you again.'

So saying, the horn-blower sounded 'wedge' and then 'advance' and we all knew what was ahead. I was at the apex of the wedge with Lazygis beside me. Could a man ask for more?

We were a massive contingent of heavily armed and armoured Sarmatian cavalry. It felt as if we flew. Unstoppable. A last charge on feisty horses, grim faced and determined. We were not charging to win, but riding to our deaths. Strangely, I had no fear. I felt no racing of the heart and there was spittle on my tongue. Battle lust had hit me already. I smiled as we gradually quickened our pace. We were attacking the Roman column halfway along its length and we knew they would swallow us up.

We hit them at incredible speed and with a crushing momentum. The sound of that clash of hooves and shields, spears and swords was deafening in my ears and it was a joy, an ecstasy. I found myself halfway through the ranks of a century of legionaries, hacking, striking and killing. Blood splashed me; it spattered my face and arms. My sword was slick with it as it ran down the blade and it flew away in showers as I raised it to strike.

Valknir reared up on occasion and I pity anyone who was near. He was a fearsome beast in a battle. He fed my pride and I his. We were killing as if we were part of the same creature, a huge, winged, killing beast. None could stand

441

before us. Blood dripped and sprayed from my sword and I lost contact with the others. I did not care. I recognised how my father must have felt before me. He too had ridden against Roman lines and died as I was going to, sword in hand and with laughter on his lips. I had a last vision of my mother, bloodied and falling and then I remember no more. I must have had a blow to the head for it seems I fought on, but much of it is not stored in my mind.

All became black.

CHAPTER XXI

"Where there's life, there's hope."

– Terentius

I awoke in darkness. There was a smell of urine and I shivered with cold. My head ached and pounded and I could feel stiff, clotted blood on my face. I tried to rise. Manacles and chains fettered my hands in front of me. I desisted and lay quiet, wondering where I was. I felt like a man who has passed through fire to emerge in some ice-bound land in darkness. Moments passed and I became aware of a faint light above me. I realised I lay on the earth floor of a tent. I seemed to be unscathed apart from a pain in my head, which throbbed and thumped as if all my battling Franks were trying to emerge. It was hard but I managed to sit up and my head began to clear. Gazing around me in the dim light I knew I was alone.

My first thought was 'where are my comrades'. The thought soon petered out for I was sure they were dead and I wished I had died too, but I suppose no one has a choice in such things. I could almost hear Chlotsuintha telling me this would happen and it was all for the good of our people. How that could be, I could not fathom. I could not even fight now I was in chains. Hopelessness and a deep despair gripped me for the first time since Cornelius had died.

Chlotsuintha's words echoed in my head. What was it she

had said? That defeat would bring victory in the end? The Franks would one day take all of Gaul for their own? I could see no way now for that to happen. The Romans had a habit of putting whole nations to the sword. I could do nothing to stop them.

I tried to stand but the combination of weariness and dizziness kept me sitting. No one came and I lay down again. I slept fitfully shivering still, until I awoke. I must have been asleep for hours before I heard the sound of approaching footsteps. Between the dreams I had wondered how they would kill me. Perhaps they would drag me in chains behind a triumph and garrotte me at the end in the Forum Romanum like some strange trophy.

They would lie to their people and say it was a great Roman victory. I knew it was not. We had beaten their army and it was only with a second army they could bring us down. I hoped I would have a chance to speak before the end. I was no speechmaker but there was much I would say to these Romans whom I hated. Much of what I wanted to tell them I had learned from them. My Master was right I was a barbarian through and through but I had pride and I had learned as much from the Romans as I had from my own nation. I would face death now without demur but I was sad for my people. They were like children. They needed a leader and I had let them down.

At mid-morning they came for me. There were two guards and a Centurion. The two legionaries picked me up under the arms and half-dragged me out into the daylight. I was blinking and the Centurion muttered to himself but did not speak to me. They took me to a large tent. It was smaller than the one my Uncle Odomir had used but it was clearly the command tent. It had wooden flooring, and braziers burned in the corners making the place warm. Oil lamps flickered shedding a yellow smoky light and there were men all around the edges of the tent. They were soldiers and there was one man seated on a wooden platform in a curule chair such as judges used in Rome. Silence descended like a curtain as they dragged me into the centre.

I knew who the man in the chair was. His face was on all the Roman coins. It was the Emperor. He had come in person to finish the Frankish nation and I had no way to stop him. Piso stood at his elbow and I felt sure they would kill me now. It would be a pleasure to die anyway. All my friends and comrades had gone before and a vision of Clotildis begging me to kill her came to mind. It was as if the same pleading as hers arose in me but it waned as soon as the Emperor spoke.

He had greying black curly hair and a thick, greying beard beneath broad cheekbones giving his face an appearance of thoughtfulness. He looked a little flushed but it may have been the warmth of the braziers and not his health. His eyes were cod-cold and steely blue in colour and he was a big man, similar in size to me. He regarded me with curiosity.

'They tell me you speak Latin,' he said, his voice deep and even.

'I do.'

'You are the leader of these people?'

'I am Galdir, Warlord of the Franks. We are a proud people.' I stood straight then, despite my chains. I had pride still. Defeat had not diminished it. I was still the Warlord of a great nation. I looked the Emperor in the eye.

He said, 'You have taken up arms against Rome. Is there any reason why I should not destroy all your people?'

A vision of other leaders, feather-crowned, standing be-

445

fore their victorious oppressors came into my head. It was part of history and I knew it was the future too in some far off place unknown to me. Words came but they were somehow not my words. They seemed to arise like some surge of eloquence to which I would never have laid claim had it not been my mouth uttering them. It was as if the very German land spoke through me. Had not Chlotsuintha told me this was my destiny? To be defeated yet win through in the end? I think that sometimes she put a spell on me; thrusting words into my mouth as a last service to her beloved nation. That is perhaps fanciful and maybe it was just the bang on the head scrambling my wits.

'Things which to us appear changeless and eternal may change,' I said speaking slowly and stumbling over the words but with my head held high. 'Today is fair. Tomorrow it may be overcast with clouds. My words are like the stars that never change. We know Rome has little need of our friendship now. Your people are many. They are like the grass covering vast hills of our land. My people are now few. Now they resemble the scattered trees of a snow-driven plain. There was a time when the German people covered our lands as the waves of a wind-ruffled lake covers its floor but that time long since passed away with the greatness of tribes like the Chatti and the Marcomannii that are now but a mournful memory.'

I paused then. The words seemed to escape me for a moment. I stumbled over the next words as if they were foreign to me.

I said, 'Your Gods are not our Gods! Your Gods love your people and hate mine. They fold their strong protecting arms lovingly about the Romans and lead them by the hand as a father leads an infant son. Our God, the Great Wuotan, appears to have forsaken us. Your Gods make your people wax stronger every day. Soon they will fill all the land. Our people are ebbing away but they will return one day. The Roman Gods cannot love our people or they would protect us too. My people seem to be orphans who can look no-where for help now. You give your laws but you have no word for us Barbarians. No, we are two distinct races with separate origins and separate destinies. There is little in common between us.'

I looked the Emperor in the eye. My words seemed enough to challenge any leader of men. It gave me strength. I still knew deep inside me they were not my words, but I used them as they came into my head. In the back of my mind, I could hear Chlotsuintha, her high pitched voice almost coaching me, pushing the words out.

'Our religion is the traditions of our ancestors—the dreams of our old witches, given them in solemn hours of the night by Wuotan. It is written in the hearts of my peo-ple. Day and night cannot dwell together. The Frank's night promises to be dark. But a single star of hope hovers above his horizon even though now sad-voiced winds moan in the distance. Grim fate seems to be on my people's trail now and ever they hear the approaching footsteps of their Roman destroyer and prepare stolidly to meet their doom, as does the wounded doe that hears the approaching footsteps of the hunter. It is the order of nature, and regret is useless.'

The Emperor shifted in his chair. I could not read from his expression whether he was impressed, bored or angry with my apparent temerity. That my words were having some effect was clear but I could not stop. It was my only chance to tell Rome who the Franks were and what they might one day become if only they let us live.

447

'Your time of decay may be distant but it will surely come for even the Roman Gods cannot exempt you from the common destiny. We may be brothers after all in that. We will see. One day you may need us. When your need is dire and all your world is threatened we will come to your aid. These things I swear before my Gods and yours.'

The Emperor looked at me. He frowned a little but said nothing, so I continued.

'When the memory of my people shall have become a myth among the Romans these lands will still swarm with the invisible dead of my people and when your children's children think themselves alone in the field or in the silence of the pathless woods, they will not be alone. At night when the streets of your cities and villages are silent and you think them deserted they will throng with the returning hosts who once filled them and still love this beautiful land. The Roman will never be alone.'

There was silence when I finished. I wondered if the knock on my head had released something unstoppable from my mouth. I had never heard the words I spoke and they arose in me like a wellspring and that is all I can say.

Marcus Aurelius gazed at me in silence for a long time. He had a puzzled expression on his face and he said, 'You speak well. Even if what you say is true, I cannot simply erase your actions. I have had to come here myself to subdue your uprising. Surely you knew you could not win?'

'I knew Rome would fight. We had no choice. We tried to sue for peace and our emissary was taken prisoner. Hostages were held and your Legate refused to parley. What could I do? I hoped that by harassing the supply lines you would leave, but I underestimated how much Legate Licinius Piso hated us. It was his hatred of my people and his wish for war making us fight. We wanted only to live in peace. We did not even wage war on the Eburones when we came. We negotiated. Rome does not negotiate and we knew it. I knew you would come, so we prepared as well as any Barbarian nation can. Not enough it seems. I ask only for the lives of my people. I will sign any treaty, any terms of peace in exchange for their lives. I will pledge them to Rome so when you have killed me they can live. They make poor slaves, but they can fight for you. I ask nothing for myself.'

I knelt then. I hoped it was enough.

I glanced upwards and saw Piso whispering in Caesar's ear. Marcus Aurelius frowned and turned then to scowl at Piso. I did not catch what he said to his legate, but Piso turned pale and walked to the back of the tent.

Caesar spoke, 'Nobility is not a trait I see in many Barbarian leaders. To recognize when it is there, can sometimes be hard. I see in you a savage, an educated savage, yet a man who kills without conscience. I also see deep within you a nobility and strength rarely apparent in your countrymen, who are crude and vulgar, uneducated and with no grasp of any philosophical concept. I admire the courage of the Franks who have fought my army for so long. I have decided their fate. I have long believed one should accept the things to which fate binds one, and love the people with whom fate brings you together, but do so with all your heart. I can see you speak with reverence and from the heart. It would indeed be a heartless man who would refuse to listen to your pleas. I am also impressed you ask nothing for yourself. It will be thus: I will let your people live here as vassals of Rome. The land will be annexed and your men, all of them, will serve in my armies abroad. All of your nation will swear never to take up arms against my armies again.'

449

I looked up. I was not smiling outside, but inside I knew I had won. I wondered what my fate would be now. I would face my end with calmness. I had done much that was bad in my life and much that was weak but I would face my end as my father had faced his.

The Emperor said, 'There is one matter in which you will obey me. Several hundred Sarmatians escaped into the forests after the final battle. If they do not capitulate and become my auxiliaries as well, all your people will die and the Frankish nation will be erased from our world. You will find them and convince them or your subjects will face the consequences.'

I looked again at the Emperor. He had a faint smile on his lips. I knew then he thought he had nothing to lose, whatever the outcome. I knew he was a clever man, but his deviousness lowered my opinion of him. The chance of convincing Lazygis or his men, if they still lived, was remote and the Emperor knew that as well as I did. Still, I was surprised he had spared me.

'How can I send word to the Sarmatians? I have chains about my limbs and no horse.'

The Emperor said, 'That will be taken care of; you have two days in which to return with the Sarmatians.'

He turned to one of the guards, 'Take him away,' he said.

They dragged me to the same tent, but it was only for minutes. A smith came and he removed the manacles. As I rubbed my chafed wrists, a Tribune briefed me on what the future might hold if I was successful and what would happen if I failed. Five legionaries escorted me to a fenced area where there were horses.

'Pick one,' a surly and unprepossessing legionary on my right said.

450

I saw my horse. I whistled to him. He pricked up his ears and galloped across the paddock. He shook his head and stood as near as the fence would allow. I walked towards him and the same soldier said, 'Not him, I've got my eye on him. Take another.'

'He is my horse and he won't respond to any other rider. He won't be of value without me,' I said.

The soldier looked at me with disdain expressed in his face and acquiesced with some reluctance, I know not why. There was no one else in the camp who could ride him. They saddled Valknir for me and I used my stirrups to mount. They had given me my own saddle too. It was a wonderful feeling and it was tempting to ride away and never return. I knew Caesar meant what he said and I knew also my people's only chance was for me to bring back the Sarmatians. I guessed where they might be. There were hills all around and the one where we had camped before releasing Lucia to her husband seemed a good starting point for my search.

It was midday when I saw the hill and crossed the ford. A flock of crows flew north above me as I walked Valknir up the grassy slope. I whistled giving the call sign we had used on our forays against the advancing Roman supply lines months before. No sooner had I reached halfway up the slope than fifty Sarmatians appeared on the summit. They recognized me at once and whooped for joy. They called my name as they approached. I was home in some strange way. I was among friends and allies but I knew it would be hard to tell them the truth so I kept my counsel at first.

'Brothers!' I said, 'Who leads you?'

Panador, one of Lazygis' lieutenants approached and smiled. 'Lazygis of course. He was wounded but he waits on the top of this hill for news of his brave Frankish allies.'

'Wounded?'

'Yes, a foolish little wound in his leg. It will mend but it is no matter, now we have you too to lead us, Galdir.'

I smiled and walked Valknir gently up the steep slope. The wet grass was soggy under his hooves and a soft rain began to fall as I reached the summit. I was damp but not cold as I had been in that tent. I remembered what the Romans had told me to do. I thought of my people and it gave me courage. I still did not know if I was unwittingly leading my friends into a trap of Roman design. Could I trust Rome or her Emperor?

Lazygis sat on a blanket under a hastily erected awning made of woollen cloaks and I could see a bandage of grey linen wrapped around his leather-clad thigh. A bright red spot adorned the middle of the dressing and I wondered how deep the wound might have been.

He looked pale, but he struggled to his feet when he saw me approach.

'Galdir, is it really you? You return from the dead and all alone. What became of you? My men make a legend of the way you and Valknir fought. None could bear your charge. You fought a path through those Roman ranks none would have thought possible. The dead lay all around. Valknir turned in circles and bit them and kicked them. No Roman dared to approach in the end. It was a wonderful sight but Panador saw you fall and we thought you were gone to your father's side.'

'Yes, I fell and there is much I cannot recall. Much of it seems hidden from my waking mind. The Romans captured me. What became of my brave Sarmatian comrades?'

'We fought like you did. We emerged with blown horses

and wet blades on the other side of the Roman Legions. They sent their heavy cavalry after us and I confess we left the field of battle firing arrows behind us. We could do little more with blown horses and following Romans. We escaped through the woods and came here. You were always right about this place; it is unassailable by an enemy. We saw you approaching miles away. Come Brother, sit with me; standing is painful and I cannot remain upright for long.'

'Lazygis, I need to talk to you.'

'Talk?'

'Yes, Marcus Aurelius has come in person with the fresh army and they occupy Sicambra.'

'I know that,' Lazygis said. 'I do not know where we shall go. We considered going to Dacia and sheltering with Duras, if he has regained his kingdom.'

'Duras will be allied to Rome if he sits in his father's hall. You cannot go there. The Emperor has offered my people peace and will annex the territory and wants all my soldiers as his auxiliaries.'

'It is as I feared.'

'He wants you and your men to come back with me and become his soldiers too, in far off places.'

'We did not capitulate when he destroyed our people and we have lived for death fighting the Romans ever since. We have not found that end yet but we will never give up. We will never fight for Rome. What has happened to you? Did you really think we could be so weak?'

'Lazygis, if you do not, they will put all my people to the sword; every last man, woman and child. I care not what happens to me, but my whole nation will die like yours.'

'No; I am your friend, your brother, but you cannot ask this of me.'

453

'I must. Many months ago, I thought only of fighting and defending my walls. Now I have to make decisions that will end my people forever or not. I beg you Lazygis, come with me.'

'And if it is a trap? Do you trust Romans to keep their word? I don't,' he said with a wave of his hand.

'I have no choice. We will all die sometime and in some fashion, does it matter how? If they betray us then it will at least have been a death for a noble cause. Please save my people. You could not save Ayma or Panogaris, nor could you stop the Romans killing all your people. This time you can do something. If we are betrayed I swear I will die by your side.'

Lazygis sat looking at the ground for a moment. The sloping rain had hardened and droplets ran down his nose, dripping onto his knee.

'Where will they send us?'

'The officer said Britannia.'

'Is that a hot place or a cold place?'

'Cold I think, and misty.'

'Better for our horses if it is cold. We are used to cold, but hot weather is no good for us. I need to talk to my men.'

I took his arm as he stood up. We looked in each other's eyes and smiled. The drooping tips of his moustache widened and the creases at the sides of his eyes contracted. That smile said much. He called his lieutenants.

There followed a long discussion in true Sarmatian style. Each man had his say. Sarmatians do not speak concisely, something I had learned since I had met Lazygis all those years ago. Their speeches contain references to the grass and trees and moon and stars and ramble around before they say the important words. It took a long time.

My mind began to wander. I sat by the rock where Lucia and I had made love and I thought of her. It aroused me. I could almost feel her fingernails as they tore at my back, her moist lips and the contours of her body.

The Romans had told me Piso was to be deputy Governor of Britannia and would travel with us and I wondered what he would do to us on the way. He hated us. I knew this. I was condemning us all to a life of oppression but somehow I did not care. I wanted my nation to exist and I wanted to see Lucia one more time before I went to my father's and mother's sides.

At least Lucia would be in the same land to which they wanted to send me. Perhaps I would see her again. I wondered vaguely whether I felt love for her but it was a passion borne of circumstance and it could hardly have been love. The 'what if' thoughts continued and I reflected upon how I had changed. I was no longer a slave. I was a defeated King, fighting desperately to preserve a nation. And where was Frija? Had they taken her? Had they raped her and taken her power? I needed her and her view of the future. The present was all too frightening I thought.

'Galdir,' Lazygis said drawing me from my reverie, 'My men have decided.'

'Yes?'

'We will do as you wish. Did they say we could keep our weapons and our horses?'

'The weapons will be given up until we reach Britannia and we can keep our horses as well as any spare mounts we have in Sicambra, they said.'

'Then let us go before darkness comes and hope these Romans can be trusted.'

'Lazygis, we can trust Marcus Aurelius but as for Piso, I

do not know. There was some kind of dissent between them. You know he hates us.'

'Well he doesn't know you killed his father does he?'

'No, no one but you and Duras know about that. I don't think he will ever make that connection. Who would possibly believe an escaped slave could lead a nation?'

'I do,' he said and we mounted our horses and rode down that hill to whatever the future was to bring us. Britannia? Death far from our own lands? The Gods move us in any way they wish and perhaps for their own amusement. The illusion of freedom may just be that, but as we rode in the rain across the river, I felt sure I would return one day.

EPILOGUE

Dawn shed a gentle yellow light on the town and there was birdsong in the quiet, cold, rain-filled air. Long shadows reached restlessly across the muddy street at the man and woman who stood facing each other in silence beside the Great-Hall doorway.

'They are sending me to Britannia with the Sarmatians,' he said.

He was a tall shaven-headed warrior and she a small dark-haired woman of no more than twenty years.

'Yes,' she said looking up into his face. Her gaze was piercing, her deep blue eyes had a knowing quality and her face was impassive as ever.

'What will you do?'

'I cannot go with you. I will remain here to watch over our people as Chlotsuintha instructed me. I will always keep faith. I swore to be your witch and nothing has changed for me.'

'You kept your powers?'

'I kept my powers. The Romans did not find me.'

'I must go. I am sorry to leave but I had no choice. If I had not agreed to the terms, our people would have been destroyed.'

'I close my eyes and I see a boy too frightened to take on the responsibilities thrust upon him by his destiny.'

'You remember?'

'Yes I was there in the council hut when you came. When I open my eyes, I see before me a Warlord. A man who can now make regal decisions and whom his people will remember and wait for.'

'I don't ask for that. I do not think I will ever return.'

'You will return for your people will have need of you before the end.'

'Do you see that?'

'No, I have not dreamt for days. I did have one thing to tell you. Chlotsuintha often spoke of it.'

'Yes?'

'There was a woman with green eyes in her dreams and she said to beware for she will play you false. It is her words that will matter.'

'Yes I remember her saying that. What of it?'

'You know of whom she spoke?'

'I can guess.'

'Then know this, Galdir Warlord of the Franks. A time will come when you will be faced with hard choices. When the time comes, remember your people and all will be well.'

'All will be well? I will be in Britannia and so far away nothing can bring me home. The Emperor has decreed it.'

'Emperors do not live forever. Remember.'

She turned then and walked towards a hut. She lifted the leather flap and when she had entered, it swung gently in the cold air.

The warrior turned and mounted his horse, a large grey steed with a battle scar on its back and it trotted towards the gate where an ala of heavy Sarmatian cavalry awaited him. As they departed north, fading into the sloping rain, none of them looked back.

GLOSSARY OF NAMES AND PLACES

Aretium: City in north-west Italy.

Ariminium: City in north-east of Italy.

Ayma: Wife of Lazygis.

Chlotsuintha: Frankish witch.

Clotildis: Odomir's young wife and 'aunt' to Galdir.

Cornelius Nepos: Retired gladiator and Sextus' / Galdir's mentor

Donar: German version of the Norse God Thor, the God of thunder. They believed that when it thundered, Thor used a mighty hammer to battle giants in the sky.

Eudes: Frankish king and old friend of Galdir's father

Flavia: Wife of Valerius, Cornelius' friend.

Frija: Witch and Chlotsuinta's apprentice.

Gaius Licinius Piso: Galdir's master in Rome.

Galdar: Galdir's father Warlord of the Franks.

Galdir: The German name of the story's protagonist.

Gladius: Short sword, used as standard issue in the Roman Legions.

Guntramm: Galdir's cousin, Odomir's nephew.

Lazygis: Sarmatian king.

Livia: Niece of Cornelius.

Loge: German name for the Norse God Loki. He was a trickster and the God of fire.

Lovosice: Town in northern Bohemia 60 Km south of Prague.

Lucia: Wife of Marcus Licinius Piso.

Lucius Licinius Piso: Youngest son of Gaius.

Maroboduus: Marcomannii King.

Marcomannii: German tribe at war intermittently with Rome from 9 BC onwards.

Marcus Aurelius: Roman Emperor.

Marcus Licinius Piso: Eldest son of Gaius Licinius Piso, later commander of the besieging troops.

Medana: Niece of Moscon, the King of the Dacia.

Moscon: King of Dacia and father to Duras.

Panogaris: Infant son of Lazygis and Ayma

Pannonia: Roman province north od Italy, bordering on the Danube. Much of modern Hungary lies within it.

Pipin: Horse master of the Franks (Pipin was a common Frankish name).

Ranulf: Clotildis' cousin.

Raetia: Roman province to the west of Pannonia. It encompassed Switzerland and Bavaria.

Rugio: Brigand

Raetia: Province north of Italy

Sartorius: Brigand

Sextus: Galdir's name in Rome.

Stator: Frankish soldier sworn to protect Galdir in childhood.

Tyr: God of war

Valerius: Friend of Cornelius, owns a farm.

Verus Aurelius: Co-Emperor with Marcus Aurelius (died in the East, leaving M.Aurelius sole Emperor).

Wuotan: German name for the Allfather. Also known in Norse mythology as Odin. He gave his left eye in exchange for knowledge of all things and was served by two ravens.

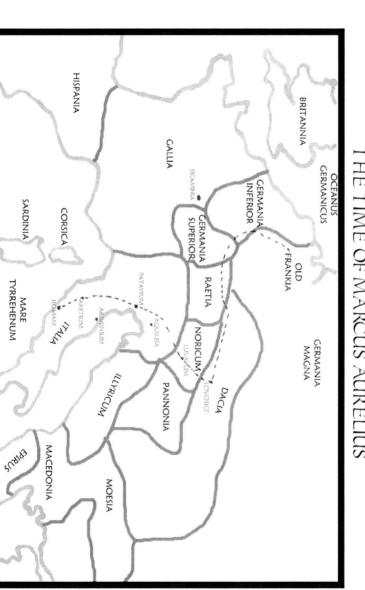

THE WESTERN ROMAN EMPIRE IN THE TIME OF MARCUS AURELIUS

OCEANUS
GERMANICUS

BRITANNIA

HISPANIA

GALLIA

SARDINIA

CORSICA

GERMANIA
INFERIOR

SICAMBRA

GERMANIA
SUPERIOR

OLD
FRANKIA

MARE
TYRREHENUM

PATAVIUM

ROMAN
ARETIUM
ARIMINIUM
AQUILEIA

ITALIA

RAETIA

NORICUM
LUVAVUM

GERMANIA
MAGNA

DACIA
LOVOSICE

PANNONIA

ILLYRICUM

EPIRUS

MACEDONIA

MOESIA

ALSO BY FREDRIK NATH FROM
FINGERPRESS:

THE CYCLIST

A World War II Drama

"Brilliantly executed... Nath's biggest success is the sustained atmospheric tension that he creates somewhat effortlessly."
-LittleInterpretations.com

"A haunting and bittersweet novel that stays with you long after the final chapter—always the sign of a really well-written and praiseworthy story. It would also make an excellent screenplay."
-Historical Novels Review—Editor's Choice, Feb 2011

www.fingerpress.co.uk/the-cyclist

FAREWELL BERGERAC

A Wartime Tale of Love, Loss and Redemption

François Dufy, alcoholic and alone, is dragged into the war effort when he rescues a young Jewish girl from the Nazi Security Police.

Then the British drop supplies and a beautiful SOE agent whom Dufy falls in love with. But as the invaders hunt down the partisans in the deep, crisp woodland, nothing works out as Dufy had hoped.

www.fingerpress.co.uk/farewell-bergerac

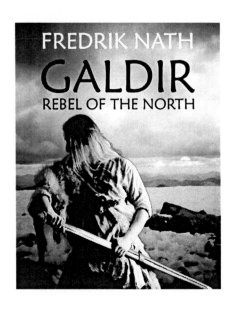

GALDIR: REBEL OF THE NORTH

Barbarian Warlord Saga, Volume II

A dark tale of Celtic mysticism, grief and battle.

Forced to serve the Roman Emperor as an auxiliary commander of cavalry on Hadrian's Wall, Galdir faces increasingly fierce attacks from hostile Celtic tribes north of the Wall.

www.fingerpress.co.uk/galdir-rebel-north

Lightning Source UK Ltd.
Milton Keynes UK
UKOW041056091212

203352UK00001B/1/P